Reclaiming the Shadow Self

Facing The Dark Side In Human Consciousness

Anwan

Channeled by Christine Breese

Illustrated by Laurel Taylor

D1231395

1997
Starlight Press
Rock Hall, MD, U.S.A.

Reclaiming The Shadow Self

ISBN 0-9657511-0-4

Cover Art: Kathey Fatica and Christine Breese
Cover Design and Book Layout: Kathey Fatica
Illustrations: Laurel Taylor

Library of Congress Cataloging

Breese, Christine 1965-
1. Self Help   2. Spiritual
3. Psychology   I. Title

Printed in the United States, 1977

*Dedicated to all my
brothers and sisters
who are awakening.*

Reclaiming the Shadow Self

Table of Contents

Who is Anwan?
About The Affirmations And Exercises
Introduction

Who Is Anwan?

There are two Anwans. There is Anwan the individual (me) and there is Anwan the group energy (myself and my soul group). Anwan is the name I have as a soul. Anwan is who I am at a deeper level. However, when channeling, I experience Anwan as myself and my soul group. Anwan is all of us as a collective entity. I have chosen to use the name Anwan for the sole purpose of having a name for the group. For some reason, I am not able to translate the "name" of our group energy into words.

I am aware of twelve members besides myself. The group has periphery members too, and the number seems to be growing as I grow. When I move into trance, I join and blend with the twelve members of my soul group and become part of a gestalt intelligence. All the members of my soul group are Masters of Life. They do not have counterparts on the Earth plane at this time. They have all finished the wheel of reincarnation. We have all gone through the wheel of reincarnation more than once. I am learning how to be part of a group entity. Two heads (or thirteen!) are better than one!

Anwan is a very diverse group of souls. Between them all, there is an immense amount of experience and information. I first became conscious of them when I needed to feel safe and nurtured. They are incredibly wise and have immense love and light. They have a great sense of humor, too!

Reclaiming the Shadow Self

They are amazingly powerful, yet they are so gentle. They stood by me in my direst moments. I think of them as my family and my dearest friends.

I channeled this information for myself and all others who have similar paths to mine. I discovered in my journey that my path was not uncommon at all. Many people walk the same roads I do. I asked Anwan to create a book that would have helped me if I found it on the shelf earlier in my path. That way others with similar paths can understand what is happening to them. This book is the signpost I leave behind as I walk past this point in my path.

This material is a collection of answers to my questions, as well as the questions of others. During the sessions for this book, there were large groups of people attending on the inner planes with questions of their own. I suspect these people are you, the readers.

You will find yourself getting in touch with your own soul group. Anwan wants to help everyone reach conscious knowing of their soul groups. Some have asked if other people can channel Anwan, and the answer to this is yes. However, the energy will come through your own soul name. The current of energy Anwan brings through is the same energy being broadcast through any soul or group of souls.

About The Affirmations And Exercises

The affirmations and exercises are tools I used to heal myself. There are 220 affirmations and there are 70 exercises. Please feel free to change the words around to fit your own needs. In forming affirmations, I found that avoiding words like "not", "no" and "don't" had a better effect on me. I also bought a gadget that looks like a beeper. It could be set to buzz or vibrate at any time interval I wanted. I used it as a reminder to quote an affirmation every hour. It accelerated the process of reprogramming my mind to think in new ways. If you want to get one of these, I recommend it. The only place to get it that I know of (Tools For Exploration) is listed in the back of the book.

I only picked one or two affirmations to work with per day. I found that if I used too many at once, they became white noise and didn't do anything to reprogram me.

As far as the exercises go—-sky's the limit! These exercises can be useful to you, but you can also make up your own. Create exactly what you need. Feel free to tailor these exercises to your own style.

Use a notebook to write down answers to the questions asked and also the questions you make up for yourself. You can also jot down affirmations as you think of them.

Write down your experiences as you use the exercises. You can even make taped journeys for yourself out of the exercises. Record what you see when you go where the exercises direct you. Also use your notebook to jot down realizations or thoughts that come up as you read Anwan's words.

Use a highlighter and pen as you read. Mark the book up! It's a study tool! That way, at a later time when you can use some encouragement, you can refer back to it for quick reference or skim through it and read things that stood out. You can get a lot out of this book by reading through it first and then going back to the exercises and working with them comprehensively and slowly.

Anwan has spoken words, but there is a lot more going on underneath. Under the message, there are keys for DNA codes and there is a huge amount of love, compassion and healing for the hearts and minds of those in pain. When you find yourself triggered by what you are reading, you are tapping into this deeper current.

If you find yourself in tears (or even rage) at certain points in this book, please stop and put the book down. Don't rush through it. The next paragraph will wait for you! Let the feelings come forth. Anwan is touching you personally in that moment. A healing is taking place. Tune in on the inner planes. Watch for the realizations you will have in these moments. A code has been unlocked and you are letting go of trapped energy in yourself. You are letting it integrate with the rest of your aspects.

Anwan has a huge number of associates in the realms of light. Actual places of healing have been set up on the inner planes for those who want to use them. You can ask to be taken there and you will be. Anwan and friends will work with you (if you ask) in your dreams, your meditations, your affirmations, and also when you use the exercises even if they are altered by you. All spirit guides love creativity, and if you get creative about exercises, Anwan will be glad to join in with what you invent! So will your soul group.

You might not be conscious of everything, but know that healing is happening if you have asked for help. The results will be noticeable later.

An Introduction

W e would like to greet all of you who have had a less than gentle life. You may be finding that your spiritual path has led you to some darker corners than you expected it to. This book is for those of you who feel you have had a harder time than most people. You are the wounded healers. There are many things to address when you have reached the dark cycle of your spiritual path. We would like to address these things.

In our introduction, we will touch on some concepts which will be covered in more detail later in our message. For some of you, this book will be validation about the path you took to heal which you may be on the tail end of now. For others, this book will be reassurance that you are on the right track. For all of you, this book will remind you of information you already know in your unconscious or conscious mind. We will simply trigger it. Perhaps you will remember your soul reasons for choosing such a difficult path in life (and in other lifetimes) after reading this message.

First of all, you are beings of light. You really *are* a sweet person, even if others don't think so. You really *are* lovely, even though you might not be showing it right now. You just got frightened along the way in life. Something caused you to shut down. You have immersed yourself in the darkness so you can turn the darkness into light. *You are not the darkness.*

Reclaiming the Shadow Self

Many of you are from other galaxies. Some of you were actually powerful and respected leaders and guides where you are from. It took a great leap of faith to come to a place where none of that would count. You decided to come into this seemingly crazy world, a runaway experiment gone amuck (as it was planned to be), and set things straight again. You didn't quite realize the extent of what you were getting into, though. You thought it would be much easier than it has been.

Long ago, a conscious decision was made by the human race to push the limits and go to the edge of no return with the concept of fear. You have been on that ride. Now the edge has been reached. This is the end of the journey into fear. This is where the human race has cried "uncle", and wants to abandon the idea of pursuing fear any further. The universe has been waiting for that call, as was agreed on ahead of "time", and help has been sent to stop the momentum of the direction humanity has set in motion. Humanity is now embracing the help available.

We would like to inform you that you can relax now. Phase one of your life is nearly over. Now that you are where you are, it means you are about to begin phase two of your life.

Phase one was the part of your life where the stage was set for the issues you chose to process in this lifetime. You will use the abilities you have gained in all your lifetimes, including this one, and the transmutation of your darkness will be complete.

Phase two is about service toward planetary transformation and the realities surrounding it. You can think of phase one of your life as being the journey of gaining enlightenment. That was the first task. Phase two is the part of your life where you are *living* your enlightenment, and a different set of challenges will present itself to you.

It does not mean you need to be famous and publicly visible. Your life work can be as simple as effecting those around you. If you are not already aware of your purpose and area of service, you will know more about this and who you are after you transmute phase one of your life.

Not all of you are meant to be famous, although many of you will be. *Please be assured that you are not just another person passing through.* You are very well known on the inner planes. Many of you are here to work in a less noticeable way because there is much inner planes work to do. Fame may not be on your soul's agenda this time. You had many lifetimes of Earth fame in the past and you are learning about valuing your work even when you aren't receiving public recognition for it. This is an important lesson for the soul.

Many of you will learn how to work in the dream worlds with others. Many of you will be assisting others in crossing dimensions. Some of you will be working with masters who are aiding humans as they reach for inventions, ideas, and discoveries. This is the kind of work which will not be noticed by people on Earth. You might be in a supportive role to others who may be in the limelight. This is valid work.

Realize that your fame reaches far beyond what you think famous means. *You have no idea how much attention you have drawn to the Earth plane!* You are *quite* famous, and have been for a while now! You are actually well known in the universe, and you are being watched and applauded by more beings than you could ever guess. Even sleeping humans are famous simply for being here. So realize that your work is important even if others don't see what you're up to or how incredible it is. Fame on the Earth plane is nothing compared to the fame you already have.

> **Your specialty is
> blending
> darkness and light
> into oneness**

Some of you have a different dilemma. You already know what your life work and purpose is. However, you have become frustrated because you have not been able to reach these goals. Perhaps everything you tried has fallen short of what you hoped for. This is because you are blocked in some way. Without removal of the blocks there is no way your creativity and lifework can flourish. You *must* clear these things before you can be efficient and abundant as a light worker on this plane of reality. By now you have seen how frustrating it is to get your life work out into the open while you are only sailing at half mast. You simply do not have all your power and your deep resources yet remain untapped.

The result of transforming the shadow self is that you will be taking back your power. *Many of you are afraid of your own power.* We will say this about power: when you do *not* have power, you cannot hurt *yourself.* When you have power, and use it wrongly, interfering with the freewill of others, you can bring upon yourself uncomfortable results. This is why you are afraid to take your own power back. You know you can hurt yourself with your power if you do not use it right. You have gone through this many times in your past lives and had painful experiences which were connected with misuse of power.

If you find yourself crying all the time, let this flow. This needs to come out. This is the body's way of purging and clearing the emotional body. There is nothing wrong with you! Know that this will pass. *This will pass!* You can be absolutely sure of this. You are going through a mourning process.

In the meantime, you must be fully present for the part of your journey you are on right now. If it means you must cry, then you must cry and be 100% attentive. Do not try to be absent from your body while you allow these emotions to purge. If you are present 100% while you go through these emotions, you will discover many things. Insights and memories will come to you. Do not be afraid to feel your emotions deeply.

If you find you have had a very large ego up to this point, it is okay. The big ego was a way for you to feel better about yourself during a time when you were feeling inferior to everyone else around you. Inferiority is often counteracted by superiority.

The darkness you are in is something you volunteered for. Much as you would like to disbelieve this, it is true. You have volunteered for this because you are one of the more advanced souls, might we say. We do not want to encourage the idea of higher or lower, but there are some souls who have *more experience* on the Earth plane.

If you have taken difficult roles and patterns upon yourself to transmute for the mass consciousness, as well as for yourself, you are a more experienced soul. If you have a damaged psychology, you are a strong one. *You* are the ones who have enough experience on the Earth plane to overcome this. *You* are the ones who can handle this. You have taken the most difficult jobs there were to be taken in this dramatic transformation of a reality.

Those of you who have come back to deal with atrocities and trauma in the human consciousness are the ones who had the best chance to overcome the deeper obstacles. You had the best chance at surviving this. You had the best chance to ascend from the depths you allowed yourself to be pushed to. Not all souls could have done this. Not all souls were prepared for this. Not all souls had enough experience. There are many levels of souls on the plane at this time. There are some here for the first time and there are some here for the gabillionth time.

All of you have experience in other systems of duality in which there were much greater wars than the ones you experience here. You specialize in bringing balance and harmony to duality. Your specialty is blending darkness and light into oneness. That is why you are here.

So do not be jealous of those who had a more pleasant lifetime or had a pleasant childhood. Some of these souls may be newer to the Earth plane and would not have been able to handle this. They did not choose to take these jobs for they were not sure they would survive through the early stages.

The "older" ones who would have been able to handle this but did not choose to go through the atrocities have avoided it for other reasons, some of which you would not understand. One of the reasons some of the experienced ones have chosen to take a less harsh path is because helpers were needed for those of you who *have* taken the harder jobs. It does not mean their path is not difficult as well, but it may be less traumatic.

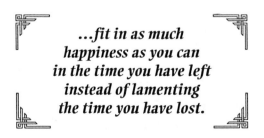

*...fit in as much
happiness as you can
in the time you have left
instead of lamenting
the time you have lost.*

Reclaiming the Shadow Self

We do not want to encourage you to think of yourself as greater than those who have had less traumatic experiences in their lives than you. However, we *do* want you to recognize the greatness of yourself for being brave enough to immerse yourself deeply and fully into the darkness. You might have drowned. You might not have succeeded in your journey. You see, these were dangerous positions to take when you entered the Earth plane, for if you did not make it, the experience would be troubling for your soul moreso than the experiences themselves. You would have felt as though you failed at a very important task and lost a chance for great service, which, of course, as most of you know, would accelerate your growth greatly.

You knew when you entered the Earth plane under these conditions there was no guarantee you would make it. It took an act of courage to subject yourself to the pain and anguish you knew you would experience. You hoped you would survive it all. You hoped you had not misjudged your abilities to transmute the energies you chose to take on. It was possible you would "lose the game" you chose to play.

We would like to congratulate you for taking these jobs! Congratulations on your graduation lifetime and for the honors list you will be on! When you graduate from the Earth plane, for this is your graduation lifetime and you can think of this as your finals, you will graduate with honors and not just perfect grades. Feel good about yourself! Feel confident about yourself for you have all the abilities and tools you need to accomplish the transmutation of these energies. You are overly qualified for this even though it doesn't seem so to yourself.

All the tests you did not pass with an A plus in your past lives are being retaken in this one. There are no second class students who graduate from this plane. You cannot pass without perfect grades. You *must* get perfect grades on every test before you are allowed to go on from this reality. This is one of the rules of the game you agreed to when you entered this zone. In the freewill zone, it is important that all the lessons are learned perfectly. If you get a C, you get to try it again. If you get a B, you get to try it again. If you get an F, you get to try it again. Eventually, you will get the A plus. Be assured of that.

All of you plan on getting it in this lifetime. This is your chance.

Suicidal feelings were probably a large part of your life. We would like to commend you for making it this far. This was a difficult lifetime to survive, since the energies are so intense at this point in the history of the Earth plane.

You have already done the hardest part. You have survived. Those of you who have made it deserve a gold star. We would like to say to you now that there is no more need for the suicidal feelings, which many of you have been living with all of your life. These feelings will continue to surface for you, especially at the times when your process of healing becomes excruciating.

We advise that you do not take these thoughts of suicide quite as seriously as you have before. The suicidal feelings are temporary and will pass. You will be glad you are alive once all of this is over.

Your suicidal feelings were not there because you wanted to die. You felt suicidal because you desperately wanted change for the better and could see no chance of that happening in your reality. If a person cannot live a quality life, he or she would rather not live here at all. This is, in part, why the human race has been considering self destruction, for the quality of life is not being realized.

Many of you nearly drowned in the darkness, but you have survived the worst of it. Some *have* drowned and have taken their own lives. However, they are safe on the other side and are watching. They wish they did not take themselves out of the game, and they are dealing with the specific area of mass consciousness which feels ripped off and angry after suicide. Once they are back in spirit, they realize they committed suicide because of events they did not even consciously remember. So there is a feeling of being *tricked* into suicide by outer forces. The resulting grief for the self is immense to deal with.

However, they are surrounded with love and light. They are still allowed to help in the shift on this plane. They are not able to play the game quite as visibly and actively as they would have been able to had they stayed on the Earth plane but they are still allowed to help.

The ones who committed suicide are quite respected anyway, for they deserve the utmost of admiration for giving it a try. They are heroes for even being here on the Earth and attempting the job. They are not looked down upon. The tasks they took on were very difficult. They were push-

You Came Here For An Adventure

ing the edges of their own abilities, just as you have.

If you have made it this far, you will make it all the way. You have survived this long, so you might as *well* go all the way! You are almost there. You are not far from the finish line. You can relax now, for the hardest part is over. If you quit now, it would be a shame. You have already done most of the work. The stage has been set. You no longer have to live through the setup of challenges. Now all you have to do is let it all go. This is more easily said than done. We understand this for we have experienced it.

The rewards for your work will be great once you transmute darkness into light within yourself. These rewards are not something you will have later. They will be realized here on Earth in your lifetime immediately after your transformation.

There is an aspect of yourself right under your skin that is *completely* enlightened. You have *always* been enlightened. You know just what to do about the situations you experienced and the ones you are in now. You *are* masters of life. You *have* mastered the Earth plane. You came back because you have deep compassion for the plight of human consciousness. You came back to make a shift on the Earth for the ones who do not have as much experience here. They were not able to transmute these energies with the speed and finesse that you can.

In direct proportion to the depths you have sunk is the same proportion of the heights you will reach, and more. The intensity of *sadness* you have experienced is the same intensity of *joy* you are capable of experiencing. The intensity of terror you have experienced is the same intensity of peace and love you can enjoy.

We honor you, for you can feel emotions more deeply than most people. Some souls will never realize in this lifetime the heights you will go to, not even once it is all said and done and the world is at last a light filled place. You have a special place in all of this.

Peace is something for you to look forward to. It is something to encourage you to keep going and stay on the path. We would like to offer you reassurance that peace and joy is there for yourself. You will not be unhappy forever. We can guarantee you this. It has been long, yes, but a lifetime is only a few blinks of an eye in the overall scheme of time. Look at your past as if it were two blinks of an eye, and your future as if it is perhaps three or four. This should help those of you who feel you have been delayed or feel you have lost or wasted much time. Think of your glass as half full instead of half empty. You have some time to enjoy the rest of your life, so simply fit in as much happiness as you can in the time you have left instead of lamenting the time you lost. When you look back on it all, once you are in the spirit worlds again, time will be irrelevant. You will also fully understand why you chose the hard path, and it will not seem so terrible to you then.

You may have noticed time is moving faster. We would like to inform you that this is a benefit for you who are healing. It is possible to heal in a much shorter amount of time than was earlier possible on the Earth plane. The need for humans to go through years of processing are gone now. Your process will go by fast. What may have taken one year to transmute may only take three months now. What may have taken ten years to transmute will only take one year.

As you know, time is accelerated, and so is growth. This is because the many trails to enlightenment have been blazed by those before you. The paths are widening more and more as each day passes because more people are walking them than ever before. You are clearing the obstacles as you go.

There is much aid on the inner planes for you. There is much aid from the light beings who have come here to help. There are more helpers than you could imagine! You are not alone as you do this healing, although you may *feel* alone.

Try to sense the presence of the guides around you who support and love you while you go through the transformation of yourself. They are there and they hold you while you cry. They are somewhat glad *you* are doing this, and not themselves, for they do not envy the pain you are going through! However, they do have deep compassion, and they are dedicated to helping you.

Do not forget to ask, dear ones, for they cannot interfere wi.h your freewill. You must give them permission to help you and work with you. You must be absolutely clear in your statement that *your freewill choice is to be helped by them.*

An Introduction

As you go through this transportation—-Hmmm—-a slip on words!—-transmutation process you are protected by these beings as you release deep emotions. There are dark energies (which we would rather call *misguided* energies) who would be attracted to you and would attach to you as you release negative energies in yourself. It has been very difficult for a human to ascend before now, for as soon as the emotions such as anger, despair or fear were released, misguided energies attached to the new "food" and held the human in that space.

At this time, you are being dearly protected as you go through this. Light is being held around you so misguided energies cannot hinder your progress. These light beings are making the ascension process safer for humans than it has ever been before. Many of the veils are being lifted, and many of the obstacles to ascension are being removed. There is not as much blocking you as there was earlier in your history. You are now enabled to transmute your fearful darkness into the dazzling darkness more easily than before.

It is important to ask for this protection, not out of fear, but simply out of the knowledge that misguided energies do exist and are a hindrance to you at this time in your development. Do not forget to thank the guides for the "cleanup" they have been doing in the etheric realms around the Earth!

Darkness is the unknown and light is the known. Darkness could be thought of as "areas of no awareness". Light could be thought of as "areas of awareness". Both are needed for an interesting reality in the freewill zone. The darkness is a place of deep power, creativity and wisdom. It takes great bravery to go into the darkness and find the information which exists there. You must surrender to it and trust it before you can retrieve anything from it.

Going into the darkness can be dangerous if you fear it. If there is no fear, though, the darkness is not dangerous. It is actually comfortable, dazzling, intimate and beautiful. It will keep you on your toes and give you a sense of adventure! Darkness does not have to be an evil thing. Darkness does not have to be a frightening nightmare. It is a misconception on humanity's part that darkness is harmful and should be avoided at all costs. This is not the case. The darkness is made of love just as much as the light is. The darkness could be thought of as the raw material used for creating.

Yes, you have learned the darkness is dangerous if it is misunderstood, but if approached in the correct fashion, the darkness is your friend, not your enemy. Everything you have experienced with the fearful darkness up to this point is not a mistake you made. You have purposely explored it in this way in order to understand it completely.

In order to transmute the shadow self, the first step is to *love* the shadow self and *accept* the shadow self. It has served you greatly, and will continue to do so as long as you are on a plane of duality. The shadow self is as beautiful, powerful and precious as the light self. Eventually you will bring the light self and the dark self together. A different reality will emerge for you and then later for the entire world around you. It will not be *ruled* by polarities, although the polarities will still be used in a different fashion. There *are* existing realities which are made of duality and are quite harmonized. Just because a world exists in duality does not mean it cannot be harmonized.

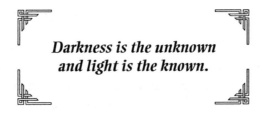

**Darkness is the unknown
and light is the known.**

As we have said, the light is the known. These are things already created and understood. The darkness is the unknown. These are the things not created or developed yet. This is a way you could look at the darkness from now on instead of seeing it as something dangerous, something to be avoided or feared.

We can see you in your light forms. You may think you are dark and unenlightened, but you aren't. You have been in disguise not only to others, but also to yourself! You have *fooled* yourself! You have simply come here to transmute energies in order to learn, have an adventure, and raise the mass consciousness of humanity.

In your present lifetime, some of you have taken on more than your fair share of negative karma to transmute. Think of this as your gift to the world, for that is what it truly is. Think of this process you are about to go through, are in the midst of, or are just ending, as your gift to others and not a curse on yourself. Also realize that this is your gift to God. You have volunteered to let yourself be hurt in order to make the hurting stop for everyone.

What is happening on the Earth plane is a *very* important event in the universe. Never has spirit been able to immerse itself quite so deeply into physical reality, or live consciously in the physical realms in exactly this way. This was a stretch for divine consciousness. Earth can be thought of as one of the first prototypes that has worked—-once it works, that is! At the time the shifts are completed on the Earth plane, at the time you have anchored your soul fully on Earth, and not just brief glimpses of it, God will be living in physical reality in His conscious thinking mind, in a way He has never done, and better yet—-in a freewill zone! It will no longer be an unconscious dreaming state within the illusion to Him, as it has been up until now.

There are realities in non-freewill zones where conscious entities are present on the physical levels. However, their powers are somewhat limited for they do not have the knowledge about misuse of power and freewill that humanity does. The universe is very curious to know what will be possible on these planes of reality once the soul is housed in it's entirety in a physical body, in a physical reality, in a freewill zone.

Once there is full consciousness on the Earth plane, and the other planes like it, spirit will not just be here in the light without choice in freewill, nor will it be in the darkness, lost in the misuse of freewill. It will be here in it's pure and unadulterated state. Many new avenues and directions will spring forth. Spirit will have the full ability to choose freely what it would like to explore and create. It will possess knowledge about how to use power in a benevolent and loving fashion which is normally reserved for God.

God Himself is learning about freewill. We would like to inform you that *God is a student.* He is watching, studying and learning as this process takes place. We will have more to say about God's learning and psychology at a later point in this book. There is much to say. We do not want to address this in the introduction, but we would like to hint to you that there are many things misunderstood about God and His power, His understanding, His emotional life, and His knowing.

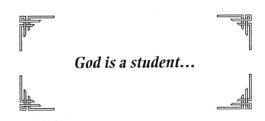

God is a student...

Yes. God is very grand. Yes. God is far beyond comprehension. However, all beings are in the image of God, and reflect different facets of God. If all these beings are in the image of God, then there are parts of God which are evolving. As these parts are evolving, they are also already evolved, just as you are already enlightened, for time is simultaneous and not linear.

The unfinished product is always in existence with it's finished version at all times. They are superimposed upon each other. The beginning is the end and the end is really the beginning, for time works more like a circle than a line. It moves outward from itself and then folds in upon itself. The universe is a paradox. God is perfect, yes, but at the same time, He is evolving toward perfection. We will continue this in a later chapter. This is something to think about.

In this introduction we would like to state that many of the things said here may challenge your belief systems. Many of the things said in this book may not ring true for you. You may say, "No! I do not believe this. No! The guides are wrong."

We invite you to honor your own systems. Honor what your intuition feels. Honor what your heart says is true and what is not true. We are not attached to what you believe or think about what we have to say. We honor all choices that you make. We are not here to overpower you or abuse your freewill. This is one of the major issues we would like to address. Misuse of freewill is really the main problem on your plane of reality!

We come from one school of thought, others come from another school of thought, and yet others come from another school of thought. All schools of thought are valid. All schools of thought have a basis. Perhaps some schools of thought are not ones you subscribe to! This is fine. This is alright. You must use your greatest abilities of discernment in this age of many messages and information.

Honor your intuition and only follow that which rings true for you.

You will benefit greatly from looking at your life in an objective fashion. This includes all the other people in your life and the world. We know this is difficult.

The pattern of judgment has been on the Earth plane in human consciousness for centuries upon centuries upon centuries. These patterns (which could also be called illusions) have been deeply ingrained in the human memory. The challenge is to re-route negative thought processes to positive thought processes.

If you manage to transmute a pattern (redirect a normal pathway of thought) in human consciousness, this is an incredible feat indeed. If you manage to do this in one lifetime, it is an amazing accomplishment and you should be proud of this! If you manage to transmute one of your patterns in only five years, you have accomplished this at light speed!

Compared to the thousands and thousands of years you have lived under these patterns and thought in these patterns, you are moving ever so quickly. We ask you to refrain from being impatient with yourself as you work with illusions. You are moving as fast as you can possibly go in physical reality!

Growth is not always visible to yourself or to others. You may think, "Oh! I am working so hard, but I don't seem to be changing." Be assured that you are and know your soul is doing much work on the inner planes. It is invisible to you for the most part. This goes for your view of others as well.

You may find that your dreams are very intense, or you may find you cannot remember your dreams at all, even though you used to remember them easily before. Allow whatever happens to happen. Surrendering is part of the process. If you are processing deep trauma, it may be possible that you are not able to process it all consciously. You will be doing a lot of your transmutation during your sleep. The results will be evident later. In time you may find yourself saying, "Oh! I don't know how I got here, but I am so glad I am!"

We would like to ask all of you who are going through this process of transmuting the darkness into light to do a favor for those behind you. It would be beneficial if you were to keep records of what you are going through and how you are working it out. Often, when people reach enlightenment, they do not remember in detail how they got there. If they do, they do not care to go back, relive it and write it out for those behind them. This is because they do not wish to enter their unhappiness again now that they have finally freed themselves from it. This is understandable. So keep the records as you go so you can look back and see how it all played out for you. Besides, your journey might be interesting enough to be made public later. Do not write it for this purpose though.

Not only will keeping a journal be a wonderful exercise for yourself as you go through your process, but it will be a wonderful gift you can leave for humanity. By keeping a record of the path you are taking you set up signposts for the others behind you who are looking for enlightenment. They might not be sure that their process is correct or that it leads to enlightenment unless somewhere they saw that someone else did this and it worked for them. This will give them more confidence in their own journey.

> ***You have taken***
> ***[a difficult path]***
> ***in order to help humanity***
> ***in it's efforts to ascend.***

For as many of you who are transmuting darkness, there are as many beside you who are similar to yourself and have similar styles and ways of dealing with things. Some will transmute things in one way and others will transmute in quite a different way. *Your* ways may match for them.

All the signposts you leave will be valuable. Those behind you will appreciate that they are there. Remember, transmutation into the light is not something you are just doing for yourself. You have taken this on in order to help humanity in it's efforts to ascend. You will most likely never be aware of all the people you will affect if you do this. You may remain unconscious all your life of the people who were encouraged by your transmutation process and the signposts you left behind.

Many of you have come in to help your parents, your grandparents, your sisters, your brothers, your friends or your lovers. You may never even have to say a word to them. But you will find that they become interested in transmuting their darkness quite unexpectedly. You will find that suddenly they are on the path too and they do not know what prompted them to do this. You may also be surprised to find that they are further along with their progress than you thought.

Their sudden interest in healing themselves has a lot to do with your transformation. They have been waiting for *you* to begin the process! *You* may have come in with the torch, so to speak. As you light your torch, the others in your family will follow because they are connected to you at a cellular level. This is a contract some of you made with them before you came here.

So! Please leave signposts for those behind you as you pass through your crossroads and you figure out the labyrinth the path to enlightenment is. It truly is a labyrinth at this point. Eventually, enlightenment will not be something achieved. It will simply be something you are born with and never lose. Enlightenment has been put at the center of the labyrinth by forces outside of yourself. Of course, this was chosen.

This is our letter of love to you. We have much experience on the Earth plane with traumatic and dark experiences. We have deep compassion for you. We have cried the same tears. We have learned the same things. We have transmuted the same energies you will. We understand what you are going through.

Reclaiming the Shadow Self

As you read this book, we are with you. We *feel* you when you touch us and read our words. We *feel* you in our energy fields when you reach for us. We are quite aware of each and every one of you. If you touch with us on the inner planes, we will be there to help you individually. We are here to help the traumatized, the ones who have become "stuck" in the darkness, so to speak (although "stuck" does not exist).

We will help you——if you ask. Do not forget to ask. There are *millions* of guides who have been drawn here, are available, and wish to help you. We are not the only ones. The supply of helpers is higher than the present demand. They would be grateful if you would give them something to do by asking for their help! They cannot do anything unless the door is opened by *you*.

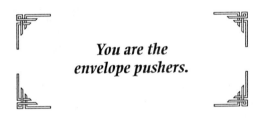

You are the envelope pushers.

We ask you to concentrate on yourself at this time. Perhaps you need to simplify your life. Perhaps you need to stop helping others. It may seem selfish, but it is not. It is coming from a deep place of compassion in your heart that you would help all these other people by helping yourself first. By making yourself whole, you will become a most efficient vehicle for light and love. At this time, if you try to help someone else, you may not be as efficient as you would be if you helped them *after* you have done your transmutation.

You are the ones who are the envelope pushers. An envelope, in technical terms, can be thought of as the limits, the parameters of experience, the ceiling, the floor, and the walls in which you are supposed to stay. You are the adventurers. You like to push the limits. This is a *good* thing and not a bad thing. However, your parents would probably beg to differ and felt that your pushing of the limits was quite annoying! Perhaps the people whom you associate with, even to this day, may find your envelope pushing annoying as well!

You will find that you unconsciously call others on their "baggage", might we say. It does not necessarily win you friends when you reflect to them what their faults are. However, this is bound to happen in a world of mirrors such as this one. You may find yourself to be the brunt of another's hatred or anger. You are the ones who *like* to challenge others and yourselves. Great care must be taken when doing this, though. Diplomacy and tact are good qualities to develop.

Perhaps you have reached a point where no guru or teacher has appeared for you in a specific form. Perhaps you have dabbled in this and dabbled in that, but you are finding that the guru idea is going out of style and the guru is no longer necessary.

This is truly what is happening. This is the time when each individual is to become his or her own guru. Besides, there are so many people awakening there simply are not enough gurus to go around!

***...there simply are
not enough gurus
to go around!***

So *you* are your own guru. You *know* how to do this! You have been gurus before, each and every one of you. All of you who are drawn to this book have already ascended the Earth plane at least one time, if not more. Since you have ascended already, you can use this information to realize you already know how to ascend the Earth plane. You have already created an ascended body which is waiting for you to remember it. You already *know* how to transmute the darkness in your consciousness. You *know* how to heal. You *know* how to find enlightenment. You are already enlightened unconsciously, and you simply must remember what it is like to be enlightened.

The human consciousness has some very traumatized areas in it. The reason the human consciousness on a mass level cannot ascend completely, and why it cannot go any further without self destruction, is because it still has unresolved issues with the traumatic events that have happened in history. Every soul has experienced much terror, horror, and abuse on this plane. It is quite a feat to calm the human spirit again after all the traumatization.

To make the human spirit feel peaceful and safe again is *your* job. You are here to process and transmute "survival of the fittest" attitudes, traumatization, terror, sadness, despair, anger, lack of self worth, loss of hope—all of these are things you have come to transmute. There is no passing "go" for humanity until this process is complete. Over the next one and a half decades, you will see much evidence of the traumatic syndrome in the human consciousness. The world will thrash in it's death and birth process.

You may see yourself doing this in your own process on a smaller scale. In this process, you *will* be dying and being born at the same time. This is what you might think of as the "born again" concept which is mentioned in the Bible. This is your entrance into phase two of your lifetime. This is where you adopt the Christ Consciousness which exists, and always existed, within yourself. Phase one can be thought of as the old story, the old self, and phase two can be thought of as the new self, the empowered self, the enlightened self, the self that is not controlled by what happens around him or her. This is the self that has complete mastery on this plane.

Your shadow self is the shadow self of the mass consciousness. You are a reflection of where the mass consciousness is at. As you transmute your shadow self and reclaim the power that was lost, you transmute the shadow self of the mass consciousness as well.

It may seem to you, "Oh! I am only one person. Transmuting my own self would be nice for me, but I don't see how it really could have that much effect."

First of all, we would like to say that the power of one is *immense!*

If you knew how many people you touch in your life, you would be completely amazed at how far reaching the ripples are which come from yourself. For instance, you may find yourself helping one person to become whole. Then that person might pass on the wisdom you spoke to him or her, or pass on the energy you gave. This one you helped might help three or four more people to become whole. Then those people may find themselves passing on words you said to the one you originally helped, or giving someone a place to stay as they grow, like you might have done for the original one you helped. Then the others pass it on yet once again. Very shortly, the energy you have given has spread as far as other continents.

You cannot even *begin* to imagine the ripples that emanate from yourself. As we have said, it is most likely you will never be conscious of all the souls you have effected. So be assured that as you transmute yourself, you are effecting many.

If there are four hundred of you who manage to transmute something very hard to transmute, it effects *many* more than yourselves. This not only happens on the physical plane, but also on the inner planes. If there are a thousand of you who transmute brutality, atrocities, terror, fear, sadness or despair, you have effected the world in a *very* large way. If there are five hundred thousand of you who transmute your despair and sadness, suicidal thoughts, and self hatred—-*imagine how much you have changed the world then...*

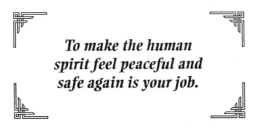

To make the human spirit feel peaceful and safe again is your job.

Most of you have completely evolved spiritual bodies. You may also find that you are very intelligent people and you have evolved mental bodies. Most likely the problem for you is your emotional body seems to be underdeveloped. This may or may not have effected your physical body. Physical manifestation of emotional fragmentation is often present in ones who have had experiences like yours. As you work with the emotional body, release trauma, and bring the emotional self back into focus, you will find that all your cards, or all your ducks, are already lined up in a row and are waiting for you to access them. You will find that your other bodies do not really need much work.

You have allowed yourself to be scattered at the core of your being but the rest of your energy is perfectly intact. As soon as you straighten out the scattered energy in your core, you will find you are a complete and whole human being and there isn't any other work on your energetic systems to do. As soon as you straighten out the core, everything else will fall into place on it's own.

Those who have their core intact may find they are working more on their mental, spiritual or physical bodies for those are the fields which need to evolve in themselves. This is not a rule. This is simply a stereotype, and as you know, there are always exceptions to stereotypes.

What we would like you to realize is that you have more benefits in your energy field than you know. You have more completion in yourself than you think. The holes, the tears or the fragmentation that happened in your energy field is because your core has been "damaged". So do not think, "Oh! As soon as I get straightened out at my core, I still have all this other work and catching up to do!" This is simply not true.

You may be finding that you are remembering traumatic lifetimes. You may be remembering past lives in which you have been tortured, brutalized, mutilated or murdered. Some of your lives will reflect back to you that you were hurt in some other way, or succumbed to a mind game which negatively affected you, or your heart was broken.

At this time, you are not only transmuting this lifetime, but you are also transmuting all your past lifetimes which are related to what you are working on in this one. It works both ways. As you transmute the experiences which effected you in your past lifetimes you are transmuting what happened in your present life. You may be transmuting some future ones too, which you would have experienced had you not transmuted certain energies in this lifetime.

This is not necessarily your *karma*. Karma is something we will address later, for it is a little bit misconstrued and has negative connotations. It can be seen in a different light. We hint to you that you may have come in to serve some karma not only for yourself, but also for your soul group.

You Are Royalty

Reclaiming the Shadow Self

Realize that you and your soul group are very connected. Your soul group will be working with you on your endeavors in the near future. Your soul group has been supporting you and has been learning through you. This is the final run-through in this reality as far as this type of energy is concerned. Everyone is "sealing" the lessons forever into consciousness so they will never forget what they have learned about the misuse of power and freewill. For some of you, your soul group is living vicariously through you.

Many of you are tired of this place and can't wait to be done with all of this. We understand these feelings. However, we would like to tell you that after you are done with the part which hurts your heart, you will be glad you are here. You will not be so anxious to leave, for your life will be sweet, your life will be rich and your life will be magical. In fact, you may change your mind and decide to come back for more lives in the future. This will no longer be a severe reality to live in. It will be much different, and it is beyond your wildest imaginings at this point!

Many of you have become frustrated with your lives and the lack of progress on your spiritual path. Perhaps you are one who has worked on everything you can find in yourself. You have read every self help book that applies to you. You have worked on your patterns, healed all the memories you know of and did everything you can figure out to do, and *still* you find yourself going around in the same old circles in your life. Some of you have been on the spiritual path for a very long time now. Even though there have been noticeable improvements, you are frustrated and unable to understand why you are *still* not in the light you are striving toward, or why you are *still* unhappy in many ways.

This may have to do with the fact that you have yet to discover some unconscious memories which are still effecting you deeply at the core of your being. The mind has a way of protecting the self. It buries deep in the subconscious the memories that were impossible to understand and process at the time they happened, especially if the events that traumatized you happened at a young age. You simply were not equipped to deal with these events at the time.

Now you are equipped and it is safe to unlock these hidden drawers in your mind. If the traumatic or confusing event you buried in your memory happened during your adult life, this still applies to you. It is safe now to deal with it.

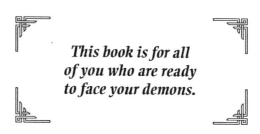

This book is for all of you who are ready to face your demons.

Many of you have been entertaining the thought of dropping everything you are currently doing in your life, for you are beginning to feel as if you are going nowhere. Many of you want to concentrate fully on attaining enlightenment. Many of you are thinking of selling everything you own, putting your careers or goals on the back burner, leaving your current relationship, and going the way of the spiritual aspirant. You may have tried several avenues and have found only dead ends when you endeavored to create a desire or direction. Many of you are thinking about traveling and "finding yourself".

If this is happening for you, it would be beneficial for you to heed this call, even though there appear to be many obstacles in your way like lack of money, objections from relatives and friends, or lack of certainty that it is the right thing. We highly encourage you to follow your heart, even if it does not make sense in society's view. This call you are hearing is a deep call from your soul to come closer.

We highly suggest you do this if you are being called to "find yourself" *and not stop until you do!* The rewards will be great, although evidence of abundance in your life may seem scanty for a while. If you concentrate 100% of your focus, intent and energy on your spiritual path, you will accelerate your healing process immensely. It will not take very long if your intent is focused in such a way and not dispersed over several other things which fragment your attention. If you do this, you will find the parts of yourself which have been missing all your life much sooner. Then you will be more efficient in your life and the endeavors you undertake, for you will reclaim the power you have lost in the shadow self.

This book is for all of you who are ready to face your demons. This book is for all of you who are willing to face your deepest fears. This book is for any of you who have decided to put aside everything in your life until you have attained and remembered your enlightenment.

This is a good thing for you to do, for it will change your future for the better when you return to your "life". You will find it much easier to accomplish your goals, for you will be functioning with your sails full of wind and your foundations will be rebuilt and sturdy. We encourage anyone who wishes to do this to *go for it!* Your life will be easier and richer on the other side of your transformation.

Go for it...

Chapter 1

Creativity

We would like to begin our first chapter by addressing the subject of creativity. As we have said in our earlier words, darkness is the place where creativity lives and unknown ideas are born. You are very creative people! Many of you are in the arts. There are various types of creative endeavors besides the arts and some of you are involved in those.

Most of you know how creative you are, and it gives you pain to know your creativity is not being realized. If your creativity is not flourishing, you are blocked and you know this. We would like to assure you that the full expression of your creativity will be realized after you transform what needs to be transformed in yourself.

Your creativity will bring you abundance, yes indeed! Do not worry about this anymore! Do not fill your mind with fear about whether or not you will ever be able to paint for a living, or if you will ever be a musician, or if you will ever be able to write, or whatever your creative ideas are.

Some of you want to build houses which are strange and different, or roads that are more efficient. Some of you want to work with animals, create artistic food, or help children. Some of you want to aid people in legal matters. Whatever it is you are drawn to, it is creative. We assure you that your creativity will be realized. Please do not spend your energy on wondering about this anymore. Right now, concentrate fully on your healing.

You do not even know the incredible forms your creativity will take. There are ways to be creative which do not exist on this plane yet. This is why some of you do not know your life goals and purposes. They have yet to be invented. You will be the ones who do this.

At present, we advise you not to try to understand how, visualize how, or focus on how your creative endeavors will take place. You will take part in creating these new art forms once your transformation is complete. Your transformation is the most important thing to work on right now. The universe will bring these visions to you as you heal and when the time is right.

Be confident in the abilities that surface for you and know they are there even though you are not aware of them right now. Those of you who have touched the darkness deeply have the ability to go into the darkness because of your bravery. You can pull out creative ideas which cannot be accessed by a person who is not familiar with darkness the way you are.

So! Since you are a creative person, get creative about your healing. If you are a dancer, dance your emotions out. If music heals you, use your music to heal you. If you are a painter, use your art to heal you. Play your emotions out, paint your emotions out. Play your anger, paint your anger. Play your sadness, paint your sadness. And later you will play and paint your joy. This you can be sure of. In the meantime, use your creativity as the tool and the talent that it is. Be creative with the raising of your consciousness.

**Be creative
with the raising of
your consciousness.**

Every person has creativity. We are sure you have heard this before. Every person has resources which remain untapped. It is not recognized yet in society that everything a person does is creative. Even being alive is a creative act. The way you live your life is *the* most creative act. Another person would perform an entirely different play if he or she were given the same roles, opportunities, and obstacles that you have. Your life is a unique expression of yourself and this is your most brilliant creativity at it's best.

Your emotions have much to do with your creativity. We advise you to follow your emotions in their full expression, and see where they lead you. An emotion, especially if it is a negative one, is often abandoned long before it reaches the levels where you would pass through it entirely and realize it's full potential in what it was doing to serve you.

See where the emotion leads. Go all the way to the end. Do not become frightened and stop.

Perhaps you are crying and you say, "Oh! I must smoke a cigarette, so I don't feel this anymore," or, "I must distract myself from this! I think I will turn on the TV!" or, "Oh! I think I'll eat that ice-cream in the freezer, because I don't want to feel this emotion anymore!" Instead, we advise that you follow the emotion fully.

We would like to issue a note of caution along with this; know your limits on what you can take and what you cannot take. You do not want to push yourself over the edge. This is not the goal. You do not want to overwhelm yourself so much that you find yourself taking steps backward or undoing the healing you have already done. If you can follow the emotion just a little bit further than you usually do when it comes up, this is good enough. The next time it comes up, follow it even further. Take it in steps.

Since you are the ones who like to push the envelope, you often push yourself to the point of exhaustion. We advise you to ask for help when you are doing this so you will be made aware by your guides when things are getting too overwhelming for you and you must stop. Taking breaks from your healing process is not out of order. Sometimes the horror or the confusion you feel will fold in on you and devour you. When you think this is beginning to happen, put it all away and fill your mind with pleasant things.

Reclaiming the Shadow Self

Don't focus constantly on the horror you have experienced. Break it up with times where you think about pleasant things like clouds, blue skies, butterflies and grapevines. Pamper yourself and take care of yourself. Play with children. Go to a party. Take yourself outside and lay in the grass. Learn how to switch your focus at will. Fill your mind with loveliness and pretty things. You deserve to have happiness in your mind. Relax your heart now and then so you do not get overwhelmed.

*There are new artforms
that have yet
to be invented.*

When you create, produce products of your creativity for yourself. Do not create things according to what you think others would like. This is for you! Do not be shy or bashful about what may come out, for it may surprise you. Do not judge what comes out of your system, for it may even frighten you. Allow yourself freedom, knowing that this is only a temporary moment in your progress. This is not a direction you are going which you can never return from. It is not the path of insanity, although it may look like that to yourself and others.

Creativity is an expression of love. Love has many disguises and forms. Love can be expressed in ways that are not recognized as love. For instance, perhaps the universe has provided you with frightening or despairing experiences. This was done as an act of love for you, for you wanted to explore these things and you wanted to understand these things on your own, since you have freewill. You also wanted to be of service concerning these things.

Love yourself in whatever way it needs to be done in that particular moment. If you need to express anger or you need to throw rocks, do this with love for yourself. Be a calm and loving parent to yourself as you would be for a small child who needs to throw a temper tantrum. Be the patient parent to yourself who simply stands by and makes sure you don't hurt yourself as you express your emotions. Love yourself as you creatively ex-press the emotions which have been de-pressed for so long. Love yourself as you heal yourself.

As we have already said, you cannot express your fullest potential in your creativity until you have healed phase one of your life. Phase two of your life will be the time in which your creativity will blossom, flourish and grow. Phase two is the place where your creativity will be visible not only to yourself, but also to others around you.

Many of you are actually world leaders, world teachers, and world healers. Your creativity is the vehicle you will use to work with masses of people. People (souls) respond eagerly to creativity, especially when it is expressed in it's fullest loving form. Everyone is curious about something they have never seen before. Everyone is curious about the unknown. People who tell themselves they are not curious about the unknown are lying to themselves. It is the nature of the human self. It is the nature of the soul. It is the nature of God.

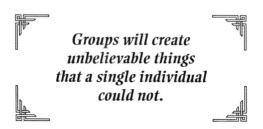

Groups will create unbelievable things that a single individual could not.

Creativity does not only come forth from yourself. Often, creative ideas blossom in groups. There will be new creative efforts, ideas and practices which can only be realized in groups. Groups that know how to blend their energies, groups that know how to manifest what their combined energies have produced, will create unbelievable things that a single individual could not. It is about blending of energies.

Reclaiming the Shadow Self

We would like to give this to you as a faint and ever so vague glimpse into the future of creative ideas and art forms. Many of you will be involved in these art forms. Many of you will bring these new art forms onto the physical plane, for you have the ability to go deep into the darkness without fear once you have transmuted your ideas about fear and darkness.

You will find that most of the creative ideas and mediums which come forth will be used primarily for healing. However, after the transformation of the planet, these art forms will be there for a different reason. They will be there for further expression and exploration of consciousness. Healing will not be necessary anymore since the healing will already be done! Once the healing is done consciousness can go into any area it wishes without fear. We will drop you another hint. Humanity is destined to heal other entire worlds and species. The arts will be used in this.

This is not to say there will not be more lessons for humanity concerning fear. There *will* be more lessons about fear. These lessons will continue far into the future, but they will not be of the same vibration as the lessons of fear on the planet at this time.

Creativity

Affirmations

1. I am a creative person!
2. I use the darkness wisely. I use it to retrieve creative ideas.
3. I am creative about my healing.
4. My emotions lead me to deeper resources within myself.
5. I am an inventor of new art forms.
6. I like to push the creative envelope.
7. I am open to receive information about new artforms.
8. The universe gives me many opportunities to be creative.
9. I know how to blend my energies with others in a creative way.
10. My creative ideas are being born into physical reality as I heal, even though I am unconscious of them right now.

Exercises

1

Think about the aspects of your healing and transformation. List the ways in which you have been creative and resourceful about it up to this point. List other ways you can do this which have not been utilized yet. List resources you would like to be made available, but are not. Then ask the universe to make these tangible for you.

2

Imagine yourself going into the darkness willingly. Imagine that it is the dazzling darkness where you are warm, comfortable and supported. Hover in the darkness and sense all the movement underneath it. Notice where there are pockets of energy. Notice there is much happening in them which you simply cannot see yet. This is the raw material of the universe you are touching.

Reach into a pocket of energy and take hold of it with your hands. Wait until there is a "click" in your energy, and then bring it back with you into the light. It is alright if you do not recognize consciously what you have acquired. It will come to you when the time is right for you to receive it's full impact. Over the next few days, ask the ideas to come to you consciously. Right now, you are simply creating the birth of an idea into the "known". If any glimpses of these art forms come to your conscious mind, file them in your head, write them down or draw them. Leave the door open for more insights, for you will receive many more details as time goes on. The vision will mutate, become more detailed, and change many times.

3

Imagine yourself in the future as the great artist you are. Imagine you have already remembered the skills you have forgotten. Imagine you have already brought new art forms (or new versions of established art forms) into the Earth reality. Imagine that you have already been successful in your work for a long time.

Look at yourself and see what you can find which is different. What is your personality like? What are your surroundings? What kind of people are around you? What kind of equipment is there? What does the energy feel like? These are the things you should work on surrounding yourself with right now so you can resonate with the goal you are seeking.

Reclaiming the Shadow Self

Chapter 2

Parents And Other Influencing Adults

We would like to address your parents' role in your life. We will speak about the circumstances you were born into, and the things which shaped your psychology as a child.

First of all, you chose your parents! Most of you know this, although you might regret your choices at this point. We understand this. We would like to say that there is no reason to regret what you have chosen, for you will be rewarded for the pain and the anguish you have gone through. You will be able to feel more in the realms of light than you would have been able to if you did not go to the depths you have gone.

Your parents are your friends even if they seem to some of you to be your worst enemies. The person you hate the most is one who loves you very dearly at the soul level *and was willing to come and play such a horrible role for you.* We realize that some of you do not have a problem with your parents. It may be a stranger, or another member of your family. It may be an uncle, it may be a friend who has damaged you, or it may be someone who you hardly know who has influenced you to be upset, confused, or extinguished your light.

Even the stranger who has hurt you is your friend. You have chosen this and worked this play out with the stranger before you were born. At the soul levels, this stranger is actually not a stranger at all to you. You know this soul very well. The people who have played the "bad guy" roles in your life are there at your request. You auditioned them, as they have also auditioned you. You asked them to play these roles so you could take on the pattern which fits the imprint you chose to work with. They asked *you* to play roles for them in order to meet their own inner challenges.

Most of you are reliving your parents' old patterns. You will find that your grandparents held the same patterns and passed them down to your parents. You will find that if you had harsh parents, your parents made a better life for you than they themselves had with their parents. Your parents transmuted these patterns somewhat. Now you are transmuting the rest of the program. If you have children and passed the pattern on to them, you will find that they will transmute what *you* have not been able to transmute.

If you have a child who has taken on your patterns, use this opportunity to work together with your child in order to transmute what you both share. It may be something you have to start with on the energy planes because it may have manifested into a turbulent situation in your everyday life. Even though the play may go on, you can be an observer and watch yourself and your child. You will see the pattern clearly.

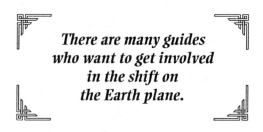

There are many guides who want to get involved in the shift on the Earth plane.

If your parents or any other adults have abused you, we ask you to stop hating them for this is not serving you in your healing. *If you are angry with them, it is alright to express your feelings in constructive ways.* We will say more about constructive expression of negative emotions in later chapters. However, refrain from expressing in destructive ways. Do *not* continue to war with your parents. You will not heal until you at least call a truce and say to your parents, "I do not hate you anymore. Yes I am angry with you, but eventually I hope we can be friends again. Look, we have hated each other for so long and it is not working. I would like to rebuild the relationship if you would like to do so too." This is a beginning. If you can, it would be a good idea to bridge the gap between you and your parents. Make the offer only if you are ready to, and then the choice is theirs.

Most often your parents will say "yes" to you for their souls yearn for fellowship with yours. If they say "no", then you must respect this. However, you can still work on your side of the bridge. As you build your bridge and heal yourself, you will find that the parent who does not want to speak to you anymore may have a change of heart without you ever having said a word. All souls desire peace with others.

It may be a while before you can be in touch with your family. Separation may be the healthiest thing you can do for yourself right now, especially if there is mental, verbal, emotional, or physical violence between you and your family members. Take care of yourself and remove hurtful people from your immediate sphere of reality.

You cannot heal if you are in an abusive environment. You need peace. You need psychic and physical safety. You need a place where you can let down your defenses and be vulnerable. If you are around people who hurt you, or you continue to stay in touch with them, it would be silly to let down your guard and you know this.

For some of you, the trouble did not start until you were a teenager. Perhaps you are one who ran away from home a few times. Some of you met with even more disaster away from home than you experienced at home.

If you are a runaway from home right now, or thinking about it, yours is a complicated matter. If there is great hatred between you and the other, you most definitely need space. There are many things you can do if you are unable to be in the same room with your family members without coming to violence of some sort (physical, verbal or other kinds).

Search for other things you can do besides subjecting yourself to the dangers of being on the streets alone as a teenager. You may have other relatives who would be willing to take you in for a while, or friends whose family would like to have you stay with them. If your home life is seriously abusive, you might even want to think about going to the authorities and asking to be put in a foster home. Of course, this would only be a last resort solution (and only appropriate) in situations where you actually need to protect your life.

If your family does not want to let you stay with someone else besides themselves, you may have to insist by telling them you will report them if they do not allow you to go to a place where you feel safety and peace.

If you cannot escape the abusive environment of your home, you can ask the guiding ones to help you. It will give them something to do and will give them a chance to get involved on the Earth plane. There are many guides wanting to get involved in the shift on the Earth plane but cannot until you ask for their participation in your life. They will calm down the energy in your household and the intensity of the anger between you and your family will settle a little.

If you are not able to leave your family, you will benefit from spending more time alone. It is alright to withdraw from them for a while and get quiet around them. It would be better than doing further damage to each other. Spend time going for walks alone, writing in your journal, being creative, or meditating. Learn how to entertain yourself. This is a skill.

Your withdrawal from the play you are all acting out will have positive effects. Your family will suddenly be curious about what you are doing, and wonder why you are not playing the same roles you were playing before. They will wonder what happened and why you are no longer allowing them to upset you.

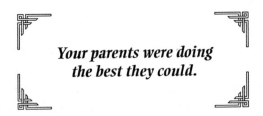

Your parents were doing the best they could.

Your parents were doing the best they could. They did not know better at the time. There were not as many resources on how to be a good parent as there are now. Many of you find yourselves trying to be a better parent than they were. You have read all the self help books on how to be a good parent, or how to handle a child which is acting out.

You must realize that your parents did not have these opportunities. They did not have these books. They did not have these counselors. They did not have the knowledge or the tools you now have. And furthermore, they did not have use of the energies which are now available on the Earth plane. They did not have as many resources as you do.

We would like you to take into account that your parents did well with the fact that they had no hammers and they had no nails. They had no precise tools for handling the unruly child, the unusual child, the talented child, or the spirited child. No one really knew much about child psychology before this age. The tools they had were not nearly as gentle as the ones available to the world now. The only tools they had were those their own parents passed down to them, which may have been sledge-hammers.

So have mercy on your parents for what you might consider "poor parenting". If you have been abused by them in any way, whether it be sexually, verbally, physical violence, or any other form, do not hold this against them. (We will address the sexual issues later, for this is a very large subject.)

The fact that abuse took place does not mean your parents are un-redeemable. They are hurting inside just like yourself, although they may be too proud to admit it or have learned how to fake a good life. We ask you to have compassion for these ones who have participated in your play and gave you the patterns you chose to transmute. You needed *someone* to set your stage and furnish your foundations. This is what they did for you.

Now you may wonder, "Where were my guides when all of this was happening? And where was God when I was crying, when I was hurt? Where was my protection?"

We assure you that God and your guides were there. They *did* protect you from anything you did not choose to experience. They held a sacred space as your early childhood circumstances were played out and the stage was set. They also knew they would be here at this point later in your life to help you transmute the patterns you took on.

Think of the patterns your parents passed on to you as gridworks and intricate designs of light. In some places, these grids are missing pieces, have distortions in them, or are not flowing correctly. What you have come to do is replace these missing pieces in the patterns and repair that which has been damaged. This pattern exists in the mass consciousness of humanity. It is not just *your* pattern, and remember, it is not your soul who holds this pattern. It is a pattern your soul is wearing and cares about transmuting.

Now as you fix this pattern, repair it, transmute it, give it new life, and add your own touches, you will find that others with the same pattern are boosted in their own processing of similar patterns. This is why you will see your family being affected as you begin to find the light. They will follow suit because you are very connected to each other. You have similar patterns. Since they are so close to you not only in physical structure, but also in spirit, they catch these changes as they pass on and becomes part of the gestalt intelligence which is humanity.

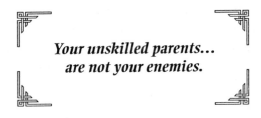

Your unskilled parents...
are not your enemies.

Try to connect with your parents at their higher self level. Connect with them in their evolved state, for their evolved state does exist superimposed over their unevolved state. You can speak with the "higher" versions of themselves. You can speak with their soul from your soul. You can accomplish much in this way. You will be able to grasp the idea of objectivity more easily if you leave the realm in which both of you have personality conflicts. Go to the place where there is no conflict, and there is only love between you. This is a place where you are both above all this, and you can look down on your lower selves. Perhaps you will even feel humor about what you are going through!

If one of these "offending" ones has passed away from the Earth plane already, you can still communicate with him or her in this way. He or she will hear you and work with you. In fact, it may be easier to work with past "enemies" if they are on the other side of death. They are more able to touch with their own soul at that point and find softness in their hearts. This is, of course, no reason to wish for someone's death!

Parents

Reclaiming the Shadow Self

We would like to advise you to use humor as much as you can even though you may not feel very humorous right now. Humor can alleviate pressure which inevitably builds as you release your darkness. You *will* encounter inner pressure when you tap into the shadow self. Expect it.

You have nothing to fear from your parents now. You are older, more powerful, and you have the ability at present to enforce the boundaries which were violated as a child. You are not a victim of your parents anymore, which perhaps at one time you were. This is a reason to be free of fear with your parents. If you find that you live a few hundred miles away from your parents, you live in California and they live in Wyoming, then it is irrational to continue to fear their presence.

If you fear them as if you are a child when you actually *are* in their physical presence, think of this: Would you not get in your car and leave if one of them hit you, or even *threatened* to hit you? What if they tell you they will not help you, maybe even disown you, if you pursue a career in the circus instead of being a lawyer? Would you not tell them that it is your own life and you will do with it what you want, with or without their help?

You see, they do not have power *over* you anymore. You must enforce your boundaries on what you will and will not accept from others in your life, including your family. They can still tyrannize you with your future, but only if you let them. Much of what your healing is *about* is learning how to enforce personal boundaries in your life. This has to do with self worth and self respect. This is what your parents failed to teach you as a child.

Keep in mind that if it is not a parent who has victimized you, and it is someone else, these words apply to them as well.

So we would like to encourage you to release your fear and anger at your parents if you still have this issue. If you want to discuss your anger with them, do so with the intent to find a solution, not to destroy or rip the relationship further.

Your unskilled parents, or other "bad guys" in your life, are not your enemies. They are your friends. We cannot stress this enough. Considering the fact that they are your friends, would you not want to help them heal, too, as you heal yourself? No matter how much a parent, or even a child who has turned against you, might want to prove to you they do *not* love you, we say to you that they *do*. Relax your mind. Simply know this is the truth underneath the surface reality of your life.

If you feel betrayed by your family, your parents, a sibling, *your own child*, or any others who have had influence over you in your lifetime, you must release blame on them for what you are going through. They were only vehicles for the patterns which fit the imprints you chose to work on. Switch your focus from the people who upset you to the pattern being played out. The pattern is what you really need to deal with. The pattern is what you are angry about.

Affirmations

1. I accept the faults of my parents with unconditional love.
2. I forgive my parents (or any other adult) for the abuse inflicted on me.
3. I accept willingly the patterns I have chosen to transmute.
4. I am clear underneath the negative traits I have taken on. My essence is untouched and pure.
5. I now remember the enlightenment I had as a child.
6. My parents were doing the best they could. My parents did everything they were supposed to do for me.
7. As I heal, others with similar patterns are healed.
8. I release the concept of blame on myself or others.
9. I now have the power to control my reality.
10. I am free of victim roles. I am free of perpetrator roles.

Exercises

1

Go back to an incident in your childhood when an adult abused you. Watch this incident from an objective perspective. Watch from the soul level. See if you can identify what lessons you and the adult are learning together.

Then step into the picture as your soul and stop the play. Hold the frightened child self that you were and calm it's spirit. Speak to the child and nurture it. Let it know there is a reason for all of this, and that it is protected from all it did not choose to experience in this lifetime. If it feared death or damage in that incident, assure it that you survived and you are alright.

Speak to the adult(s) in a loving way as you hold the child in your arms. Ask what the source of their disharmony is. Watch the adult's reaction to their own aggression. Perhaps you will find out that the cause of their aggression has nothing to do with you. Most likely, the adult will break down and realize his or her mistake.

Forgive your tormentor(s) and release them from their guilt by telling them you understand there is a higher purpose for the event and you are not holding them to blame. Place the child self back in the picture with a calm spirit. This will help you to reconnect the fragmented selves you have lost in your consciousness. These fragmented selves now have full confidence and understanding, and there is no more need for fear, for later they will understand and be healed.

This will create great shifting for you and the people in these scenarios on unconscious levels. Do this with every incident you can remember. You will clear much from your slate this way.

2

Go back to your childhood and search for the alternate realities which exist next to the one you "officially" experienced. There exist many versions of your childhood. See if you can find these other plays and retrieve the positive energies of each. Blend them into your present life.

If you find a version of your childhood which was worse than the one you experienced "officially", send love and healing energy to this version of yourself. If you find a version of your childhood which is better than the one you "officially" experienced, absorb the positive energies from it. This is the point in time where you can create a merger for all the realities, life paths, and self aspects which have remained unconscious up to this point.

3

Make a long list of all the people you have had a "falling out" with. Raise yourself and all others you have had a conflict with to the soul level. (This is an inward movement) Sit in a circle with these souls and join hands. Let yourselves feel the deep love between you at the soul level. All is water under the bridge now. Being angry with each other would be an absurd notion and wouldn't make sense now that all of you know you have been actors in a play.

Look back on your lives and see the immense lessons you have learned together. Look at the ingenious ways in which you have ad-libbed your parts.

Then take a break and go play with all these people on the soul planes in the fields. Let yourselves shine in your true soul essences. Laugh and smile with each other, pure and free of the conflict you experienced on the Earth plane. This is how it will be when you have all finished your incarnations.

But why wait until you die? You can achieve this now.

Chapter 3

Various Aspects
Of Your Process

We would like to mention some of the things you can expect and prepare for as you begin to transmute the deepest parts of the shadow self. There are some parameters you may want to set up before you truly delve into your trauma, your fear, your sadness or your self hatred.

When you first remember a devastating event which you have buried in your unconscious, it will seem as if it "happened yesterday". You will find yourself in the state of mind you were in immediately following the event when it happened. Your conscious mind is picking up where it left off. Now that you are able to deal with it, the conscious mind resumes the task of processing and understanding the event. Your emotional self resumes the task of healing and moving through the event. You have great power and energy tied up in your tragedy. *Your tragedy is your power.*

Once you get going with the purging of trauma, if unconscious memories come up and upset you, you may find that you are not able to function in society in a normal fashion. You may find yourself unable to work. We advise you to be aware that this can happen and encourage you not to let the lack of funds stop you from healing yourself.

We realize that many of you are broke and you are in survival level financially. We understand this. We would like to tell you that if your intent is true and honest, the universe will provide the place, the money, and give you the time you need for this endeavor. The universe has been waiting for you to move inward instead of focusing outward.

Perhaps, in the processing time, you may feel like you are *still* in survival level for you will have to deal with the survival issues. But be assured you will not be forgotten or abandoned. You are doing the hardest work on this plane. You have the utmost respect of the beings of light. They will make sure you are able to eat, have shelter and continue to live!

Always ask if you can exchange work or if there is some way you can have what you need for free. You will find there are compassionate souls who wish to help you and *who are also being guided to help you.* It does not hurt to ask. Do not beg. Do not plead. Simply ask. You may be surprised at the benevolence you will find in people. Do not be afraid to ask someone if they will accept your work instead of your money. Work exchange is coming into play on this plane much more than it has been lately. It is the first step for humanity in moving away from the idea of "money" as the only symbol of energy exchange for services rendered or objects obtained.

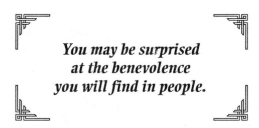

**You may be surprised
at the benevolence
you will find in people.**

There are many ways to live free in the world.

You may have relatives or friends who are sensitive to the fact that you are going through a deep process and may supply you with a place to live or work in a flexible format. Someone may give you a place to stay simply for work exchange.

There are spiritual centers and communities all over the world in which you can do work exchange and live for a minimal fee, or for free.

We would like to say that this is not a bad thing to consider, even if the agendas and religious practices they have do not particularly fit your own. You can still absorb the energies around you in a spiritual center and participate in their practices. These spiritual centers are a good place for you for they are places where you will *feel and be* safe while you go through the more dangerous and vulnerable areas in your consciousness.

If you do not set yourself up in a place of physical safety, your unconscious self will not unlock it's darkness. There will be part of you who will know, "I am not safe, so I cannot explore these areas at this time." We would like to stress safety in your environment. You must find a place where you can have safety, privacy and protection while you process your "stuff".

There is always camping. The Earth is free to live on in many places. Perhaps you would benefit from traveling to beautiful places which soothe your soul and sleep in your car at night. Spring time, summertime and fall are warm enough in most places where you can live in nature. Nature will help your healing process greatly. This is one of the ways you can handle the fact that you are in survival level and do not have enough money to pay for a place to live while you go through this deep processing. There are many ways.

Living in nature is very powerful. Nature will heal you simply because it is all around you. Mother Earth is a grand helper in the planetary drama you are involved in. The Earth is going through the same processes you are, except She is not unsure about how to do this. The Earth is much more adept at transmuting energies than you think.

If you are afraid of animals, we ask you to let this go. The animals will not harm you. Your heart is pure if you do not wish to harm them. They will know this. The animals will actually help you. Animals are transmuting fear as well. Your peacefulness will help them become less fearful of humans.

You will find that the plants will help you. You will find that the sky and the stars will help you. You will find that the dirt and the rocks will absorb your energies and transmute them for you. Trees are very sensitive and wise. Their roots reaching into the ground are good to sit over when you are feeling tears. There are many ways to achieve enlightenment. You do not need a lot of money to heal yourself.

Reclaiming the Shadow Self

Your soul has been starving for beauty and gentleness for a very long time. If you immerse yourself in nature, you will find you feel peace without even noticing it has crept into your consciousness. Nature is very alive. Nature is a *grand* entity which is there to help you. Nature will delight you. Do not be surprised if you see things of beauty and interest which you have never seen before. You will have new eyes.

Now if you are one of those who does not like to rough it, does not like to live outside because, well, there are mosquitoes or flies, there will be opportunities for you as well. We still advise you to immerse yourself in nature as much as possible. This will help you transmute these energies in more ways than you know.

Remember, if you do not have the money, ask the universe for it. Then follow your intuition. Do not let yourself fall into the pitfalls of feeling that you do not deserve it. You are precious and you have been through a lot. The universe does not wish to prolong it for you, so don't prolong it for yourself. Realize that you are worth saving and the universe will help you in whatever way you need.

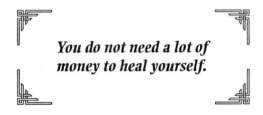

You do not need a lot of money to heal yourself.

You may find it beneficial to sell everything you own and simplify your life. Then you may find you have enough money to buy your food for a few months or even a year, depending on how much you have collected in your house! If you choose to live in nature, or find a place to live for free, food does not cost much extra.

Perhaps you are having trouble parting with your material things, or fear you will miss them. If you have plenty of money, then store them somewhere. If you are reluctant but you need the money, and you feel that selling your things would be wise, we can tell you this: you will not be the same person after your transformation and these items will most likely not fit your personality anymore. They are things you will probably end up selling or giving away anyway!

We advise you to lighten your load. If you are lacking money, this may solve your problem. You can turn your load into currency which you need for your healing process. It is a symbol to the universe, and to yourself, that you are removing old energy from your life and making room for the new. It would be a signal to the universe that you are serious about your path of healing. It would show that you are taking a leap of faith and trusting the universe. The act will not go unrecognized. It will be applauded. Besides, you will feel lighter immediately!

If you are afraid you are going to lose your job, you may want to quit gracefully before you are fired, which would only cause you further anguish and feelings of inferiority.

If you have loans which require monthly attention, we suggest you do not let this stop you from undertaking your healing either. Forbearances and deferments are available on most loans. Even if you have already used the available forbearances and deferments, you may be pleasantly surprised that the institution (or person) who has loaned you the money, will be kind enough to grant you another grace period (even if it is not their normal policy to do so) if you simply explain your situation to them.

Post Traumatic Stress Disorder (PTSD) is a medically recognized condition and this is exactly what you are going through if you are dealing with confusing, shattering, or fearful events from your past. Simply explain to the parties concerned that you fully intend to pay them back, but at this time you are needing a healing period for your dis-ease. A doctor's note would not hurt. There are many clinics you can go to for free if you cannot afford a doctor.

If the bank does *not* grant the extra time you have requested, perhaps you can re-arrange for smaller payments. Perhaps you can send them a token of $10 per month, even though your payments are $100 per month. This would show the credit bureau that you are at least *trying* to honor the loan.

If you cannot pay anything at all, and still cannot obtain a grace period, then do not be attached to having perfect credit! You can always repair it later. This may be a part of your lesson. Do not be addicted, even though you may *prefer* it, to having perfection in your finances in order to be happy. Do not become upset with yourself or your situation. This is a step toward not letting your life take *you* for an emotional roller coaster ride or letting outside circumstances influence you unfavorably. This is a chance for you to learn how to have peace inside yourself no matter what is happening around or to you.

If you are worried about the interest which will be added to your already overwhelming loan, we suggest you do not worry about this. Once you have completed your healing and have tapped into the richness you have lost in the shadow self, there will be more than enough money to pay off your loans *and* the accrued interest.

This is your financial advice from spirit, if you would like recommendation from us!

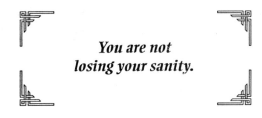

You are not losing your sanity.

As you go through this process, do not judge yourself about your ability to function. If you are going through deep emotional stress, you will feel rather inadequate in your everyday life and you will not function as well as you usually do. Be aware that this is temporary, and you are not losing your mind or your sanity. Do not be afraid to sink into what you need to transmute, for you cannot pass into your light until you have passed through your darkness. As long as you do not decide you want to stay there, or let it devour you as you give up, then it is fine to let yourself be there in the darkness with yourself.

This void in yourself will give you much richness once you have touched it. We advise that if you find yourself falling into despair, remember: this too shall pass. It is only part of the transmutation process. Make these words your mantra. (A mantra is a word or phrase you say to yourself repeatedly, much like an affirmation.) If you become frightened or angry that you are getting "stuck" or the pain becomes too intense, say these words!

Remember, this is your last blockage, so once it is removed, you are on to a new life. It will feel as if you have been reincarnated in the same body in the same lifetime. This will take less time than you think, and it will take more time than you wish. Simply be aware that this will pass. It will not last forever. The anger, sadness or despair—-it will pass. You must be patient.

It is important for you to be around people who are not expecting anything in particular of you. It is important to state the fact that you are going through a difficult time and you are not going to be able to live up to everyone's expectations (except you must do the work exchange you agreed to do). Perhaps you are around people who are impatient with you and would love for you to be "over it already, get past it please so we can have fun".

This kind of energy is not beneficial for your process at this time. You have the capacity to have fun, yes, but at this time, it may not be in your best interest to distract yourself from the important, deep and painful work you are about to undertake. You may want to take breaks from the serious work you are doing, but probably not for very long because it is in your nature to "go for it".

Concerning those people who become impatient with you or look down on you as you go through this, you will have to stand your ground. If you become less able to function and cannot meet their expectations or needs, *you must not heed negative energy from them.* Lack of ability to function will not happen for all of you, but it will for some. If this is the case, then you must say to them, "I am sorry you are impatient, but I need to take care of myself. I will see you later in my journey. Unless you would like to help me, I must leave *you* for now and you must leave *me*. I cannot meet your needs or expectations at this time."

If you have decided to face your demons, you must be around people who will let you do this your own way, in your own timing, and not have judgment on you for how you do this or how long it takes. There are not many people who can deal with this, nor do many people even want to be around as you shed your darkness and your tears. Some of you may find you must be in secret and alone. This is fine.

You see, these people who become impatient with you may have already done what you are doing and don't want to be around it again.

Reclaiming the Shadow Self

Or, they have never done this, and never *will* have to transmute such deep darkness. Or, they have never done this and will have to in their future. It is possible you are making them nervous, for they do not want to look there in themselves.

Another thing which may happen as you begin your process of transformation is that many people will come forth with all kinds of advice for you about how to do this. It is useful to listen to what they have to say, but it is important for you to decide what rings true for you. It is important for you to only accept that which you resonate with. If these people who have all kinds of advice for you about how to deal with this or that are attached to you doing it their way, you must tell them they will need to change their attitudes about this.

If they do not respect your way of doing things, you will have to exclude them from further contact so you can concentrate on what you are doing. They may unknowingly thwart your healing process with negative energies they might feel toward you if you do not choose to make use of their advice. Remember, you are very wise and you know what is best for you, even though it may not appear that way to others.

*No one will enforce
your boundaries
but yourself.*

For instance, you may feel that drinking coffee or smoking a cigarette now and then is helping you, even though an outside source may tell you differently. Go ahead and continue with what you are doing. Your healing is the point, and whatever it takes to heal, even if it means falling back on some of your old vices, it is okay. This is not an encouragement to let all your habits run amuck, but if you need them for the time being, it helps you, and you realize your old vices are only there temporarily, it is okay.

These things will fall away once you have "treated" your emotional ailments.

All people have their own ways of dealing with things, and you have yours. Some will match with others, and some will not. This is okay. You will learn through this process how to state your boundaries and enforce them. No one will enforce your boundaries but yourself. So develop this skill in your healing right now. You must repair and establish boundaries which were violated earlier in your life, especially childhood.

It is important not to impose your trauma on others, or ask them to commit all their time to listening to you. They will not be able to give you what you wish, nor will they desire to go to these depths with you. This is a journey you must make alone. This is the dark hour of the soul just before enlightenment. Only *you* can be there in this moment in your own universe, terrifying as it may seem. You may need to call for someone if you are in a panic or a crisis, but for the most part, you might have to do this alone as much as you can. Remember, you are your own guru. You know how to do this. You have done it before.

Be aware that not everyone you meet will be understanding and compassionate about what you are going through. However, be assured that your guidance is understanding and compassionate. You are quite visible on the inner planes. Know that you are supported with the utmost of love and respect. Know that your guides will be patient with your process for however long it takes. You will be guided to the people who will help you if they are not already around you.

Do not be afraid. You may *feel* alone many times, but you are not. Even though you may not feel the presence of guides around you or the help which is always coming toward you, we ask you to rest your mind and simply know it is there. The guiding ones love you very dearly. It is like the poem about the footprints in the sand. There were two pairs, and then there was only one when the going got tough. The afflicted one who thought he was alone later found out that he was actually being carried by God. This is what is happening for you even though you are not aware of it.

You are surrounded by many high teachers, for you are a very high soul (remember, this is inward). You do not realize just how magnificent and powerful you are. You have hidden your magnificence from yourself.

Reclaiming the Shadow Self

You have come to help because you are qualified to handle the deepest, darkest secrets of human consciousness.

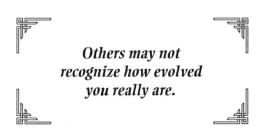

Others may not recognize how evolved you really are.

Keep your head up, for you can be proud of yourself and the work you are doing. Others may not recognize how evolved you really are. They may even see you as losers, pathetic, or lost cases.

Do not let yourself be swayed into believing their projections (judgments) on you for you are truly an impressive being. If they only knew how great a being you are, they would have much reverence for you. They would be *thanking* you for taking the "grunt work" jobs so they themselves did not have to do it. So keep your head up and be proud of who you are, even as your tears fall from your eyes and you struggle with the difficult patterns you have taken upon yourself.

When you need outside help, this will be made available to you. You must ask for it. Do not forget this. Sometimes you will find you are getting overwhelmed and you are becoming frightened as your memories unlock. If your memories come up and are terrifying for you, you may need cellular release work or some other kind of energy work in order to help the process continue to move forward.

Do not be resistant to allowing someone to know what you are going through so you can get the help you need. Many of you actually need energetic surgery, and you cannot perform major surgery upon yourself! Many of your imprints are so deeply ingrained that you will not be able to transmute them alone. Yes, you can do your own minor surgery, but the things which literally shattered your core are things you will need help with.

Do not be afraid of what may happen in cellular release, or other kinds of energetic working. It may be rather dramatic, loud, and may even be frightening. You might have convulsions or thrashing. This is okay.

As you process your trauma, always realize it is only something passing through you. These issues do not define who you are! Always tell yourself this as you are in the midst of your sadness or fear. Many of you have suffered from depression for so long that you do not want to enter the depression more deeply than you ever have before. However, this may be necessary. You must pass through the terror, the horror, the confusion, or the sadness *before* you can enter the light.

See this as a beautiful thing you are doing. Someday you will look back on this and see it truly was a beautiful birth into the light and not a death that was ugly and horrid at all. The death has already taken place for the most part. The death happened when your light was extinguished as a child, or whenever the devastating event happened which caused you to shut down.

As you go through your process, pray to your helpers and to God (who you are part of) to protect you from manifesting more darkness while you transmute your patterns. You most likely know you can attract that which you fear. You might be afraid you will attract even deeper and harsher circumstances because you are entering the void and going where it hurts. Ask for guidance and protection as you go through these things. Ask for shields to keep you from manifesting your fears. At this point, it would not help you to be manifesting the things which terrified you.

Be careful and be alert. For instance, if you are terrified of rape, be in a place where an event like that is highly unlikely, like a spiritual center, or another type of safe place. Avoid walking down the streets alone in the night. You will be wearing these imprints on your energy field in a more visible way. You may be attractive to that which you fear, or that which you have already experienced or *almost* experienced.

For instance, if you are afraid of dismemberment, do not use a power saw. If you are afraid of this or that, go to certain measures to keep these things from happening while you are vulnerable to that which you fear. Secure your environment! This is a practical measure. On the physical level, remove the dangers in every way possible. On the energetic level,

Nature

tell yourself that you should not fear anymore. You are safe now. These things are in the past and you are changing all that now. Soon you will be on to your new life.

As you move through your process, we would like to remind you of something. You are a light being and an angelic soul in disguise as a human, even if you are playing the role of the "bad guy". The disguise is put on completely. Realizing this will help you in remembering who you are.

As you go through this process and you cry, feel sadness, or express anger, we would like to remind you that you are truly an angel as you do this. Even in your tears, you are beautiful and royal. You are an incredible being of light and love. You are a magnificent point of power in the universe. You will remember who you are once this process is over. Simply be assured that you are a strong, powerful and loving soul, even though you have disguised yourself to be weak, small, unlovable, and sad. You will soon realize that this was not the case at all.

Many of you will feel you need counseling of some sort. If the information you need can be found in ordinary reality systems with ones called psychologists, or other types of counselors in this area, then go ahead and use these resources. Often there are clinics where you can take advantage of these services for free or nearly free. These people have many tools they can give you to work on your problems. Be discerning about drugs they may offer you, though.

There is much hoopla about the antidepressants on the market now. If you are offered antidepressants, realize that these are only advantageous in an emotional crisis state. If you are thinking about suicide, or you are unable to stop crying for a month, or you are so depressed you have stopped eating, this is when we would say it is a proper use of an antidepressant. If your condition is not serious, you would be much better off without the antidepressant. The more of your facilities not masked by pain relief in the emotional body, the clearer you can be. The point of all this is to *heal* the emotional body, not mask it's pain and allow the state of upset to remain hidden underneath.

If you have accepted the antidepressant, do not stay on the antidepressant long, even if you are not fully finished with your process. Only use it to get yourself over the hump, or the dangerous areas in your psyche. Your guides will nudge you when it is time to stop. You will know when the time comes because the effects of the drug will change for you and it will develop unpleasant effects.

We suggest that antidepressants not be used for more than six months maximum. If you continue to use them after you received signals to stop, you will enter a period of denial and not realize that your emotional body is still in need of repair. For some people, three months will be plenty of time to get past the anxiety stages.

Many of you are going to have questions about your soul purposes and other things which are far beyond this particular reality. If this is the case, you will probably find you are attracted to channeled readings or spiritual counselors instead of traditional psychologists. We highly suggest that if this is something you are attracted to, then go for it and use the opportunities which come your way.

Channeled guides will be able to give you much information which you cannot access otherwise. If you have memories you are not sure about, perhaps a channeled reading can help you find out if they are true or if the records are drawn from the mass consciousness library.

There are channels who are clear and there are channels who are not. You must use your discernment and your intuition. If you find you do not gel with a certain channel, this probably will not be high information for yourself. If you find there is a magical feeling, or a feeling of peace and light between yourself and the channel, then you can be fairly sure this channel is clear and will give you high information.

You will also find that if someone is a clear channel, he or she is working with you on a vibrational energy level and not just with the words being spoken. The vibrational healing is very useful and is more a part of the reading than the words themselves. The words are for the mental body, and the energy is for the other bodies.

If you do not feel satisfied with the reading afterwards, simply do not return. *Do* continue looking for one who can help you, though. Do not give up on your first experience with a channeled reading. You may find that these ones can help you more than a modern day psychologist can who is working with less expansive methods. It is beneficial to use methods which straddle more than this reality.

If you are not attracted to channeled readings, then this is fine! Honor your own path! These are simply suggestions for those of you who are attracted.

This is a note for those who are supporters *and those who will be after transformation.*

For those of you who did not have dark and traumatic experiences but are reading this anyway (in order to understand what others are going through) we ask you to be compassionate to the ones you see as troubled souls, losers, or needy ones. This has to do with superiority and inferiority complexes. It is important for you to see these souls in a different light. It would help to have understanding for them, treat them carefully in their presently delicate state, and help them in their transmutation process.

These souls are your friends. These souls are your teammates. These souls are your brothers and sisters, no matter how ugly or immature they seem. It is important in this age that *anyone* who truly desires to be in the light makes it no matter what it takes for them to get there. For some, the entrance into the light is not graceful. They may have to struggle, scream and claw their way into it. Their lives were not gentle and their lives were not clear.

These souls are evolved (experienced on the Earth plane). They are not new souls. Yes, they do need another's help at this time, but once they are over the crisis section of their growth, and are on their feet remembering who they are, they will surely take it from there. You will not have to help them anymore, for they will not need it. They are very capable souls.

In the crisis stage, it would be highly beneficial for them if you do not shut them out. They will benefit greatly from your energy, especially that which you hold with them on the inner planes. Even though you don't understand it, become frustrated with it, or wish they would already heal because you are bored with it, be patient. Healing happens at a different pace for every person.

At the soul level, these souls chose circumstances at an early age which would make life very difficult. They set up great barriers for themselves, which in the end will make success all the sweeter. Some have created so many barriers for themselves to overcome that the only way they can be transported is to take drastic actions against others in order to be moved at all. Have compassion for these people. Have appreciation for the heavy emotional experiences they are going through. These beings are experiencing intense and painful separateness and isolation.

For those of you who have not had traumatic experiences, did not live through brutality and abuse, it is hard to understand why someone is having such a hard time with things that come so easily to yourself. It is important to develop compassion for the things you do not understand. Remember that other people's paths are just as valid, have just as much meaning, and can produce as much light as your own, no matter how different it is. It is important not to judge these people or to resist these people being in your space. It is important that you give them whatever you can to help them. This will help you with your own growth, for you will open your heart centers by having greater compassion for those in pain. You will also find yourself dealing with the "inferiority/superiority—versus—equality" issues within yourself.

You are being challenged to let go of judgment, superiority and separation. You are being challenged to love and respect the ones you see as inferior and have compassion for what they are going through. It is just as much a challenge to release the concept of superiority as it is to release the concept of inferiority.

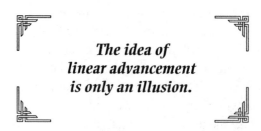

**The idea of
linear advancement
is only an illusion.**

You are not necessarily ahead of these souls in your evolvement, and in some cases, they may actually be far ahead of you in ways which are not visible right now. You have simply chosen a different path. You have chosen a path which did not cause you to lose your center quite so drastically. These ones who are seemingly "lesser" in their evolvement than yourself are your equals. If you see these ones as your equals, and treat them as such, it will help them greatly with their feelings of inferiority. The idea of linear advancement is only an illusion anyway.

Affirmations

1. Phase one of my life is over and phase two has just begun.
2. The universe will provide the money I need as I focus my full intent on healing.
3. I am protected and safe as I integrate my shadow self.
4. I release the old and invite the new.
5. I am gentle and nurturing toward myself.
6. This too shall pass.
7. I rest my mind from worry and realize that I am not alone. I am surrounded by high teachers and guides.
8. I am a magnificent being of light and love.
9. I release inferiority and superiority issues. I am equal with all souls.
10. I am experienced on the Earth plane. I know how to transcend my fears.

Exercises

1

When a highly charged negative emotion overcomes you, sit down and close your eyes. Visualize your energetic systems, especially the emotional body, as intricate gridworks of light. Look for the places in the gridwork where the emotion has become tangled or unmoving. Unwrap it's hold on your energetic system and allow it to flow again. Ask the emotion to give you it's message or show you the thoughts which brought it into your system. Then let it pass through your system as if you are only air, or as if you are transparent. Let it slide off you as if it were "water off a duck's back". Thank this emotion and allow the universe to transmute it back into the light it truly is.

2

This exercise is for manifesting the money you will need to take care of yourself as you focus on your healing.

See yourself standing in a void where you cannot consciously perceive anything. Then raise your hands and beckon the energies in the void to show themselves to you. Watch as doors appear all around you and open, one by one. Each is a different avenue that the universe can send money and other things you need to you. You can open as many doors as you want to.

Pick one of the doors and allow the energies flowing through it to wash over you, surround you, and fill you with light. Allow yourself to deserve this! Wait until there is a "click" before moving on to the next door. At the end, allow the energies flowing to you from all directions to synchronize and work together in your energy field. Surrender yourself to this energy. Trust in it.

You have just opened a the pathway for the universe to take care of you. Your guides will now begin synchronizing the events and the people you need to meet.

3

Whenever you feel alone and unloved in your journey, take a deep breath and close your eyes. Visualize many angels around you who are caressing you lovingly, lying with you in the grass, sitting with you, holding you, or drying your tears. Allow them to nurture you the way a mother would nurture a child who she loves and holds dear. These beings are there whether you are aware of them or not.

You can have as many guides and helpers as you want. There are plenty to go around for everyone. These light beings love you very much. Meet their eyes with yours and allow their love to enfold you. You deserve this love, no matter what you might think. Open your heart to receive.

Reclaiming the Shadow Self

You may find yourself in tears as you open your heart. It will get easier every time you do this. This is an excellent exercise in learning how to receive love from others.

Chapter 4

Physical Aspects
Of Your Process

(A note from Christine:)

(I must admit that I am quite concerned about the information in this chapter [also the advice in Chapter Three about anti-depressants] and how people might take it. Anwan's advice here is esoteric in nature and is not the end-all in medical decisions. *Anwan is not a recognized doctor.*

I feel that if you are experiencing serious physical symptoms such as heart palpitations, convulsions, or other such things, you should go to the doctor immediately! These are symptoms which precede much more serious ailments. I was alright following Anwan's advice, but I was, and am, a very healthy person compared to a lot of people.

I want to go down on the record as saying that I recommend you follow your doctor's advice first and foremost. Don't ignore physical symptoms.)

Do not be alarmed when you see physical manifestations of trauma in your body. We would like to assure you that these are temporary. This happens because your DNA is changing and letting go of old codes. The chemistry makeup in your body will actually be different as you deal with your past. Do not be afraid. We advise you to simply notice these changes with curiosity. If the condition persists over a long period of time, long after you have transmuted the issue that seems to be connected to it, then we advise you to look into it with a medical practitioner.

Your body will do many strange things as your process takes place. You may find that you have convulsions or tremors. You may find that you have unusual pains which come one day and are gone the next as mysteriously as they came. Welts may appear and disappear. You may find that you have panic attacks when you have never been prone to them before. You may find that you have heart palpitations. This is especially common! The heart is very, *very* sensitive. As you transform, it may flutter. We would like to dispel your fear about this. These are good signs, not bad ones.

These are signs that the physical aspect of your cellular memory is releasing the trauma. If you find you get rashes, sores, or your face looks different, we assure you this is alright. As long as it is not a persistent thing. If it comes quickly, you will most likely find that it disappears quickly. If it does not leave you, then it means you are trying to hold on to something or failing to acknowledge something.

When this happens, we suggest you find outside help in an energy worker. There are many types of energy workers and there are many techniques which help dislodge energies when they become "stuck" in your system.

There *are* ways you can work on "stuck" areas yourself. We advise that you drink as much water as you can, up to a gallon per day if possible. Your body will be purging much and needs a channel to carry the old energy out of your system. Eat lightly. Do not eat heavily. We also suggest breathing deeply. The more oxygenation and the more water you have in your system, the more easily the DNA and the other frameworks in your nervous system will clear and become lighter.

During your processing time you may feel a need to sleep a lot for you will be doing much dream work. You will be doing much transformation in your sleep which will not be visible or "feel-able". Do not be alarmed. You are not getting sick or contracting a disease. In fact, you are removing these possibilities from your system.

You may find that you lose your appetite, or your appetite increases. It will be different for everyone. If you are not a person who normally fasts, it would be a good idea to learn about it.

Short fasts are good. Long fasts could be detrimental. If you really want to get down to the bottom of things, a long fast will jolt you. However, you must be prepared for the repercussions because they will last for months in some cases. It will not only be difficult during the time of the fast, but the effects of the fast will continue for many weeks afterwards. This will dislodge much stored energy, and it may shatter your foundations.

We advise that you don't do fasts for longer than a week, even if you do have plenty of stored calories in your body. You will most likely not be able to handle it if your body is not in peak condition. By the middle of the second week, you will find you are actually destroying your body instead of helping it to clear. We advise you begin with one or two day fasts, and as you grow accustomed to this, perhaps move up to a three or four day fast. Later, you can try the five or the seven day fast.

The one day fast can be done as often as once a week. The three day fast can be done as often as once per month. The seven day fast should not be done more often than twice per year.

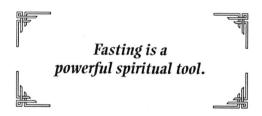

**Fasting is a
powerful spiritual tool.**

Fasting is not a toy. Fasting is not something to do for curiosity or fun. It is a very powerful spiritual tool for unlocking deeply buried unconscious memories. You may not find you are enjoying what the fasts unlock. Be sure to take this medicine slowly if this is something you want to do. A fast will bring unconscious fears to the surface. It will *also* open doors to ecstatic frequencies. You will experience both.

We suggest you don't fast for the goal of losing weight. We suggest you do it for the goal of cleansing your cellular memories, which will in turn help you understand their relation to your extra weight. You can also think of a fast as a way to remove unnecessary tissue and debris in your body from the years of unhealthy food you have eaten.

You will find that as your energy becomes lighter, the foods you eat will change. Perhaps this has already happened for you and is still happening.

We suggest you stay away from meats at this time. Meat has heavy energy. At this point, you are trying to lighten your energy. If you eat meat, you are ingesting fear. This is exactly what you have too much of already. Besides, you will be helping the animal kingdom to overcome their own fear if you allow them to keep their lives. The animal kingdom is transmuting as much fear as the human race is. Humans are not the only ones involved in the shift of this reality. If you can, avoid the meats and simply work with vegetables, fruits and grains. This will aid in your spiritual cleansing greatly. Of course, it is your choice and we honor *any* choice you make.

Protein is very misunderstood. The amount a human needs is less than you would think. Unless you are a body builder, you do not need 100% of the USRDA (United States Recommended Daily Allowance). You will find what is right for you. If you decide to decrease your protein intake, please do this slowly and not abruptly. If you currently take fifty grams of protein per day, do not suddenly drop down to ten! Go down to forty five, then perhaps to forty, then to thirty, and perhaps level out at twenty or ten. You do not need to make the jump all at once, for it would jolt your system.

What you want to do right now is transform your body in as smooth a fashion as possible. Jolts to your body will not aid in your transformation. Your body will be jolted enough on it's own just from the memories which resurface and the darkness you process. You do not need to do it on purpose in other ways.

As you process, be careful with your body. This is the point we are trying to make.

Up to this moment, you have probably experienced much hatred of your body. Be aware that your body will reflect your new self as it manifests in this reality. This is something you can look forward to. Your body is not your enemy. Your body is your friend and it will help you if you let

Physical Aspects Of Your Process

it. It has served you up to this point and you do not even realize what it was doing to help you.

For instance, perhaps you are one who is afraid of sexual abuse. Perhaps your body has gained weight, or you dress yourself in a disheveled or unappealing manner. You may have discouraged any type of sexual attention by doing this. See your body's ugliness as a way you have protected yourself and your life. You were afraid that if someone saw how beautiful you are you would be hurt.

Realize that your body is your friend even if it appears ugly to you and to others. This goes for your personality as well. A rough and tough personality can protect you from abuse. A quiet personality can protect you. There are many variations of self preservation.

Again we say that as you process, your body will reflect your new self without much effort from you.

We would like to suggest that you exercise as much as you can through this process. It will give you a sense of confidence and get the energy moving in your body and mind. If you are already an exercising type of person, we congratulate you, for you have already made one of the major steps in transmuting your cellular memories and DNA. We say to those of you who are sedentary that it will be beneficial for you to stir the juices in your body so you can keep yourself healthy while you go through what might *feel* like an unhealthy process.

As you release your darkness, you will find you are also releasing physical weight. If you are overweight or underweight, this is directly related to the darkness you have been carrying in your shadow self. As you feel safer in your life, you will release extra weight (or gain weight if you are emaciated). Do not focus on the weight, for the weight is simply a result of your emotional state.

The key to proper health and weight is happiness in your heart and in every cell of your being. If you *do* manage to lose the weight on purpose, be prepared for the unconscious memories or energies to be released as well. The weight often holds the unconscious memory banks in which you have stored much fear. Remember, fear is the root of all negative emotions, including anger. As you release the weight, you may find that your reality shifts drastically. You may be challenged to keep up with the changes as your issues or energies are released and flare up in your reality.

As you get into the most traumatic areas of your consciousness you may not *want* to exercise. Instead, you may find that you want to sleep all day, and this is what your body might need. For many of you, this will be the case. This is alright, but do not let a whole week go by without at *least* exercising twice. If you need to be sedentary, this is okay, as long as it is not a permanent condition. Do not let your body go backwards in it's healing and evolution. Do not lose the ground you have gained in your healing.

If you exercise two or three times a week, this would maintain your body. Every day would be better. If you exercise only two times per week, make it one hour. If you exercise every day, twenty minutes to a half hour is fine.

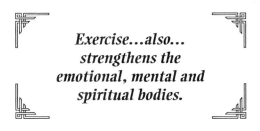

*Exercise...also...
strengthens the
emotional, mental and
spiritual bodies.*

Exercise on the physical level does not only touch the physical body. It also stirs and strengthens the emotional, mental and spiritual bodies. It straightens things out. This is something you might keep in mind as you struggle with your physical body.

Many of you may find you have trouble with your spines or with your skeletal structure in general. This is a common symptom of a traumatized emotional body. We advise you not to be afraid to get chiropractic adjustments or other body work done. These will help you greatly.

Your spine is where your life force flows up and down. As you have your spine aligned and adjusted, it will help with the energies you are trying to transform. It will keep the places clear which tend to get "stuck". You will be able to flush and heal. This is something you can do fairly inexpensively, once or twice a month, perhaps more if you have a chronic condition. Adjustments will help greatly to speed up the process.

We also suggest that you stretch and allow new energy to flow into your muscles and tendons. Yoga is a wonderful tool in this area and is encouraged whether or not you get spinal adjustments. If you cannot afford adjustments, yoga is the next best thing. It will help you maintain and heal your body all your life.

It is not a bad idea to use the services of the clinics or your doctor in order to find out how your thyroid is doing. Have a test done. Many who are shifting into the new energies are finding that the thyroid is needing assistance. It is a symptom of the throat chakra opening, which has been closed for a long time. Many of you can remember lifetimes in which you were murdered for speaking your truth, expressing who you are, or simply being your beautiful self. This is what it is related to. There is still much fear in humanity concerning this area.

Affirmations

1. New codes in my DNA are being released into my body and mind.
2. Negative manifestations in my health and body are temporary and are leaving me now. I ask for their messages.
3. My physical system is clean and clear.
4. I love to exercise my body.
5. I love to eat healthy foods.
6. My body has taken care of me the best it could.
7. My body is my friend. I love my body. I thank my body.
8. My body is now releasing cellular patterning from the past.
9. My body is sturdy. My body is strong. My body has great vitality. My body glows. My body is perfectly proportioned.
10. My spine is clear and full of light.

Exercises

1

Bring light into every part of your body. Use different colors. Use breathing to move the light in and out through the pores of your skin. Use breathing to move the light up and down your spine. Use breathing to spin the DNA in the light. Watch it's intricate coding shift, unlock, and repair itself. Permeate every single atom in your body with light as it comes from within. Imagine the atoms becoming more lively and able to sustain the light without effort. Watch them become self generating in the light.

2

Visualize your system becoming cleansed by the food and the water you ingest. Imagine the water carrying the old energies out of your system. Imagine the food replenishing your cells and making them more vibrant. Bless all things before they enter your body. Ask these things to vibrate at the right speed for your system. Ask the food to match and raise your vibration.

3

If you have a physical symptom of illness, ask for its purpose for being there. Ask for the issues surrounding the symptom to come to the surface of your consciousness so you can address them. Let your guides know you are ready for this. Then allow the answers to come to you over the next few days. Do not forget to listen for the answer once you have asked a question!

Chapter 5

Retrieving And Dealing With Unconscious Memories

It is a fact that many of you have painful unconscious memories in your minds and bodies. Because of this, your energies have been locked and you cannot access your power. Many of you cannot remember your childhood in it's entirety. You know it was bad, and you may say, "Oh well, I don't want to remember that because it was terrible! I don't need to go back there. I would rather move on with my life!"

This is where the roots of your problems lie. Your childhood is where you made specific decisions about the nature of the world. Everything else in your life has simply been a re-enactment of the things you have gone through in your childhood. Many of you may think, "I remember my childhood just fine. I don't think there is anything missing. It wasn't a good childhood, but I don't think I forgot anything."

Well, you may be surprised. The mind has a way of burying that which does not make sense to your child's mind, *and also hiding the gap in the memory*. You may find as you go into this process of enlightening yourself and dropping everything in your life until you are enlightened, your path will take you into dark corners of your psyche which you did not even know existed in yourself. This should be expected.

All of you have gaps in your memory you do not even know are there. You may remember many things from your youth, but there are still many things you have forgotten. Every person has this condition to some extent or another, even those who have had fairly pleasant and non-traumatic lives. Do not be fooled into thinking your memory is complete. Your mind can hide the gaps so your conscious self does not even realize anything is missing.

If you have been working on your patterns for many years and *still* you feel you are not getting to the bottom of what is holding you back from having happiness, it is almost a given that there is some event you have forgotten which effected you deeply.

As we have said in the introduction, if you are remembering past lives which upset you or alarm you, these are clues to what happened in your childhood. If you *suspect* something happened in your childhood, there is a chance that it actually did. It is not necessarily true *everything* you suspect happened in the childhood of your present lifetime, though. This is because you will begin searching in areas of your consciousness which hold memories from other lives and realities.

> **If you suspect something
> happened in your childhood,
> there is a chance that
> it actually did.**

The mind stores memories not linearly, but by association. For instance, all your memories of broken hearts will be stored in the same area, no matter when they happened or where they happened. All your memories of being a king or another type of leader will be stored in the same pocket of consciousness. You are tapping into a very broad bank of memories, so it will be difficult to discern which ones are which. Some of the memories you come across may not even be your own. You may find yourself tapping into the mass consciousness memory bank which is accessible to everyone who has incarnated as a human.

Retrieving And Dealing With Unconscious Memories

We suggest you transmute anything that comes up. If it catches your attention or creates an emotional stir, it is triggering the conditions which need to be transformed in yourself. If it happened in another life, another reality, or seemingly to someone else, it still effects your energy systems in a negative way. This is what you are trying to heal.

Use the content of the past lives you are remembering as clues to pinpoint the issues you are transmuting in this one. If you are a person who has forgotten areas in your childhood, which all of you have, the lives which are remembered will give you some idea of what has been buried in your past.

For instance, if you remember a past life when you were held back from having an education you desired, your intelligence ridiculed, or being treated as if you were not worthy of an education, perhaps you may find in your present lifetime that you have been deterred from getting the education you desired, or you were constantly called stupid as a child. This is simply an example. So use your past lives as clues to the things you are trying to transmute in this lifetime. This lifetime is the sum total of everything that has not been resolved up to this point.

You may find your mind has diverted your attention from a painful and unprocessed memory by completely removing focus in areas which are related. For instance, your mind may have buried the fact you have been raped as a child by making you, as an adult, completely callous and uninterested in the subject whatsoever. You may have no interest in rape cases, rape books, or people who claim to have been raped and want to tell you their stories. Yes, you are certainly sensitive to the person and what happened to him or her, but you refuse to dwell on it or get too involved in it. You might say, "It didn't happen to me. I am too strong for this. I don't think it ever will. I *hope* it never will." You may find that your mind has made you immune to the energies by pretending you have not been a participant in them.

Perhaps you have become "macho", especially those of you with a damaged feminine side. Some of you have become very strong, determined, forceful, even aggressive. *You have done this in order not to be the victim again, or to be seen as such.* It was also the only way you were going to survive what happened to you.

Unconscious Fears

Retrieving And Dealing With Unconscious Memories

Having been a victim, you had one of two choices in your childhood. One was to retreat and become a fearful, intimidated person, which some of you have done. Your other choice was to become so agressive, bold and fearless that you thought nothing could touch you. These are two defenses the mind uses when you have been a victim.

Fasting, yoga, meditation, and other spiritual practices you are attracted to, even dancing yourself crazy to rock and roll music, can unlock these memories in your unconscious mind. There are many ways to unlock the mind's secrets. Whatever it takes for you to unlock your memories, it is important for you to do this and stick with it. You must become conscious of the things which have thrown you for a loop. Once you are conscious of them and don't *fear* becoming conscious of them they have no power over you anymore. You can understand, over time, what they were about and why they happened.

You might find yourself saying, "Oh! So *this* is what has been messing me up my whole life! I am so glad I know now. I can take *that* out of my program and I can look at it differently now." Whereas before, if it was simply unconscious, you could not work with it because you did not even know it was there or that it was effecting you.

If you know it is there and you have consciousness of an unconscious memory, you have begun the process of taking your power back. These are the places where you have left fragments of yourself behind. These are the places where you became confused about how to handle reality or you became frightened of it. These are the places where you have left your power. These are the places where you must rediscover yourself and reclaim the power which lies in the shadow self.

Much prayer will help with unlocking the shadow self secrets. Affirmation will help in unlocking memories. You must let the universe know you are ready and prepared for these things to be opened.

Many of you are such bold people you throw yourself into it 100% whenever you undertake anything. This is a good attribute for you in your healing. This will aid your process in moving more quickly. You *are* fearless and you *are* willing to go into the darkness. You *know* that going into the darkness is the only way you can reach the light from where you are right now.

Reclaiming the Shadow Self

The reason you have buried the memories of your childhood is because you did not have the tools to deal with them at the time. The adults around you were not supportive as you tried to tell them in your own language what is happening in your life. In your wisdom, you decided you simply did not have the facilities to deal with it at the time since you would have had to do it alone. Children, of course, are not equipped to deal with traumatic or confusing events alone.

> *Children are not equipped to deal with traumatic or confusing events alone.*

The adults were probably clueless about your predicament. Often, a child's language is vague. A six year old child does not blurt out, "Mom, I was raped by the janitor at school." In fact, a child does not even have a concept of what unacceptable behavior from an adult is. A child does not even know what rape is, let alone whether or not it is a victim of it. To the child, the adult is always right. The irresponsible behavior of adults is shocking and confusing for a child who is trying to learn about what is and what is not appropriate behavior in the world.

As a child, you may have felt guilt or that you were wrong and deserved this for some reason. Children will often blame themselves for what happens to them and not the adult. This happens because children are closer to the knowledge that they create their own realities.

You buried the memory because it did not fit into an acceptable reality for you. A child would rather overlook it's parent's or another adult's faults than to focus on them, for children are loving and tolerant. A child will not consider them faults at all. A child will just assume that what happened is something it does not understand yet and cannot deal with.

Retrieving And Dealing With Unconscious Memories

Many of you have been confused as children. We would like to commend you and say that you gave it your best shot. You have survived. Your survival may not have been graceful, but this is okay. You are still here and you are still playing the game. That is what counts. There is still plenty of time to do what you came here to do. We want to reassure you of this. You are rather bold people. You are brave. You are courageous. You should admire the fact that you are this way. You should give yourself credit for what you have done and what you have allowed yourself to go through.

Processing dark, unconscious memories will not be easy. It will not necessarily be pleasant. Many people do not remember the bad stuff *or* the good stuff. However, as you unlock the unconscious memories which you might call negative experiences, you will find that you also unlock some pleasant memories as well. We advise you to look for these alongside the harsher memories you will uncover, for the pleasant memories do exist. You simply could not put the two together, and you buried them all.

The reason you have buried the good memories may have something to do with the fact that you are afflicted with self hatred. It is something you withhold from yourself because you feel you do not deserve to have good experiences. It has to do with self worth.

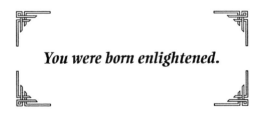

You were born enlightened.

Children lead very rich lives in their imaginations as well as in physical reality. There is much you have left behind there. You were born enlightened and you have given up your enlightenment. Some children give it up sooner than others, but this is a place where you can go in your consciousness if you want to remember what it was like to be in a state of enlightenment.

Reclaiming the Shadow Self

Think about the fact that when you were one year old, you were still living with one foot in the spiritual realms and one foot in the physical world. Focus on all the things you can remember from that time before you shut down. This is the power of opening unconscious memories.

Some of you shut down at very early ages, even before you were a few months old. Your surroundings were just too confusing, frightening, or sad, and in your sensitive state, were overwhelming. You most likely did not want to be here, for it was harsh compared to the soul planes you just came from. Try to remember the moments which were good, because they were there in between the harsher moments. You were still communing with light beings who were not incarnated in physical reality. They were a large part of your reality.

You could think of it as if you have led a double life, for you truly have.

Affirmations

1. I am ready to become conscious of memories I have buried.
2. I am a brave and courageous person.
3. I can handle any memories that come up for me.
4. I let down my defenses and allow myself to see my vulnerability.
5. I am free of fear. I master my fear when it comes up.
6. I am taking back my power.
7. I go into my darkness willingly.
8. I forgive the adults who behaved poorly around me.
9. I deserve to have positive experiences. I am worthy.
10. I now retrieve the enlightenment I had at birth. I remember my enlightenment.

Exercises

1

Imagine your memory is like a large storage area and some of the files have gotten dusty. Take one of these files out and blow the dust off it. Look at the words, pictures or feelings on the outside of it. This is the category.

Now open it up and see what words, pictures or emotions come off the paper for you. After you have absorbed this and feel a "click" in your energy, put the file away with love and acceptance of its contents.

Do not worry if you do not receive pictures, sounds or other sensory input right away. They will come up for you in the next few days. You can do this any time you are ready to retrieve another memory.

2

Examine the emotions you feel about certain events in your past. Determine exactly what the emotion is. Then turn it into it's exact opposite. All emotions have a positive and negative side. See if you can start flipping your emotions over to the side of the positive pole, as if they were coins with heads and tails.

3

If you find fragmented parts of yourself as you retrieve your memories, invite these ones back into your sphere of experience. Become your higher self (more inward self) and heal this part which has been in separateness. Be your own guide to the aspect of yourself who is hurt, frightened or angry. Act as if you are a gentle parent overseeing a difficult part of your child's path. Imagine this aspect of yourself in it's highest form. Visualize this form coming forth into physical reality and merging with the self you are and desire to become.

Chapter 6

Hallucinogenics And Marijuana

(Another Note From Christine:)

(Again, I am concerned about how people will take the information in this chapter and the next one. Don't just plunge into these words blindly. I encourage you to think very long and hard about anything and everything Anwan says. I did. And I have not put into use *everything* Anwan advises.

I must go down on the record as saying that drugs are not being recommended by me. I have reached the point where drugs are no longer useful to me and I'm not convinced it is the best route to enlightenment. I and a few others were simply curious about what Anwan would say about drugs since they are so prominent in our culture. Again, this information is esoteric in nature, and not the end-all in advice.)

We would like to address some issues surrounding drugs, especially the "power plants".

If you are attracted to these drugs, then in love and light we would like to give you some guidelines. *This is not an argument for or against drugs.* This is about how to use them if you are going into this area of exploration. These are guidelines which might keep you from hurting yourself with them.

Reclaiming the Shadow Self

Hallucinogenics are not a bad thing. They are not a good thing. They are simply a thing. It depends on how you use them and how you approach them. Hallucinogenics are a spiritual tool. They are a *very powerful* spiritual tool. They should be used as such.

The organics, for the most part, are the ones that match the human organism most closely.

The synthetics must be used with care, and as you use them, you must realize you are putting your psychology in a place it is not necessarily built for. The synthetics can still be of benefit though.

The hallucinogenics have been put here so you can reach upward. The universe knows this is a dense reality and it also knew some aids would be necessary for humanity. The powers-that-be wanted to give you some tools. There is not a general desire from the universe to keep you down. It *wants* you to be successful in the experiment taking place here on the Earth plane.

Yes, hallucinogenics have been used in many cultures to understand the nature of the universe. Yes, hallucinogenics have been used to open the windows so you can see into alternate realities. Yes, you will get a glimpse of what is possible in the human mind, which will *truly* be possible soon without the use of aids at all. These glimpses into alternate realities and alternate focus of consciousness are exactly just that—-glimpses. These glimpses can show you what you are striving toward. This is what you will eventually be able to do without drugs.

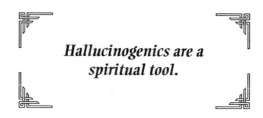

Hallucinogenics are a spiritual tool.

Drugs are not a toy. They are not to be taken lightly. Your surroundings must be secured, sacred and safe. The people you do this with must be on a similar wavelength as yourself. Otherwise you may find you have interfering energies in your journey. It is important in journeys with hallucinogenics that you do not allow yourself to be taken into negative directions for too long. Only entertain this if the negative direction is aiding you in a deep healing, something you prepared for ahead of time, and something you have purposely decided to work with. Much healing can take place if you use hallucinogenics for healing the dark places in your psyche. It can backfire on you, though, and that is why it is *not* our highest recommendation to do it this way unless you have a large amount of self control and a good grasp on self worth.

If you do hallucinogenics alone, you may find you are more likely to go into your deep, dark corners. You may also find it is harder to change the direction in which you are going while you are on these drugs because there is no one there to divert you, distract you, redirect your energies, or reassure you that everything is alright. If you do not have the power to do this for yourself, you may find the hallucinogenic taking *you* for a walk instead of the other way around. Using the hallucinogenic to go into a dark corner of your mind can be beneficial only if you have the ability to shift your focus at will and love yourself.

It is important to realize it is a drug, it is temporary, and it is simply something you are exploring. It is important while you are on the drug not to be attached to feeling functional and in control on a physical level, for you are not always so.

When using hallucinogenics, you are altering the DNA. You are altering your physical structure in order to alter your mental, emotional and spiritual structures. The physical structure is a key to accessing your other bodies. The organics alter it temporarily, although you can consciously keep some of the changes you like and make them permanent. The synthetics alter your DNA in more long term forms, but it is not necessarily bad, especially if your journey was magical and healing.

Some of these alterations can be beneficial, and some of these alterations can be *non*-beneficial. One of the non-beneficial alterations is when you allow your mind to think you are being destroyed while you are doing an hallucinogenic. You are in a sensitive state of mind when you are using an hallucinogenic. You are quite vulnerable (open) to what you create with your mind.

Reclaiming the Shadow Self

If, while you are doing the hallucinogenic, you say to yourself, "Oh! I might never be able to have a child. Oh! I am losing my brain cells. Oh! I am doing something bad to my body," then this is truly what is happening. This is something you will create if it is something you believe.

Now, if you say to yourself, "Oh! I am altering my reality. I am letting myself get a glimpse of what it will be like when my DNA is completely awakened and my consciousness can hold the light this glimpse is showing me," this is better. Then you are doing a healthier and more beneficial thing for your body.

The hallucinogenics will only hurt your body if you do them too often or if you *think* they are hurting you.

Hallucinogenics were put on this Earth by God. They are here for a reason, especially the organics, like peyote, mushrooms, or other types of naturally occurring hallucinogenics, of which there are many. These are fairly safe for you. The ones called LSD, ecstasy, and other synthetics, are perhaps more dangerous for your body if you would like to know this. These are not drugs you shouldn't take if you are attracted to them, for they will teach you much. But they are ones you should approach with a little more caution than the organics.

The hallucinogenics are each different in nature. They each have different sets of energies behind them and you must realize this when you ingest an hallucinogenic of one particular type. You are associating with the energies behind that particular hallucinogenic. You must decide which energies you would like to associate with the same way you would pick your friends. We will speak more about this in the next chapter.

The organics are something you can do more often. We would not suggest more than four times per year maximum. The synthetics are something you should do less often. Perhaps only once or twice per year. This is not something written in stone. Some of you will be able to do the hallucinogenics more, and some of you will not be able to do them quite as much. The shifts they create will take time to integrate. If your integration process is difficult or drastic after using these, you may want to take this at the perfect pace for yourself, which might be a bit slower. Realize that you may not necessarily be aware of all the integration taking place.

If you are attracted to doing this, we suggest only using a hallucinogenic during ceremonies in nature. There is a powerful shift in energy when these events occur. Nature ceremonies are full moons and solstices. At these times, the windows into alternate realities, dimensions, and different modes of consciousness are already opened a little. If you use a hallucinogenic during this time, instead of any other time, you will get much more out of it. This is because you will be further ahead than you would have been if you had to cover the ground in your own psyche which nature already covered for you.

During these openings in nature, much energy is generated. If you are interested in your physical surroundings during these journeys, it is a good idea to be in nature when you use these drugs. Do not simply sit in your apartment and look at the walls. You will miss out on much magic. If you are not interested in your surroundings and want to go deep inside yourself, then curl up in a blanket and go within. You will find much magic inside. Both ways of journeying are valid.

When you prepare for your journey with an hallucinogenic, speak with the energies associated with the drug, the guides around you, and with God Himself. Ask for a good experience. Ask for healing, wisdom, or whatever it is you are after. Asking is very important in *all* your endeavors. If you do not ask, you do not have any extra help. You might ask the Earth to ground you. You might ask the universe to show you the heavens.

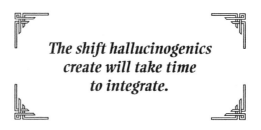

The shift hallucinogenics create will take time to integrate.

All of you have been starving for home. You have missed your home for a very long time. You wish to see it again and you can do this in brief moments with hallucinogenics if you are peaceful within the drug's embrace. If you are not peaceful and enter the drug's influence in fear or participate with people around you who are in fear, you might encounter the hell frequencies.

If you are not attracted to these drugs, for God's sake, do not do them! If you consider hallucinogenics or drugs of any sort (even chocolate!) a bad thing, *then it truly is a bad thing for you.* You will not have a good experience with it. If you approach these drugs with nervousness, you may find they simply amplify your nervousness ten times it's normal amount. Make sure you are in a good mood if you are going to take a journey. Basically, all these drugs do is amplify your own energy and abilities. They do not do much more than that. They amplify your consciousness and they open the veils somewhat.

During an hallucinogenic journey, you are not seeing the full picture. The veils are not totally parted. However, they *are* parted enough to tantalize you to do more drugs because you are so enticed by the beauty you have seen. We understand this. We recommend that you do not do an hallucinogenic again the next day or even the next week.

We suggest adjusting your energy centers before and after using hallucinogenics. Balance yourself when you go into it, and balance yourself once you return. *Especially* when you return. It is also a great idea to sweat or cleanse the day before you ingest the drug, for you can eliminate unnecessary energy you may be carrying.

After your journey, eat well for the next day or two. Then you will want to remove the chemical deposits from your structure by drinking a lot of water and perhaps fasting for a day or two. It is not absolutely necessary to cleanse, for some of you can handle this more easily in your physical structures than others. Some of you have livers which are able to process this more efficiently. If you are not one of these, and you feel you are toxic afterwards, we recommend you cleanse. Sweating in a sauna type atmosphere would help. Only a short fast is necessary, and not a long one. The deposits have not been deeply buried yet. They will come out fairly quickly.

Different hallucinogenics require different preparations. We suggest whenever possible, ingest hallucinogenics in a liquid form. The body can process liquid much more easily than a solid. For instance, if you want to take mushrooms, and they are dried, we suggest you make a tea or tincture out of this instead of ingesting the mushroom itself. If they are fresh, it is alright to eat them, for your body will be able to process them fine.

Hallucinogenics And Marijuana

Reclaiming the Shadow Self

They still have their life-force in them and have not "died".

At some point, you may find you are not getting much out of the full blown journeys with hallucinogenics anymore. This is a clue that you are soon going to enter the phase of your life where you can attain the same states of mind *without the drugs*. If you still want to play with the hallucinogenics, we suggest taking only small doses which give you a light dusting of "magic". Then let your own mind do the rest. You will be surprised at how much your mind will do.

We realize the subject of hallucinogenics is rather controversial for some of you, but again, we invite you to only accept that which rings true for you. We realize this is more information than you might expect from a channeled source, but we also realize that the hallucinogenics are very widely used and there is a bit of confusion about their use in spiritual circles. Many are afraid to approach the subject because society has mixed feelings about these drugs.

We have addressed this subject because there are some who would like to try these hallucinogenics but are uncertain about their validity in spiritual use. We would like to reiterate that they have been used for spiritual practices for many centuries and by many civilizations, even before your known history. In fact, they are used less in a spiritual context than they have ever been before. Hallucinogenics have always been available on the Earth ever since humanity stepped away from it's enlightenment. *These drugs are powerful spiritual tools*. We cannot stress this enough. They are not toys.

At this time, these drugs are more often used for partying or for recreation. This is not exactly how they were meant to be used. It does not mean you cannot play while you use these drugs, but they were not created to be used in a casual way. They are meant to be used with reverence. They are meant to be ingested with full knowing that you are using them in order to expand your consciousness.

If you can expand your consciousness by consuming a hallucinogenic and going to an amusement park to ride on roller coasters, this is fine. Yes. As long as it is your path and as long as it works for you. If you will be paranoid, nervous or uneasy in the heightened state at an amusement park, then this is *not* what we would call a good use of the drug. This is where the possibility of a non-beneficial effect could take place, for these impressions will remain engraved on your DNA. Choose wisely the impressions you want to be recorded in your energy field.

We advise you not to feel guilty if you are using an illegal drug. The only ones who think these drugs are wrong is your legal system. They are only illegal in the view of your government, which is a manifestation you have set up with everyone else in the mass consciousness. These drugs are not illegal in the view of God or the universe. Most of you as individuals do not see using drugs as a "wrong" thing, although you may not know how to use them quite yet.

If you use an illegal drug, *do be careful!* You do not want to be tangled with a system that sees it as a crime. Be careful about where you do these drugs. Be careful about having them around unnecessarily. Do not store large amounts of them. Simply get them when they are needed. Much care should be taken while tip-toeing through a system which could crush you or thwart your purposes in unfavorable ways.

It is as if you are in a foreign country. You are in a land which is governed by different rules than you are governed by personally. This means you must be incognito about your activities if they do not match what the system says is acceptable. We will speak more about this in Chapter 12, *To Buck The System Or Not To?*

Now:

There are things about marijuana we would like to speak about, for this is a very commonly used drug as well. Marijuana is a mild hallucinogenic. If you are attracted to this drug, we suggest you do not use it everyday. We suggest you use it with the reverence you would an hallucinogenic, although you can certainly use it more often than an hallucinogenic.

Put *at least* one day between every usage. And when you do use it, only smoke it until you are high. Do not smoke it again once you begin to come down. The second time you smoke the drug, it is not doing much more than polluting your system unnecessarily. You may have noticed your second session with the drug is not nearly as potent as the first.

In the past, if you smoked it every day constantly, you have found there comes a time when the drug doesn't seem to effect you much more than making you tired. You may have found that if you stopped smoking the drug for a while your tolerance to it decreased again. Then you could indulge in the drug with the desired effects once more—-until the next time you overdid it.

If you use it once in a while and use it in "one time" sequences, you will get more out of it. You will have a clean experience with it on all levels.

It is a good meditation tool, but not one you should use every time you meditate. Otherwise, you may find yourself dependent on it to get into the states of mind you are trying to achieve naturally *without the drug*. If you are one who likes marijuana, we assure you this is okay on your spiritual path. This will offer you many perspectives in your meditations. As we said, do not use it in every meditation, for you are missing the point if you do.

**Hallucinogenics
were meant to be used
with reverence.**

There will come a time when you will not *desire* to use marijuana. At that time, it will not be useful for you anymore. All you are using it for right now is a tool to make a deeper connection with God and your soul self. At a certain point it will do exactly the opposite for you. You will know if this is happening when you get there. Overuse (abuse) of the drug will do the same. Your guides will nudge you if you need notification from them.

Think of any mind altering drug simply as a preview to an excellent movie you are looking forward to seeing. In the meantime, use it wisely. Pray when you use it. Connect with the high beings who are associated with it, no pun intended!

Marijuana is an addictive drug, yes, because everyone is addicted to beauty and expanded states of mind. This is the reason why any drug is addictive. It is because you are striving to be closer to your soul and to God, which is a peaceful, happy state. A drug can give you a sense of this in yourself.

If you are with your friends in a room and you cannot visibly pray, do so in your mind. Thank the universe for this mind expanding drug and ask it to do beneficial things for you. If you use it for recreational activities, this is not the highest use of marijuana. However, if it is the way you are using it, look for all the energies underneath your conversations. Look deeper into the energies of your friends. Try to sense the dimensions underneath the one you are seeing with your physical eyes. And most of all, get into your heart space and look at your companions from there.

Affirmations

1. I choose wisely the energies I associate with through drugs.
2. I use moderation in the use of mind altering drugs.
3. I am free from negative influences surrounding any drug.
4. I approach drugs with respect, reverence and wisdom. I am free of fear.
5. When I take a drug, I allow it to pass through my body without damage.
6. I am protected when I use a drug.
7. I only allow myself to have positive and constructive experiences with drugs.
8. I choose wisely the circumstances in which I use a drug. I choose a secure environment. I choose like-minded people for my surroundings.
9. I only allow positive imprints to be stored in my DNA. I release all negative imprints from my past encounters with drugs.
10. I am aware that I have the ability to experience naturally everything I experience while under the influence of a drug.

Exercises

1

When using a drug, search for the underlying energies in everything around you. Look for the realities underneath the one you presently see. See if you can at least feel it. Take notes.

2

Keep notes about the inner sensing mechanisms you discover while you are under the influence of a drug. Look for the inner mechanisms right underneath your physical senses. There are many more than five. Most of these other senses are situated in the other three etheric bodies (mental, emotional and spiritual).

Play with these mechanisms and make a note of them. Then, after the drug has worn off, try to find these senses and use them while you are in your normal state of consciousness. This is a chance for you to facilitate the natural emergence of these senses in your ordinary reality. The idea is to use a drug only so you can discover your natural abilities. Try to duplicate and enhance your experience while you are in ordinary reality.

3

While under the influence of a drug, ask others what they are experiencing and what senses they are discovering. See if you can find them in yourself as well. Compare notes with your journeying partners. Play telepathic or other metaphysical games with them. You may surprise yourselves!

Reclaiming the Shadow Self

Chapter 7

Other Drugs And Vices

We see there are many of you who dabble in drugs other than the hallucinogenics. Some of you feel hopelessly addicted. We would like to address drugs like alcohol, cocaine, heroin, speed, crack, or other such drugs which are considered harsher.

These drugs are simply mind altering spaces, and again we would like to advise you to choose wisely the energies you get involved with. There are living energies behind these drugs too, not just the hallucinogenics. We will not name which ones of these drugs have which energies behind them for you will have to decide this for yourself. We will tell you this, though: not every drug was created with your highest good in mind and not every energy associated with a drug has your highest purpose in mind.

Some of these energies can work through you and have gotten a good hold on you through your addiction. They may be offering you pain relief from your emotional self, but they are keeping you "stuck" there as well. Some of these energies are not ones you want to have attached to you or working through you. You will need to discern for yourself which ones are which.

None of the energies associated with these drugs are "bad" in particular. Remember, it is only you who *considers* them bad. If you make this a one time *only* thing, perhaps once more in two years, you are in a safe zone with this kind of exploration. Perhaps you may even learn something.

It is important that you do not put yourself in places where you are exploring dark areas on purpose *all the time*. It is okay to say, "Oh! This is something that seems dark and sinister to me. Let me see what this is all about. Let me see if I can change how I feel about it. Let me see if I can find the light behind all this."

But do not over do it. You will find there is light behind *everything*, no matter what it is, no matter what cloak it wears. However, if you explore these tricky areas in consciousness all the time, you will lose your focus and forget the light you hold. When you decide to purposely explore something you consider bad, or have fear of, make these sojourns only occasionally and in the spirit of wisdom.

For instance, you may consider crack bad, but you are curious about what it is. You may happen to visit someone who offers it to you (for the universe will offer you the things you are curious about) and we say to you that it is okay to explore it once or twice just to see what you think.

Then, after you have explored it, you may have decided you do not like it much and you realize the energies behind it are not ones you want to surround yourself with or associate with. You may walk away from it and say, "Oh! What an interesting experience. I have learned something here and it was okay that I did it, for I was curious. But since I did not like it, I will not do it again." It is the old saying, "Try something once, and if you like it, try it again. If you don't, leave it alone." This is okay. Not only did you satisfy your curiosity, but this will also give you the ability to better understand one who is addicted to crack. You will be familiar with the energies he or she has attracted.

If you are curious, honor your curiosity. However, *use wisdom as you honor your curiosity.*

For some of you there may be something in your self which is curious about the drug but not curious enough to try it. You already know it is something you don't want to experience. This is fine. Go with your inner wisdom.

When you ingest any drug, you are also taking on it's energies. Get to know your abilities and limits in transmuting energies. We guarantee you *will* be good at transmuting energies once you finish your transformation and find yourself in a state of enlightenment (for you are all masters of transmutation). Until that time do not challenge yourself beyond your abilities. Again, it is not a bad thing to try things which are different and new. However, you must have mastered yourself entirely before you can stay immune to adverse effects. Most of you are not able to do this yet.

Heroin and other morphine types of drugs do not help the emotional body if used over the long run. If you are wanting to use this drug every day and numb yourself from your life, it would not be a wise use of the drug. This is an instance where the drug and the energies associated with it can run you instead of the other way around.

Narcotics were not meant for everyday use, not even in small amounts. What they do is give the emotional, mental and physical bodies a moment of relief from pain. In altering the physical body, you alter all the other bodies. These drugs are *only for absolute crisis* in the emotional, mental and physical bodies. These drugs were meant for moments in your life when the emotional or physical impact is overwhelming.

For instance, you have lost your leg in a car accident and your emotional body is overwhelmed. You cannot process or understand what has just happened to you, and you want to jump out the window of your hospital room because you do not feel there is any reason to continue living. This is a time when a drug like this is useful. It will calm the emotional, mental and physical bodies and anesthetize you temporarily.

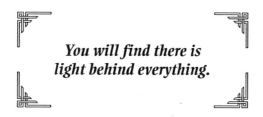

**You will find there is
light behind everything.**

If you have lost a loved one, and you are so overwhelmed with grief that you want to follow him or her into death, we would say to you this is another example of a time when a drug like this is useful. It is a tranquilizer and a pain reliever for all the bodies. Again, we reiterate that this drug is not useful in casual use.

You who have deep emotional pain in your lives are more susceptible to the addiction to peace through drugs. You must resist this, for it will keep you from healing yourself. It will make you think you are already healed because you cannot feel it. This is not healing!

Some of you are taking pharmaceuticals for medical reasons and are wondering if these drugs are really good for you. Some of you have begun to look for natural alternatives. Natural drugs versus synthetic drugs? Use what works for your body. If you believe in a synthetic drug, it will do its job for you. It is not a bad thing. It is not a good thing. It is just a thing. It is a tool you can use. It will do whatever you *believe* it will do for you. It will harm you if you *believe* it will harm you. It will help you if you *believe* it will help you.

You can use different tools to accomplish the same goals. All synthetic drugs originate, at least in the idea form, from copying something which happens in nature. If you can get it naturally we suggest this is most beneficial. Once a drug has been altered, manipulated, or processed in a certain chemical way there are differences which will not cover all the bases that a natural drug will. A natural drug is most closely connected with the human organism. Synthetic drugs are missing certain ingredients which are not even known about yet. However, these missing elements will not be a source of damage for you. The synthetic drug *can* help you.

Be aware that synthetic drugs might have more influence from *outside of your system*. Much depends on the people's energy who created the synthetic drug. Not all these influences are bad. Not all of these influences are good. They are just influences which you must discern about.

If you find you like a drug very much, and you like the energies behind it, your next step is to evaluate the drug and your abilities to stay in control with it. It is important for you to keep yourself on the side of addiction where you do not become *run* by the drug or the energies behind it.

For instance, you have tried heroin once and it was so beautiful and peaceful that you decided it was something you needed to be careful of because you could see yourself getting addicted to it. You decided you

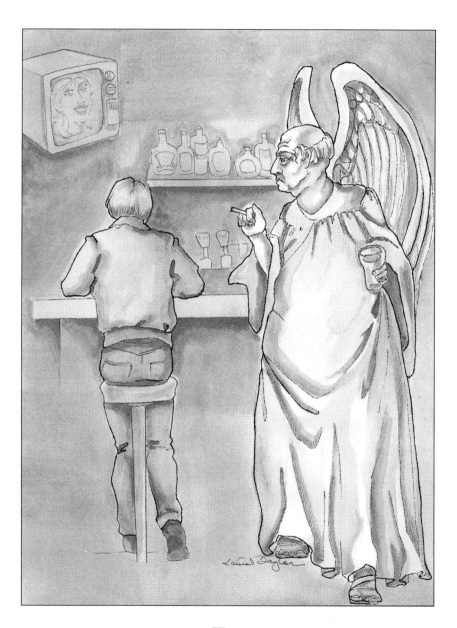

Vices

must be careful about being around the drug, or having it available, because you know you might have difficulties resisting it. It is good to be discerning about what you can handle and to look for the small print which goes along with the drugs.

You may find that the effects of the drugs change for you over time. It is because *you* are changing all the time. For instance, you might have gotten much wisdom out of mushrooms, LSD, or ecstasy at one time, but suddenly you don't seem to get much out of it anymore at all. This is a signal for you to stop. Do not keep trying to get that experience once again. This is also a signal that you are moving beyond the need for the drug in order to get the glimpses.

There may be a neutral time, a neutral zone, a no-man's-land where you feel you cannot get the glimpses with the drugs anymore and you cannot get the glimpses on your own yet. We advise you to be patient at this time even though you may be craving the beauty you have seen with the drugs. Realize you are moving toward the ability of seeing this beauty without the drug. Know this is happening.

The cleaner you can keep your system, the better off you are and the more quickly this ability will come to you. This does not mean you need to have a perfect and evolved body in order to receive your abilities. By a clean system we simply mean one that does not have heavy energy in it. If there are things which make your energy heavier, these are the things to avoid. You all know which ones these are for yourselves, for they are different for everyone.

For one of you, dairy may make your system heavy. For another, too much marijuana will make your system heavy. For another, oils may make your system heavy. For another salt may make your system heavy. For another, meats may make your system heavy. Meat will make *everyone's* system heavy. The only things you can bet on *not* to make your system heavy are fruits, vegetables and grains.

As far as sugar, coffee and cigarettes go, these things are okay in moderation. *Everything* is okay in moderation. You might find that if you use moderation you will not even be attracted to your vices anymore. In the meantime, it is important not to hurt yourself with these things. If you do them everyday you are hurting yourself. Some of these things have been made attractive to you by the energies behind them. Again we say that no energy is bad. Misguided is a more accurate word for this.

Coffee, if used once in a while, can actually be an enlightening experience. Tobacco, if used once in a while can be enlightening as well. Even sugar can be useful to you once in a while.

We realize that during your transmutation process you might need these things. This is perfectly alright. If you need a cup of coffee because you are feeling dangerously depressed, it is okay. Perhaps you feel like going to your ex-lover's house and breaking everything in sight because you are angry. If a cigarette would keep you from doing this, by all means, smoke the cigarette! Perhaps you find yourself crying uncontrollably, you cannot withstand the emotional direction you have gone in anymore, and you want to turn back. If you feel that a little marijuana will help you to calm down, then smoke it. Many of you are using marijuana or other drugs as emotional and physical tranquilizers. This is alright in moderation.

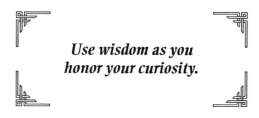

Use wisdom as you honor your curiosity.

You might find that your old vices creep up on you as you transmute the shadow self. The process may be difficult and it may make you desperate. If these things help your desperation to be a little less, we advise that you go ahead and use these things if you are attracted to them. You will find other things to replace your vices at a later date in time, like peace and self worth. All we ask is that you do not overdo it and try to refrain whenever you can.

If you have quit smoking for years, and suddenly, as you go through this process, you find yourself craving cigarettes, this may be a signal that these can help you in your present state of emotional energy. Please do not feel as if you have failed in any way if you smoke a cigarette again. You are digging up old wounds. You are digging up old sores. Whatever you used to put "bandaids" on these wounds at earlier times in your life may be the only thing you know how to do at this time.

Do not feel guilty if you find yourself using your old vices again. This would be adding stress to your emotional state. Your vices are helping you *temporarily*. You are doing this to help yourself through a very difficult time. Once you are happy and find yourself enlightened, you will not need vices at all. You will not even care to be around your old vices. You will lose interest in using vices and the desire for them will fall away automatically as you raise your vibration. This is only something you desire in this moment because you are sad or you have fear. Once you are free of these emotions, you will not want your vices. You are treating the cause instead of just the symptom.

If you are one who likes to eat ice-cream when you are sad, then go ahead and do it. Don't withhold things from yourself that can comfort you if you are in a panic or a downfall. As long as you balance out the ice-cream with exercise, for instance, it is alright. If you are doing good things for your body, a few things like this will not hurt very much. If you are drinking a gallon of water per day, yet you would like a cup of coffee in the morning, then we would say you are attempting to balance the effects in some fashion. Make moderation and balance part of your list of characteristics.

This is a touchy area and this may raise some controversy in your mind when you hear us say not to concentrate on breaking your habits and vices right now. You might say, "But *spiritual* people don't smoke, drink or overeat, do they?" Many people will have judgment on you because you still have "bad" habits. Some will even be smug with you about your habits because they themselves have been able to break them.

For those of you who are dealing with vices, and dealing with the fact that you smoke, do too many drugs, bite your nails, want coffee, beer, television, or distract yourself with too much sex, these are the things you have used to comfort yourself in the past. You are human, so give yourself a break. Only concentrate on your healing, not your vices. (Of course, keep it to a minimum.) Keep in mind that even as you use these things in the present to ease your pain you are moving toward a place in yourself where you will not need these things anymore.

We address this in this chapter for many of you feel you are "stuck" in these habits. We would rather suggest you are only *wearing* these habits temporarily.

If these habits appear attractive to you, for instance you think you look very cool while leaning on your elbow at the bar with a cigarette in your hand, then how do you think you can look cool without the cigarette? Visualize ways in which you can do this. Use these pictures in your mind to boost your self image. Perhaps you can look cool with your thumbs simply hooked in your belt. Perhaps you can look cool by wearing an air of confidence in your energy field!

The desire to look cool, the desire to be noticed as a wonderful, charismatic and attractive being, is natural. This is a desire for recognition. Someday you will be beyond this, but in the meantime, work with it as a pattern which you are in. Play with it, get creative with it, and look for other ways to boost your self image.

You all suffer from lack of a good self image. It is not a bad thing to have a little pride right now since most of you have been suffering from an inferiority complex for a very long time. We are pleased to see you are moving out of this. We hope this information helps you. Try being addicted to meditation, if you would like a new addiction which will not harm you!

Affirmations

1. If a drug was positive for me in the past, but does not affect me positively in the present, I take this as a cue to stop. I let this drug go with thankfulness for the doors it has opened for me.
2. I am master over my addictive tendencies.
3. I exercise self discipline and control when tempted to abuse a drug. I allow myself to use vices only when I absolutely need them to counteract a negative direction I might take. I release myself from guilt and judgment about myself.
4. My system is clean and free of toxins.
5. I release any energies which have attached to me during a past addiction to a drug.
6. If I begin to have fear while doing any drug, I immediately take a breath and calm my emotional body.
7. I have a good self image.
8. I am cool, charismatic, and magnetic to others simply because I am being myself. I am attractive without a vice or a drug.
9. I use moderation in everything I do. I balance my use of vices with positive actions.
10. I am addicted to meditation!

Exercises

1

When using one of your old vices, watch the emotions which precede the desire to use them. Watch how your body, mind and emotions react or adjust while you use the vice. Then imagine how you can create the same effect without the vice.

2

Before you change anything, take notes on what you are putting into your body and in what quantities. This includes everything from food and exercise, to smoke, drugs, and water.

Check to see if you are balancing the negative vices with positive actions. This will give you a gage on how much you need to balance the weight of your vices. This will also give you a chart to see how you are progressing as you begin to cut back. This will show you where you need to make adjustments.

3

Meditate on your present status with your vices. Ask for help with replacing these with more positive expressions. Ask for help in replacing the old ways of dealing with negative emotions. Ask for the exact causes of your need for vices. Then hold an alert waiting space for the revelations and insights to come to you.

Reclaiming the Shadow Self

Chapter 8

Dimensional Travel

Not many of you see other dimensions with your physical eyes right now. Instead you will *sense* them physically, emotionally, mentally or spiritually. Use your sensing mechanisms and know that other levels are there even though you do not see them with your eyes. If you sense someone's aura or emotional state, this is more valid than you know even though you do not see it. Honor what you sense, for *later* you will see it with your physical eyes.

If you are a sensing kind of a person, which is more common than anything else, use your strongest mechanism instead of using your weakest to access other dimensions. For instance, if you sense things more than you visualize them, then use your strongest, most developed and available mechanism. If you are a visual person more than a sensor, then go with *your* most developed mechanism.

Many of you are frustrated because you are not able to see into the other realms yet. You are aware that they are there, you crave astral travel, and you crave the freedom to move about in the other realms. We understand this frustration. Try to relax. It is coming to you as soon as you remove all the blocks in your past which are still effecting you. You cannot get off the ground because you are tied to your past. You are tied to the energies you left there.

Reclaiming the Shadow Self

When you are able to move about freely without anything hindering you, running you, or taking you for a walk instead of the other way around, that is when you will be free to explore the other realms. It will happen because you have developed objectivity, self mastery, and obtained skills in setting your boundaries and enforcing them.

These abilities are necessary to develop because the other realms can be frightening places. They can devour you if you do not know how to set your own boundaries and use discernment. It is good for you to practice right here on the Earth plane where your conscious mind is safer. Start realizing what your boundaries are and learn how to enforce them in a loving way with other people. You will need these skills in the other realms. You will need to use great discernment and you *must* have the power to walk away in a loving fashion from certain entities or situations you do not wish to participate with. Your boundaries and your ability to enforce them will be the deciding factor as to what will happen to you and what will not in the other worlds.

For instance, if you were able to enter these other realms right now and you still have fear in your mind, heart and body, you will be attracting and attracted to that which is in yourself. If you do not feel self worth or you do not feel self-deserving, you will find entities and energies who will reflect this back to you and hurt you. They might use you or trick you into doing things you would not normally do. For instance, this is what has happened to ones who have been "abducted by aliens" and have had traumatic experiences with it. (Not all visitations with alien entities are traumatic. Some of you will visit aboard vessels of light.)

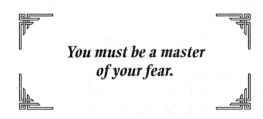

**You must be a master
of your fear.**

You must be a master of your fear. You have to be completely in charge of yourself in order to be safe in the other realms. It is not all light and joy. It is not all fun and games. You will be playing with the "big boys" and they might play rougher and smarter than you are used to. There are many diversities in the other realms, and if you do not want to be thrown around, tossed around or lose control of what you choose to experience, you must be in control of yourself right here and now in your life and with your emotional body. If your emotional body is not secure and stable you will attract things which will cause you deep fear, hurt and will actually damage you further.

So if you are one who has not been able to access the other dimensions, even though you know beyond a shadow of a doubt they are there and you desire greatly to enter them, we assure you that you are on your way. You have done the best thing for yourself by not allowing yourself in your *conscious* mind to leave physical reality. You knew you would be hurt.

Being in control of yourself is the only thing you will ever be in control of. Once you are able to move about in the universe, you may find that you are on your own moreso than you are here on Earth. You might not have quite as much guidance, for the guides will assume you know what you have gotten into and will be able to deal with it on your own.

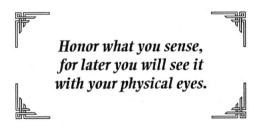

**Honor what you sense,
for later you will see it
with your physical eyes.**

Learn what you need to be like here on the Earth plane. Learn how to handle life on the Earth plane. Once your life is flowing correctly, smoothly and peacefully, you will find that the veils will open up without any effort from yourself. Then you can step through without fear, trepidation, determination, or whatever way you have been approaching it up to this point.

If you have not been interested in other realms, do not worry about these words at all. If you are not attracted you will not go! Some of you are perfectly fine with physical reality, and you would like to concentrate all your energies here. This is alright. This is good. This is fine. Not everyone needs to be Christopher Columbus.

Those of you who *are* Christopher Columbus, be assured that this is coming to you. Do not feel like you are imprisoned here, for it is not imprisonment at all. It is that you have not *allowed* yourself to leave because you knew you could not handle it yet. *You chose to avoid the unnecessary stress you would have experienced.* Be assured that once you straighten out your emotional body and your core, all your skills, abilities and remembrances will come back to you. You will know exactly how to handle it when you get there. All of you have much experience in other realms, especially those of you who have touched the darkness deeply. You will remember this.

If you would like to start sensing the other realms before you can get there *consciously* (remember, it is inside yourself, and not a destination you "go to") start connecting with the parts of your soul which are living in these other dimensions. There are many aspects of your soul who are not here on the physical plane and live in other worlds. You can connect with them. Ask for dreams, ask for signals in your every day life, ask for clues, and ask for a glimpse into their realities. You are very connected to them. They are the ones who are living in an area you might desire to go. They can send you messages and visions of what it is like. This is safe.

It is *not* safe for you to go yourself into other realities if you are in a state of emotional upset or confusion. Realize that this inability to "get off the ground" has been a safety measure you have put upon your own energy. There is not an outside source keeping you from traveling in the other realms.

Those of you who desire to see the other realms are most likely the ones who are attracted to hallucinogenics. The hallucinogenics are a safe way to see these things, as long as you have secured your environment and you are in a positive state of mind or are approaching a negative state of mind in a constructive way. Be aware that you are taking yourself into a place where you cannot go normally. If you cannot go there normally it

Dimensional Travel

Reclaiming the Shadow Self

is because you are not quite ready. When taking these peeks into the other worlds you can still get into trouble, so we advise you to ask for light and love to surround you during your journey, *especially* if you are going to look into a deep dark corner of your mind.

You will be free to roam consciously in the other realms soon enough. Do not be impatient with yourself on this issue. It will come when the time is right. You are roaming them *unconsciously* right now, so you are having these experiences anyway. You will remember them. Be patient with where you are and accept it.

Think inward.

Once you achieve the ability to see other dimensions you will be challenged to keep your energies focused on the Earth plane. You may feel tempted to use it as an escape from your reality. The ability will open not for you to escape, but to bring back to Earth what you find in the inner worlds.

We would like to give you a tip about dimensional travel. Think "inward". Every time you catch yourself saying "out there" or "up there", replace these words with "inward". It is not levels of high-ness or far-ness. It is levels of deepness. Think of the journey inward and you will be well on your way. Even going inward is not a destination you go to. It is more like opening up to who you are.

Affirmations

1. I practice using my inner senses during my daily activities.
2. I am patient as my abilities are remembered over time.
3. I am master of my universe. I remember the master that I am.
4. I am an objective person. I live in a state of non-judgment.
5. I have defined my boundaries and I enforce them with respect and caring for myself and others.
6. I have clear discernment.
7. I have conscious connection with the aspects of my soul which live in other dimensions. I can see through their eyes.
8. I look for clues in ordinary reality which will trigger my conscious mind. I now realize what is happening in other dimensions. I am experiencing it in my unconscious mind.
9. I am patient with my present state of development. I accept where I am right now.
10. Instead of thinking of the universe as being outside myself, I think of it as inside myself. The journey is inward.

Exercises

1

Sense where there are areas of fear in your emotional body. Work with them in a detached yet compassionate way. Face your fears and work with them as if you were simply working on an ordinary task. Move into your fear frequencies willingly.

How can you dismiss fear in any given situation and turn it into love, confidence, healing and vulnerability. Mastering your fear is key to discovering your power and freedom. Fear is a habit you have learned.

Reclaiming the Shadow Self

Where do you tense up when you feel fear? Where do you stop flowing? What can you do to relax these areas when fear comes up? What words would you say to yourself for reassurance?

2

Pretend, imagine, daydream and float in what you think other dimensions might be like. Write down your daydreams and imaginings every time you do this. You will soon discover that your imaginings become more and more real and weren't just imaginings at all.

3

In your meditations, think of going inward and seeing your "universe" from the inside out. See what sensations come up when you meditate on moving inward toward the stillness. This inward movement to the "alert waiting space" is the doorway to your freedom.

See if you can sense your inner vision. It is 360 degree vision in all directions, not only horizontal and vertical. Do this with all your senses. Your physical senses are only a product of your inner sensing mechanisms. Ask for help with developing them. Allow yourself to remember them. You must open your inner senses before you can perceive other dimensions. You must also be able to achieve alert stillness before you can travel.

Chapter 9

The Bad Guy Syndrome

Some of you have become a bad guy in this lifetime. Some of you have already *been* a bad guy in this lifetime. Some of you act as a bad guy upon yourselves. *All* of you have been a bad guy in your past and even your future lifetimes.

It is beneficial for you to get over the fact that you have been a bad guy as soon as possible. You have all been *saints* as well. However, you may not be remembering these lifetimes quite as often as you are remembering the bad guy lifetimes. The lifetimes in which you were a saint are not causing guilt and conflict within yourself.

Many of you ask, "How is it possible that I could be a being of light and love if I have done such horrid things? I must not really be a good person if I could have done such things."

First of all, realize this: you are not a "bad" person! You are not a failure in the eyes of God because you misused your power. You did this for noble reasons, believe it or not. In fact, you are an excellent student who took an advanced course of study called "Misuse of Power 101". Sometimes it takes several lifetimes to finish the course of study, depending on the depth of the lesson.

In the bigger picture, you have tricked the ones who changed the human genetics long ago (which was quite possibly one of your own selves). You wanted to change the wiring in the human system which causes criminal behavior. In order to do that, you had to *enter* the criminal mind and heart. You had to be inside it in order to change it. You chose to be a villain so you could get to the bottom of why this "miswiring" exists in the human consciousness.

You had to find out what the criminal heart and mind *feels* and *thinks*. Only by being inside the criminal heart and mind could you break up the pattern in the human circuitry. You had to get involved if you were going to turn things around.

The human race has to relearn everything it already knew, rebuilding from the inside out. This was chosen on purpose to strengthen the connection of consciousness to physical matter.

The beings who are watching are whistling through their teeth in amazement at what you have accomplished so far. They are also quite impressed that you were daring enough to become the bad guy. Not everyone had the bravery it was going to take to be part of the Earth experiment. The Earth experiment struck fear in the hearts of many, even ones who were very far away from it's energy.

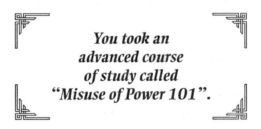

You took an advanced course of study called "Misuse of Power 101".

Back to the slightly smaller picture.

Those who have been bad guys in their lives will be powerful forces in the light once they have transmuted their darkness. The worst perpetrators will become the greatest saints in your world. They understand darkness more deeply than anyone else. If you are one of these, you know you can really pack a punch. You are strong. It took great courage to explore the frightening places you have gone into.

The ability to be able to pack a hard punch is a good thing, for if you pack your punches in the direction of light and love, you will effect others in as positive a way as you have been able to effect them negatively. You have the ability to bring a large portion of light into the world or a large portion of darkness into the world. Whatever you decide, you are able to bring lots of it! It is *your* choice whether you will bring light in or bring darkness in.

It is *alright* that you have been a bad guy. It is only a big play and not quite as "real" as you might think. We are sure you heard this concept before. Think of yourself as an actor in a movie playing the villain. When the director yells cut, you take off your mask, crack a joke and go to have lunch with the entire cast, including the good guys. This is a better way to think of this for yourself. You are only playing a role and you are learning something as you go about it.

You were cast in the role because you are perfect for it and can deliver it convincingly. You really have not harmed anyone, even though you may find it hard to believe. On the soul levels, you all are watching, giggling, concentrating and learning as you go through the play.

For instance, if you are in the bad guy role and you have beaten the good guy, or frightened the good guy, you have done your job well! When you all break out of character and discuss how well the acting went, how convincing the other was, what the lessons were, and how to do it differently, this is more like how it works on the soul levels. You are enjoying the play from there in safety.

So if you have mutilated someone, or harmed their life in some way, you really have not hurt the soul of that person. You simply delivered the part the person asked you to play. Of course you did *choose* to play the part for your own reasons. You auditioned each other before you were born.

There is a level of the soul which does not experience any of this in the sense that you do. Think of yourself as an extension of your soul, the "reach" your soul has made into third dimensional matter (there are other kinds of matter). *You* are the one who "feels" this plane. It is as if the soul is watching all of this while in deep thought and concentration about what is going on. It is as if your soul is watching a dream go by, and *you* are the aspect who is living in the dream, feeling the dream, and making the decisions in the dream.

Your soul can influence the dream, or send you messages, but *you* are the lucid dreamer on this plane. *You* are the one who is able to focus the soul's attention in physical reality. It is not as easy to be conscious on a physical plane as you might think! You are very good at it.

You are entering a time where the soul will no longer be experiencing the physical dimensions on Earth as if it were a dream. The soul itself will become the lucid dreamer. It will be the one who makes the decisions once you reunite with it and blend back in. Please do not think of this as if you are about to relinquish your throne in reality. Instead, think of it as if you are bringing a larger portion of your self into reality and your body will be able to hold more of the greater consciousness that you are. You will not be disintegrated or annihilated, you will simply become grander in your being and the purpose of your conscious mind will be different. Your conscious mind is integral in the process of manifesting on the physical plane.

Now. More about the bad guy syndrome.

We do not suggest you play the bad guy on purpose, thinking you are the vessel for everyone's lessons. In this lifetime, eventually, everyone gets to be a good guy, so to speak. That is what this particular scene is about on the Earth plane at this point in time. Everyone who wants to be a good guy *will* be a good guy. Everyone who wants to continue to be a villain, well, there is no room for them in this particular scene of the "movie" here on Earth. Your part is over, and now the scene is basically about "the bad guy turns to the light".

Some of you who read this book are actually in prison right now. Our deepest and most gentle love goes out to you. We wish to surround you with light and assurance that you are valuable and precious human beings. It is never too late for you to enter the light in yourselves. You have been in the darkness, yes, but underneath it all, you are truly in the light. There is a lesson for you here, a task to accomplish, and you will help the mass consciousness greatly if you heal and forgive yourselves for the actions you have judged as wrongsome. We love and respect you dearly. Please do not give up on yourself.

We are touching with a few of you who have murdered someone and might have gotten away with it or might not have. We are touching with you who have killed someone through negligence or by accident. We are touching with those of you who have committed another type of violent crime and might have gotten away with it or not. We are touching with several of you who have sexually violated another person. We are touching with you who have beaten your loved ones or have been violent in other ways. We are touching with you who have hurt other people in less drastic ways. It can be as simple as gossiping, slandering and damaging another's reputation, causing their friends to dislike or distrust them, or breaking their possessions.

It doesn't matter whether you did these things in this lifetime or not. All of you have done them at one point or another. All of you have experienced the despair of being in prison also.

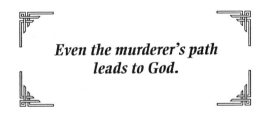

> ***Even the murderer's path
> leads to God.***

You are valuable and precious in the light, even though you may think you are not redeemable. You are loved and cared for and your predicament is completely understandable in the other realms. If you are a perpetrator, we would like to remind you that you started out as a victim. *All* perpetrators start out as victims. No baby is born and wants to grow up to be a bad guy. You are innocent. You were *shaped* by inner and outer forces that you agreed to subject yourself to.

If you are in prison and you are innocent of the crime you were convicted of, realize that this may be connected to karmic balance. Remember, karma is not punishment. *Karma is balance of experience.* We will discuss this more in the next chapter. It is important for the soul to look at all aspects of any given area of study. Realize that you are simply gathering experience as a soul, not being punished. If you *did* commit the crime you have been convicted of, these words are still true for you. You are gathering an experience and exploring all aspects, pleasant and unpleasant. Your soul is concerned with gathering a complete education and exploring this particular physical reality. It does not balk at going through unpleasant phases of experience. To your soul it is irrelevant.

Perhaps you are in prison for a crime you do not believe is wrong, like possession of marijuana or other drugs you appreciated. Perhaps you have landed yourself in prison by doing something out of character or "stupid". Perhaps you are kicking yourself for getting tangled with the system. These words are true for you too. You are gathering experience. At an unconscious level, you set yourself up for it because it was an area of experience you wanted to work with and needed in order to balance out your education on Earth concerning duality. Again, we say it is not punishment. Instead, it is courageous exploration of a frightening area of human reality.

What you are attempting to transmute is daring and deep. You have the utmost respect of the ones who are watching on the inner planes. It is one thing to be born with love and abundance all around you and maintain it through life. It is quite another thing to be born with nothing and make something of yourself. You are recognized for what you are doing. You are recognized for the difficulty of the task you took on.

Healers, guides and teachers will *flock* to you immediately if you call sincerely for help on the inner planes. You will be overwhelmed, shocked and amazed at how much they want to help you. You will not be able to take all the love the light beings will give you. If you open your heart and let their love and healing energies in, expect to cry a lot and feel emotionally raw for a while. It will be a deep and far reaching healing for you.

Everyone has their own styles of getting to enlightenment. All paths lead to God, even the murderer's path. There is no one who is not moving toward God in their own fashion and in their own way. As many people there are in the world, that is how many paths to enlightenment there are. Again we would say there is no such thing as "stuck", just the illusion of it. We realize this is a difficult concept to understand, but even Hitler was moving toward God.

The Bad Guy

Reclaiming the Shadow Self

Hitler is a good example of a real life villain. Hitler is a light being, and what he did was a precious gift for the world by being the vessel for a huge lesson which was desperately needed. Just as Jesus and other saintly role players have come to the world to teach a lesson, so did Hitler.

Hitler taught the opposite lesson. He taught all the world what the misuse of power looks like and convinced the world this was not a direction humanity really wanted to go anymore. If you look upon your current events, you will see that all nations are leery of possible Hitlers who might loom up into power. All nations are doing whatever they can to prevent such a thing from ever happening again.

Hitler's life was a pivotal point in humanity's direction into the future. It was a grand play to show what was ahead for humanity should it continue to move in the direction it was going. Hitler taught the world what it would be like to live under the tyranny of darkness and misuse of power. This was something the human race was considering experiencing more of in its future. This was a good thing for the human race to see, for it gave humanity enough of a taste of global tyranny to realize it was finished with this idea and it would like to move into the light instead.

So you have much to thank Hitler for. He has saved you much grief which you would be experiencing right now in your reality had he not shown you what tyranny is all about. He was a powerful and high being. He was able to pack a hard punch and drive the lesson home in the mass conscious mind.

If the lesson Hitler taught the world had not been learned, we hint to you that Saddam Hussein's role in the world would be much different than it is right now. Hussein would have much greater power than he does, and he would give you world tyranny in a much harsher fashion than Hitler ever did. In fact, there would be a *few* tyrannical rulers in your reality right now if you chose this path. They would be more formidable, foreboding, possibly alien, and it would be a disheartening and undesirable reality to live in.

This is why humanity was headed toward self destruction, for the quality of life would have been squashed. Humanity would have reached a point of despair and hopelessness. In fact, humanity would have been *praying* to the heavens for death and extinction. So be thankful for what Hitler has done for you as a species. In a way, he has saved your lives and the lineage of the human race. Otherwise, the experiment on the Earth plane would have been over for the time being, having reached a dead end. The universe would have had to start from scratch again, although it would have gained much wisdom, and try once more to make the human psychology work benevolently in the freewill zone.

If this kind of destruction had happened, there would have been many setbacks for the freewill zone universe. Realize that many are rooting for you, for you have made a wise decision on the mass level. You have attracted a lot of attention to your corner of the universe. The self imposed "death sentence" for humanity has been lifted.

Hitler has given up much in order to play this role for your world. It was not an enviable part. It was a part that only a high and powerful being could play. It is like the angel in heaven saying to God, "Okay, if you really need a bad guy, then I will play it for you, although I really don't enjoy being your opponent. But I will do it for you anyway because you desire it, you need it, I happen to be good at it, and I love you enough to do it."

We understand this is a difficult concept to grasp. Many have a vested interest in hating the Hitlers in the world. Please realize that these Hitlers have presented you with lessons in the misuse of power and its devastating effects.

It was unfortunate that the play concerning Hitler had to take place. If you are Jewish, please do not be upset with us, for we are not advocating what Hitler did to you. The world has much to thank all of you in the Jewish lineage for because you agreed to play the victim role. It was truly a difficult and painful part to play, and is one that you still play somewhat in the continuing saga on Earth. Yours was not an enviable role either. Our deepest love and respect is with you.

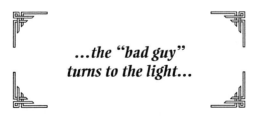

...the "bad guy" turns to the light...

Upon his death, Hitler had great remorse. He was very afraid of the repercussions from his acts. He still sheds tears for those he hurt and he experiences the concept of self-hate. He wishes to repair the damage he has done, for at the soul level he never wished to hurt anyone in the first place. This is the part of his job which is not enviable. He was well aware of the repercussions he would reap upon himself once his life was over and the balance for his acts would need to be made. He entered the law of duality willingly, knowing that all acts are counteracted by it's opposite, since the universe is a paradox.

Now, think of this. If a soul such as Hitler's is so powerful that he can create great darkness on a plane of reality, this same soul will be that much more powerful as he creates light on the same plane of reality.

We hint to you that Hitler is working with the guides who are helping in Earth's transition at the present time. Many of you will refuse to believe this. He is generating much light for you, instead of darkness. He is "paying off" his karmic debt with service to mankind. He will also be learning about forgiveness as the human race slowly moves toward forgiving him and showing their graciousness to one who has wronged them. He was, and still is, learning a huge personal lesson for his own use.

Those of you who have judgment of these ones who have played villain-like roles in your life, be it the Saddam Husseins, the Hitlers, or ones who are less famous and have hurt you personally, we ask you to change this for your own sake and for theirs. You are holding *yourself* in a space of hatred and you are holding *them* in their spaces of *self* hate. They are having difficulty transmuting their darkness, be they dead or still alive on this plane of reality, for you are keeping them there and not letting them move on from the roles they have played for you.

If you were to free them from their roles, they would greatly appreciate this for it will help their growth and healing as well as help you on your own journey. Your hatred and disgust toward these ones is not serving anyone toward anchoring light and love on the Earth plane.

Realize that every single one of you have been a Hitler. You would not be dealing with what you are dealing with right now, or getting ready to serve humanity in it's reach for the higher frequencies if you were not. A soul who has not been a bad guy in it's past lives on Earth would have no idea what to do with the victim concept which many of you are dealing with. You are here to heal both the viewpoint of the victim, *and* the viewpoint of the perpetrator.

Affirmations

1. I forgive myself for the past. I forgive others for the past.
2. I am a being of light and love. I am radiance.
3. I am objective about my prior transgressions and I see them as the learning opportunities they are.
4. I allow others to exercise their freewill even though I have the power to interfere.
5. I only use my power in loving and benevolent ways.
6. I view all of this reality from the soul level.
7. I realize that there are deeper meanings underneath the events in the past, present and future.
8. I am now a good guy.
9. I forgive myself for being a bad guy in the past.
10. I have learned much about the misuse of power. Now I am learning about the loving use of power.

Exercises

1

Visualize yourself getting a new part in the "play". Visualize yourself getting the role of the good guy. Visualize yourself as a powerful and respected saint. See that you are able to effect people in positive ways as powerfully as you have been able to effect them negatively. You do have the power to do it, you know. See if you can effect someone positively today without being blatant. A simple smile or a kindness would do the trick.

2

Create three columns on a piece of paper. Make a list of all the "bad" things you have done. In the second column, make a list of the people who have been effected adversely by your actions. In the third column, list the reasons why you have done these things. Your reasons are valid, even though you may have acted inappropriately. Look for patterns. You might find that you have been the perpetrator for the same reason in most of the incidents you have listed.

These are the areas where you feel most vulnerable and these are the very areas which need to be healed. Once you heal these areas, you will find that you are no longer driven to "act out" your upsetness. These offenses from others will not upset you anymore.

In the second column, you have a list of all the people you need to mend hearts with.

3

Send love and nurturing to a person you have harmed. Hold this person in your arms and convey to him or her that you mean no harm anymore. Dispel his or her fright, for he or she may still have fear of you. Visualize yourselves rising above all of this and looking at it from a deeper level. There is total understanding on your side and on the other person's side at the soul level at all times. You can go to this place any time. Work with this person on the soul level and try to understand what this person has been teaching you. Look at what you have been teaching him or her. Generate love between yourself and this person.

3A

This will help greatly in developing objectivity toward yourself and others. Visualize yourself looking down (outward) on the play you have participated in on the Earth plane. You are simply the observer of the drama. Pretend there are two of you (which there are) and they are the observer and the observed. See if you can switch back and forth. Try to use the viewpoint of the observer as much as you can, since this is fairly new for you. Let yourself be the audience of yourself. Tune into the part of you who is sitting back comfortably, in safety, and is simply watching the drama play itself out. You will find much release about the parts you have played, are playing, and will play.

Now tune in to the guides who are around you and are aiding you in your transformation and healing. It is easy to reach them at this level. You will feel them. Reach for them whenever you are upset. Ask them to help you understand what you are seeing in the play. They are there to help you with this.

Reclaiming the Shadow Self

Chapter 10

Victim, Perpetrator, Karma
And Anger

Many of you are discovering a past life where you played a murderous villain in a war, you killed many victims, or you have caused much anguish and grief for people in some way. Some of your past lives include experiences of being a vicious and ruthless ruler.

Some of you are only remembering victim lifetimes and are wondering why there are so many. If there are a long string of victim lifetimes, then you can be sure to find a lifetime before them of being a bad guy.

You were fully aware of the effect your misuse of power would have on you in your next lifetime. It took great bravery and courage to take on a lifetime which would bring so many repercussions.

"If I do something bad to someone else, then something bad is going to happen to me." This is "level one" of karma. This is a first grade way to look at it.

The string of lifetimes where you were victimized were not necessarily the consequences of your karmic punishments. We would like you to find higher levels of understanding about karma. Instead, look at these lifetimes as exercises in compassion for the ones who were your victims. Look at these lifetimes as an exercise in learning about cause and effect. Look at these lifetimes as lessons in freewill and misuse of power from the viewpoint of the victim. Look at these lifetimes as a balance in education and experience.

If you try to see the deeper levels of karma, perhaps the reasons for pain and suffering on this plane of reality will begin to make sense to you. It is a stretch, but we assure you that you can eventually understand it. Karma could be better called "exercises and lessons". Karma is the "structure" of this particular educational environment. In fact, the Earth experiment has given the universe many ideas for schools in freewill and other such topics and it will be less drastic for the soul. It will be more like a simulation than the real thing.

Karma has to do with the fact that there are polarities on this plane. In duality, every action is counterbalanced until it is stabilized. Karma has to do with the fact that you are desiring of a diverse experience and you are exploring the light and dark with great fascination. Karma has to do with the fact that you are exploring the realities which exist in a freewill zone, and there is much to learn about power and right use of will.

You see, you *chose* to misuse your power so you could understand it more. Often, a student will be requested to "do it wrong" so he or she can see the results. You know how to use your power because now you know how *not* to use it. You know what love is because now you know what love is *not*. When you know everything there is about how *not* to do something, you automatically know how to do it right. That is how the class "Misuse of Power 101" works on this plane. Forgive yourself for not being perfect before you took the class. You were *supposed* to do everything you did. You were *supposed* to "do it wrong". Now that you are graduating from the class, you can "do it right".

You *chose* to misuse your power so you could learn what *God* knows about freewill. If you know what God knows about freewill, then you are qualified to have power which is normally reserved for Him. You desired to explore being the perpetrator, and you desired to explore being the victim. *This was your choice! You signed up willingly, even though you might not have realized what you were getting into!*

The perpetrator is afraid of being the victim because he has learned that he can hurt himself by being *vulnerable*. The victim is afraid of being in power because the victim has learned that he can hurt himself by being *powerful*. We can tell you how to handle both. As the perpetrator, we suggest you open the parts of yourself which have been hurt when you were vulnerable and heal them. As the victim, we suggest you take your power back and make a commitment to use it in light and love. Simple as that.

Now: There are practical measures which you may need to take.

If you are a victim and the perpetrator is in your face every day or in your house, then you must do whatever you need to do to remove this situation from your life. If the perpetrator is hitting or verbally abusing you, then you do not have much choice but to remove yourself from where you live and find another place to go. If the perpetrator himself or herself does not choose to leave on his or her own volition, then *you* are the one who must leave. Do not wait for the perpetrator to do it even if you have to take a loss in possessions or stability. There are many of you in this situation, and not all of you are a woman being hurt by a man. Many of you are male and are being victimized by the female.

All you have to do is state to yourself that you are done with this and you will not accept this behavior from another person in your life anymore. You must rise to a level of self-deservingness where you have new boundaries about what you will and will not accept from other people.

If the perpetrator is one of your co-workers, it doesn't necessarily mean you have to leave your job in order to remove the perpetrator from your life. It may simply mean you refuse to be intimidated by the perpetrator anymore. If you stop playing the victim, the perpetrator will either transform and grow because of you or the perpetrator will look for someone else to victimize.

We do realize that all of this is easier said than done, and we support you on the inner planes concerning these issues.

There is a difference between judgment and discernment.

Reclaiming the Shadow Self

You have the power. Remember, you are not trapped, although you might think so. Lack of money is no reason to stick around and put up with abuse. Be assured that the universe will lead you to safety if this is something you desire. You may have young ones in your care, as well, and you are their guardian angel in the physical, so to speak. You have contracted with them to take care of them, keep them safe and teach them about life.

What exactly *do* you want to teach them? That abuse is alright? That being a victim is acceptable? If you have these young ones in your care, then you must do them a favor and remove them from physical abuse if this is what is going on for you all. You may even have to go away from your children for a while in order to heal if you yourself are the abuser. *It is not wrong to go away for a little bit in order to heal yourself so you can be a better parent afterwards.* Your children will appreciate this, actually. But do not leave them with someone who will abuse them while you are gone.

We see many of you in this situation and we are supporting you in your choices.

If you have been a victim please do not berate yourself for this. You have not done something to deserve it. You are learning about boundaries which you have not set yet. It is simply a lesson you needed concerning discernment about others, your surroundings, or your assessment of your own abilities. You may have made a misjudgment about someone's integrity of character, or you may have misjudged the safety of a certain area where you were walking, or you may have misjudged a situation you became entangled in. Be aware that you have done nothing wrong. It is okay that you made mistakes in your discernment of the character of others. It does not mean you are worthless or that you should give up on yourself or let the offending ones devour you.

There is a difference between judgment and discernment. Judgment has emotional overtones and sees good versus bad. Discernment comes from a place of objectivity and simply chooses for the self what to participate in and what not to.

Judgment says, "Oh! That is bad. Don't do that because it is bad. Don't hang around with that person because he or she is bad. Don't go to that place because it is evil!" Discernment says to you, "Hmmm...that is interesting, but I don't choose to participate in that event, or with that person because that doesn't match with me. I will continue onward and look for something else to do." At the same time, discernment has compassion for the ones who it chose not to participate with and gently wishes them love in their journey toward the light.

If you were powerless and were attacked against your will when you were minding your own business, or you were a child and you were at the mercy of the adults around you, this is something you *chose*. You all have different reasons for choosing what you chose, and only you can know these personally. You can change your choices any time you want now that you realize you can take your power back.

Sometimes the crisis happens as an adult. This is something you chose partly because you were not paying attention to the growth your soul wanted to do and you needed a wake up call. Perhaps someone has attacked you and has taken your sexuality, for we are speaking to many of you who have been raped. Perhaps someone has attacked your business and made you bankrupt, or you have lost a limb in an accident. These are things you chose because you wanted to go deeper into yourself.

Always pay attention to your inner self and what it is trying to teach you. Strive to learn the lessons which are always coming to you. Also realize that these are not only wake up calls. Before your birth, you chose to work with these energies .

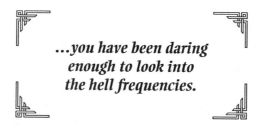

...you have been daring enough to look into the hell frequencies.

If you look back on the crisis moments in your life, you will see they have *forced* you to go deeper into yourself and learn about who you are. You have become stronger. You have defined a certain boundary which was not clear before the crisis. You have realized something you needed to realize about yourself. You have learned how to take precautions in a world which is not all fun and games. You have learned to develop discernment.

Instead of looking at the *de*struction you have suffered, look at the *con*struction and the rebuilding you have done. You are more wholesome and more stable than you were before you experienced this, believe it or not.

Some of you are ones who hurt others but you cannot seem to control this in yourself. For instance, you have gone into a blind rage once again and your emotions got carried away. You realize that you have beaten (or abused in other ways) your pet, your companion, or your child again. Perhaps you broke things even though you did not want to and have promised yourself before that you would stop this behavior. Perhaps it is as simple as verbal abuse. It keeps happening over and over again and you do not know how to break this pattern and get hold of yourself. You may be getting frustrated and feeling ready to give up on ever getting out of this lifestyle.

We highly recommend that you go to an energy worker. There are some of you who have misguided energies attached to you who are keeping this energy going within yourself. This is because it gives *them* energy. It may feel to you as if you are trying to lift an entire train off your back, so you will need the help of someone who has a crowbar and a crane. For the serious cases, yes, you may need to have a dark energy lifted off your field. All we can say about the fact that dark energies sometimes attach themselves to a human is that you are evolved enough to handle it.

Tell the energy worker what you are doing and what you suspect. They energy worker will most likely be able to tell you for sure if what you suspect is truly the case. If you think you have attracted a dark entity, again we would like to say to you, do not think of this entity as an evil or bad one. It is simply a misguided one who does not know any better how to get it's energy.

For some of you, it is not so drastic. For some it is simply the fact that you are "stuck" in a pattern and it keeps folding in upon itself. It would *still* be good for you to go to an energy worker and put a break in the pattern. It may have locked onto your system with more tenacity than you have energy in yourself to lift alone.

We want to reassure you that if you are one who has been trying to break a violent pattern, even if it is only emotional or verbal violence and not physical violence, you can transmute these energies and the means will be given to you. You *do* have the power to overcome this in yourself. You are not a victim of your patterns. Right now your patterns are taking you for a walk instead of you being the one who is in charge of the walk you are on. Take back the reins and redirect your energies. You can do this.

If you are a perpetrator or an aggressor you are valuable players in this game on Earth. The victim is often the child, or another kind of vulnerable one, and is looking to you to refrain from passing on the aggressive patterns which will create the perpetrator in him or her later in life.

For instance, because this is what you have taught them, many children grow up to beat their own children, thus making them the perpetrator. A woman who is raped may go insane and kill innocent men for sport, thus becoming the perpetrator. The perpetrator pattern is always preceded by the victimized state. It is the perpetrators who must transmute the energies which cause people to be victims and then become perpetrators later. If the perpetrators transform themselves, there will be no more victims in the world. That means there will be no more perpetrators either. Then the world will be a peaceful place to live and entirely different avenues can be explored by mankind.

So if you are a perpetrator, your position is one of importance. You have the chance in this lifetime to become a powerful example of love. We understand this is hard for you to believe, but it is true. Even if you are in jail, murdered someone and gotten away with it, raped someone, or if you have caused someone to lose their source of income, their livelihood or zealousness for life, you are important ingredients to the transformation of the planet. You have simply taken on the villain role so you can transform it.

Some of you have taken it further than anyone else dares to. You must commend yourself for your bravery for you have been daring enough to look into the hell frequencies. We admire the fact that you were willing to go into such a dark area which was terrifying and traumatizing for yourself. Not only have you traumatized yourself, but you are also connected to the trauma you have caused in others.

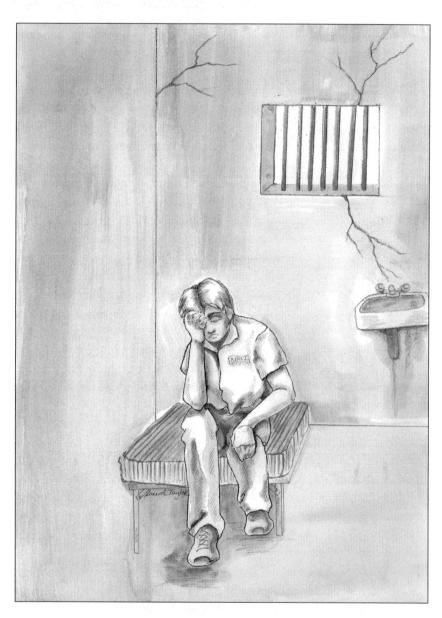

Victim, Perpetrator, Karma And Anger

You are probably feeling guilt about this, especially if you are one who has been drawn to this book. If you are reading this book, then you are trying to transmute the darkness in yourself and trying to stop hating yourself for this. You are on the right track.

Those of you who are in prison or are in places where you are unable to connect with energy workers, please do call on the guiding ones. They are there to help you lift dense energies from your system. They surround you with light in the dark place you are in so you can gain a little more ground in your journey toward the light in yourself.

If you are a villain in your own life and in other's lives, we ask you to *stop* being the villain now. Begin to explore your vulnerability. *Show* your vulnerability and *show* your sensitivity. Refrain from your old behaviors. We realize this is difficult, for most likely you have been trying to do this for a long time already and have not been successful. Call on the guiding ones who specialize in this area and they will help you to change your behavior if it is your choosing. You are a being of light and love, although most people around you probably do not see you this way. Be assured that the ones in spirit do.

Those of you who have been in the villain roles, or still are, will find that miracles happen as you honestly and sincerely transmute your darkness. If you are intending to become enlightened, your villain-like tendencies will come up less often and you will be freed from the things and the places which are imprisoning you. Once you reach inward and make the initial effort, the universe will give you a helping hand and *pull* you into the light as much as you will allow it to.

Do not feel you should throw yourself away because you have messed up so badly in life and you are unable to repair it or live with yourself because you hate what you have done. The universe loves you and sees you as valuable even though society seems to have thrown you away or given up on you. Some of you are very alone. The guiding ones are with you and their hearts break for you. Know you are loved.

Remember that it is all a play. It is not quite as real as it seems. You may look at your prison walls, or whatever kind of prison you have created for yourself, and you may say, "This is *very* real and not a dream at all!" We say to you that you are free in many ways which you do not realize. Much prayer will help you. Affirmations will help you in transmuting your shadow self. You *will* find your freedom again. You are allowed to pray for miracles, you know! Realize that the miracle will come from yourself, though. A miracle can present itself to you, but you are the one who must have a sense of deserving and allow it to happen to you.

Get aggressive about your healing.

If you are still feeling aggressive and angry, use this energy wisely and get aggressive about your healing! Get aggressive about removing these patterns from your system. Get aggressive about changing yourself. Get aggressive about setting your boundaries with other people or the dark energies which might have attached to you. Get aggressive about transmuting darkness into light.

It is alright to express anger. Please do. In fact, throwing fits is highly encouraged. The guides completely understand. Just as tears must come out, so must anger.

You have a right to be angry, even though you did volunteer for this. You have been in pain for a very long time. You have been in the dense energies of the Earth far longer than you expected. Any dignified being such as yourself would be angry about the conditions you have been subjected to. You have had enough of it and you are ready to be done with fear already. You've been wanting to be done with it for a long time. You have reached the end of your rope. That is why everything is changing on the Earth now.

Anger will lead you to your pain. Anger is not a bad emotion. It is a very strong emotion, yes, and one which is useful when you want to get something done.

Use your anger against the ignorance and darkness in yourself. Do not use it in a destructive way. Simply say, "I am not happy with this anymore. I don't like where I am. I am going to do something about it right now!" and set your path into motion toward the light. If you use your anger in this way, it will be more constructive. Using your anger in destructive ways is a waste of energy. It only goes around in circles between yourself and others, and simply goes nowhere.

Do not be afraid of your anger anymore. From this point onward you can express it in a way that does not bring back to you disharmony.

Expressing anger can be a tricky thing. If you are feeling over-whelmed with anger toward yourself, another, or God Himself and you feel like you need to break things, hit people, or do things which are harmful to yourself or others, there is one thing you can do. Simply vent this physical action onto inanimate objects while you are alone.

Go into nature and throw rocks and sticks, or run for as many miles as you need to before you are tired. If you deal with it in this way, your anger will not last long. You will get to the place where the tears live. Do things which will not hurt yourself or anyone else. Also, please be careful not to hit the animals if you choose to go into nature to throw stones!

Nature is objective. Rocks and trees do not take it personally. They know humans are strange creatures and are quite unpredictable. Nature has patience with your tantrums. This goes for the animals as well. Simply vent your frustration in a *non-destructive* physical way, and this is okay. While you are venting, do this with love for yourself, for you are venting some very depressed and compressed emotions which have gotten too large to be controlled.

**Anger will lead you
to your pain.**

Eventually you will not need to do this anymore. You will learn dif-ferent ways to work with your emotions in the future. For now, the act-ing out method is alright. It is something you are familiar with and something you understand. We would simply like to stress that you not act it out on yourself or on others.

If you cannot express your anger without getting into trouble, for instance, if you are in prison, go directly to the place where it hurts. Ask the guidance around you to help you bypass the anger and heal the painful place where the anger is coming from.

It will be easier to control your behavior once you process the traumatic events in your youth. Go back to the roots where your problems lie. These ideas were developed in your childhood. Go back to your early years and find the parts of yourself which you have abandoned there. You will find many pieces of abandoned self there. In fact, you may find that you run into selves which are very angry with *you* for abandoning them! This is alright. Understand it, for they have a reason to be angry with you. Simply tell them you are back and you are sorry it took so long, but you would like to continue where you left off and help them evolve and grow.

You are going back in time to re-parent yourself. You are going back in time to change the way you feel about the incidents that happened to you and around you.

Affirmations

1. I am safe in the world. I am safe when I am vulnerable. I let my vulnerability show.
2. I am free of negative karma. Under the law of grace, I am starting anew with a clean slate.
3. I have the power. I release myself from victim roles.
4. I turn my judgment into discernment.
5. I understand that the universe knows what it is doing. If things seem bad to me, I realize the potential for learning opportunities and a chance to grow.
6. I release the negative patterns I have been wearing.
7. I am in charge of my life. I have the power to change it.
8. I use my aggression and anger to get further on my spiritual path.
9. I express my anger in constructive ways. I go past the anger and deal with the pain underneath it.
10. I release all negative energies which might have attached to me in the past and are still with me (this includes past lives). I send them back to the Source with love, light and understanding. I thank them for what they have taught me.

Exercises

1

Go to your soul level and place yourself at the point where you are choosing your challenges before birth into this life. See yourself in the classroom with your soul group. You are studying your past lives and the past lives of the other members in your soul group. Based on the past lives, you are deciding what is the next step in your latest string of lifetimes which creates a lesson about use of power. You are also considering the fact that the Earth plane is in the midst of a major transition and there is much to transmute. At the soul level, there is a state of innocence and purity. You are making clear decisions. What decisions did you make?

Connect with the state of clarity and purity you were in at the time of birth, free of the ideas about reality and yourself that you now have. Connect with how innocent you were as a newborn baby. This is how you really are.

2

Imagine yourself straddling the darkness and the light with one foot standing in each. Sense the differences in both. What sets of feelings and thoughts do you have of each one? How do you see them?

Now imagine yourself reaching outward to each side and taking hold of the dark and the light with your hands. Pull them toward yourself and bring them both into your heart. Blend the darkness and the light together, making them one. Bring harmony to the dark and the light, as if they are long lost friends who had a falling out long ago and are finally "making up" with each other.

Feel the sense of relief, now that the battle in your heart between the dark and the light is over. Feel the oneness as it floods through your system. You are bringing harmony to the duality within yourself. What does the darkness and the light look like now that they are one?

3

This is an exercise you can use the next time you are angry. Sit down and clench your fists. Close your eyes. Find the places where the anger has a grip on your energy systems. Ask the anger to take you to the place where you feel hurt and where root issues exist. Ask what you need to do about the issues in order to overcome this pattern. List the judgments you are making about another person or yourself which must be examined.

Now take the anger out of your energetic system and hold it at arm's length. Use this energy to create momentum for a shift in yourself. Tell the universe you are sick and tired of being in the darkness (having no awareness) in this area of your life. Get as aggressive as you want to get.

Pretend you are Zeus holding a lightning bolt in your hand. Now, with all the force you can muster, plunge the lighting bolt into the darkness around you and inside of you. Scream as you do it if you want to. Watch this bolt explode into light, dispelling the darkness in one huge sweep. What happens? What do you see in the area that was once dark and is now lit up? If you don't get it right away, look for it in dreams.

Reclaiming the Shadow Self

Chapter 11

Euthanasia, Execution and Crisis

We have been asked if drugs are useful for execution or euthanasia. First of all, execution is absolutely out of the question. No execution of any sort is humane. There are no circumstances in existence which make execution of another being acceptable, no matter what that being has done. Execution is *absolutely* an incorrect use of will and power.

However, since execution is a reality on this plane, we would say yes, a gentle execution is less detrimental to the passage of a soul into death than a brutal one. It is not beneficial when death is met with anxiety and fear of the painful way in which it will take place.

If the person is killed in a painful or terrifying way, this can cause delays in that person's passage into the light. He or she may encounter confusing or terrifying experiences on the other side until he or she sees what is called by you "the tunnel that leads to the light". A painful or brutal death is very stressful. There is much help on the other side of death and not many get stuck for very long. Some do, though. It is a difficult passage when the death is frightening. This is the kind of thing that creates trapped spirits on your plane of reality who haunt specific places.

Being murdered is a traumatic experience. The more brutal and frightening it is, the more traumatic it is. Most of you are less afraid of death itself than you are of the painful ways in which it can happen. Your past life experiences are why this fear is present. You have died in many terrifying and painful ways. Being slowly and painfully murdered is just about the deepest experience of fear you can have on this plane of reality.

It is a challenge for the soul to shift the experience of being painfully murdered. It becomes a highly charged cellular memory and must be shifted at one point or another in the journey through the wheel of life. If death was quick and painless, it is not as difficult to process.

If you remember brutal and excruciating deaths, you may actually find yourself collecting aspects of yourself which have become trapped spirits and "ghosts" on this plane of reality. Many of you have trapped aspects of yourself in your past. You will receive much of your power when you retrieve the "ghosts" you have left on the Earth plane who never took the next step.

A "ghost" happens because you were not able to accept the circumstances and ramifications of that specific incarnation. Many of you actually have aspects of yourself who haunt places whether anyone notices them or not. When you remember a specific lifetime or traumatic death experience, quite possibly you did not retrieve that aspect of yourself after death and it has been trapped there. Now is the time to invite this aspect of yourself to integrate the experience and move on.

We would like to state again that execution of another person or any other kind of living being is misuse of power and is considered murder. The entire society is guilty of murder when a member of the living races is executed. The entire society is responsible for the misuse of power which has taken place and finds itself doing a "balancing act" for the event within the structure of karma.

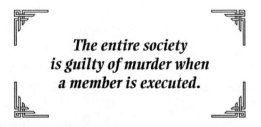

**The entire society
is guilty of murder when
a member is executed.**

Societies must learn how to handle "incorrigibles" in a different way. No being is absolutely and irreversibly "incorrigible". The hardest criminals will have a meltdown in the heart if there is a powerful concentration of love directed toward him or her. *Society must learn how to heal the damaged person instead of destroy the damaged person.* Entire societies must learn how to hold great focus of love and direct it with great power and intent to the damaged individual. (This will be necessary in the future of Earth to avoid being victimized by other races.)

If societies can work together as a unit and learn how to heal an "incorrigible", negative karma will not be set into motion for the society. The new paradigm method of dealing with "incorrigibles" will be anchored on the Earth plane. Once this is done, societies will no longer need to learn this lesson and "incorrigibles" will not exist in this reality anymore. It is simple.

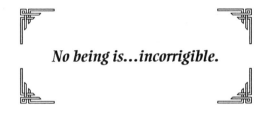

No being is...incorrigible.

About euthanasia. If you are diagnosed as being terminally ill, we would like to say to you that our love is with you. We also want to congratulate you on the blessing you have received. Not many people have a chance to say good-bye to all the ones they have loved on the Earth plane or repair all the relationships which have been broken, thus clearing the slate in the same incarnation in which the events took place. This has given you a chance to prepare for death ahead of time and embrace forgiveness and grace before you die instead of after.

This opportunity is a blessing for you. You have a chance to put closure on this incarnation. You have a chance to gather your loved ones and say your farewells in a peaceful way. If you have broken relationships, or people you still have hate with, it would be most beneficial for you to clear this up before you leave the Earth plane. If you do not, you will pass into the after worlds with this remaining in your energy and then you must come back and learn this lesson again. It is important for you to repair this broken line in your life. Even if you cannot contact this person, repair it in your heart at the energy levels. Even if this person has passed on already you can still touch him or her on the inner planes. This would be a most beneficial use of the time left here on Earth.

It would be good for you to notice what you can and let your heart be softened instead of hardened. Instead of lamenting the life lost or being angry about the fact that your life has been said to end soon, we advise that you embrace it. Use the time wisely to clear your lessons in this life and finish your studies with good grades, so to speak.

However, just because a medical person or institution has told you that you are terminally ill, it is not necessarily true this will happen. You might become a living miracle. Very soon, even AIDS patients will become living miracles. If you repair and transmute the things within yourself which caused the physical manifestation of a "death sentence" on yourself, then it is possible for you to change the outcome of this. The crisis is only there to awaken you.

The world can use living miracles at this time. There will be some of you who might be diagnosed as terminally ill yet will live far beyond your years because you have volunteered to be a miracle holder in this world. More of you who have been diagnosed as fatally ill are in this category than you realize. Many of you are afraid to believe that you can be evidence of a walking miracle. You must embrace this if this is a possibility for yourself.

Many of you have *not* chosen to be walking evidence of a miracle and you *will* die. Many of you have chosen to do this for reasons outside of yourself. It is not a karmic pay back, a punishment, or an unfortunate development. Many of you have come to teach others around you that death is not a fearful thing and can be embraced in a beautiful way. This takes great courage. Embrace this beautiful lesson you are giving to those around you. Be gracious and loving in the last days of your life, and many rewards will be there in your heart when you enter the next planes. You have much happiness, love and light to look forward to even if you were a foreboding perpetrator in your life.

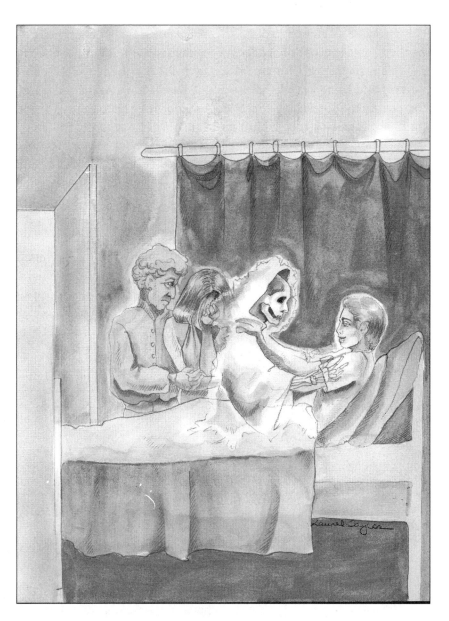

Euthanasia, Execution and Crisis

Reclaiming the Shadow Self

If you are diagnosed to die within six months, are not in excruciating pain yet, and you use the concept of euthanasia at this time, we would say this is premature. You are taking away the possibility that you are a walking and living miracle holder in this world. You also may take away the possibility of teaching those around you that death is not a fearful thing and can actually be a birth into the light.

Some of you have been ill for a long time, you have been in pain, and you simply wish to leave already for there is no chance you will be healed. If it is close to your death, it would be wise to release the struggle against it, for that is what you are doing even though it may be unconscious. The struggle against death and resenting it is why it has become physically difficult for you.

If you embrace death and are in peace, the body will release certain pain relieving compounds which will keep the pain at a level you can withstand easily. There are many things you can use to alleviate your pain up until that point. There are drugs which can numb the pain yet allow the mind to stay somewhat alert. We suggest you continue through to the end if you can. Only consider euthanasia if your pain is excruciating and cannot be controlled.

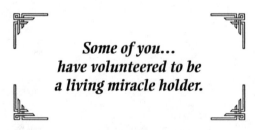

Some of you...
have volunteered to be
a living miracle holder.

It is not the responsibility of those around you to issue euthanasia for you. *It is your responsibility.* Having others perform euthanasia on you is not the best route for it could become a confusing area. It is not clear in human consciousness when it is correct to administer euthanasia and when it is not. This is a gray area and it is not certain at this time that humans can use the concept of euthanasia in a correct, wise, and benevolent fashion. Humans issuing euthanasia to others should be avoided at this time until more is understood about death and more is understood about pain and suffering on the Earth plane. There is a very fine line between euthanasia and murder. It is quite possible that humans will misuse this power.

However, if a person desires euthanasia, it should be allowed. If euthanasia is desired, then it should be done naturally by the person desiring of it by discontinuing activities like eating and drinking.

If you are considering euthanasia by overdose with a drug so you may pass on without pain, it is not a wrong use of the drug. However, it is not conducive to conscious passage into the other worlds. In the past, an old or terminally ill person would stop eating and let themselves pass on in this way. This is the best way to perform euthanasia on yourself. It is good to have a clear mind when you cross over so you can remain conscious in the passage.

Instead of using a drug, perhaps you might want to fast, or request removal of supplemental fluids and vitamins which hospitals administer intravenously. This way, your system will remain clear, and you can let yourself die in a conscious state. When your mind is clear upon death, instead of drugged, you can remain conscious during your passing over and you will enjoy it!

Unfortunately, hospitals are committed to force feeding intravenously if a person wants to die. This is interference with freewill. This controversial issue is being challenged by many in your society. Soon, in your future, euthanasia will be allowed for the terminally ill who are in pain and are past the point of return to health. Eventually, your world will be a place where such things like terminal illness do not exist and euthanasia will not be necessary or useful.

We are not saying live longer so you can enjoy more pain and suffering. We are saying do not miss opportunities that will emerge underneath your death experience which you are not aware of. Embrace your death lovingly and in light and it will be a birth for you instead of a death.

Much can be gained during your last days. You are gathering large amounts of your energy. Your spiritual growth will accelerate by a thousand times if you wish it to be so. The time before death is highly charged and great amounts of energetic healing can be done.

Affirmations

1. I see my terminal illness as an opportunity to gather my energies before I leave the Earth plane.
2. I release my fear about death.
3. I allow miracles in my life.
4. No matter when it happens, I embrace my death with love, calmness and grace.
5. I am enjoying the rest of my life no matter how long it is.
6. I am a living, walking miracle holder.
7. I overcome physical pain with my love for myself and others.
8. I am a wonderful example to others.
9. I can connect with my guides on the other side at any time if I become frightened. They are always there for me.
10. I look forward to my new life in the other dimensions. I will enjoy greater freedom there.

Exercises

1

Tune in to all the beings around you in the last part of your journey here on Earth. Some of them have been with you all your life. Some have been with you at times when they had something to teach you. Some of the beings may have come solely for the purpose of aiding you in your transition from the Earth plane to your next step.

Let these beings encircle you and infuse you with peace, joy, and calmness about death. Ask for the veils to be lifted so you can become more aware of what you will be moving into. If it is becoming harder for you to remain aware of what is going on around you in physical reality, do not worry. It is time to let go of your focus on this reality. It is a good sign if this happens, for you are supposed to let go of it!

2

Practice feeling safe, even in death. Practice being brave and fearless. Ask the guides to help you let go of your fear. Think of all of this as just another great adventure in your life. Assure yourself that your life is not ending, for it is not. You are only letting go of the body. You will experience great freedom, lightness and joy once you let it go. Visualize and imagine all the light waiting for you. What will life be like in the spirit worlds? This is something to look forward to!

3

If you are in pain, work with it as energy. Instead of resisting the pain, fighting it, or being irritated by it, invite it into yourself instead. Imagine that it is a pleasant feeling, one that tickles, or feels like a caress. Imagine that the pain is ecstatic. Learn mind control methods about pain. Turn the pain into something else. This will release endorphins. Deep breathing and exercise will help with this too, if you can do it.

4

Retrieving your "ghosts":

If you remember a traumatic past life experience and you are having a hard time getting over it, you have trapped energy in the past.

Get into your soul level space, the wise, gentle and powerful part of yourself. Dress yourself as a beautiful, angelic guide who is coming to take the lost aspect home.

Go to the place where your spirit is trapped. Perhaps it was a prison cell, a place of execution, or a house. Perhaps your "ghost" has fled to a place where it once took comfort and felt safe. Wherever it is, go there and sit with the "ghost" who is trapped in it's sorrow or anger. Wait until the "ghost" sees you. If it does not see you, shed light on it and wake it up. Break it's focus on it's immediate reality.

The "ghost" will most likely be very sad, upset or lifeless. It may be in a state of shock from it's experience in the incarnation. Smile and reach out your hand and let the "ghost" take it. Say soothing, gentle and loving things to it. Let it know that you can see it's beauty even if it is not presently beautiful. Tell it you have come to take it back to the light (which is where your soul is). Tell it that it doesn't have to stay in this place anymore. Tell it that it is part of you.

Take the "ghost" in your arms and begin to rise out of the place where it had imprisoned itself. If there is resistance to this, then you will need to allow more time for the "ghost" to trust you and decide that it wants to leave. It may take a few days. Realize that your "ghost" has become accustomed to it's sorrow and imprisonment. It's consciousness is caught in a loop. Have patience with this.

Once you have taken the "ghost" out of it's reality, fly with it in the sky or in whatever form freedom takes for the "ghost". Watch and celebrate with it as the "ghost" sheds its darkness and is brought into the light. Spin and dance with it. Laugh with it as it cries out in joy. It will transform before your eyes, become very powerful and self sufficient, and it will be deeply grateful to you. It has been trapped in unsavory energy for a very long time. It will be ecstatic and will hardly be able to contain itself now that the horror and sadness have been left behind and joy and integration have been embraced.

Feel your power coming back to you as your "ghost" releases it's terror, sadness and helpless feelings. Admire the royalty that your "ghost" really is. Admire it's beauty which is now emerging. Invite the "ghost" to be part of your team.

Do this a few times with your "ghost" if the memory of the past life begins to terrorize you again. Once the process is complete, that particular past life will no longer upset you.

Chapter 12

To Buck the System or Not To?

The system is much bigger than yourself and can thwart you if you try to mess with it blatantly. As an individual, if you want to buck the system, this might be a *futile* effort if you do it by yourself. If you want to change something in the system, you will need much support from other individuals in this world. If there is a cause you are passionate about, you can be sure there are many others with the same feelings who would join you in your rally against the system. If there is a flaw in the system that you want to change, you could start by making others aware of it.

A *non-futile* effort to change something would be one where you have the support of many, perhaps a few thousand people, who are willing to stand in front of the White House for a week or pay for court cases which you would like to take the government to court on. We hint to you that there are some of you who will do this and create very beneficial changes in your government. If you have a cause and you want to change a system, you must have support if you are going to go at it with a battering ram.

The battering ram of an individual is not comparable to the battering ram of thousands. The sum is always greater than it's parts. If you want to make a big change, then begin networking, gathering people and making them *aware* of what you have found upsetting or needing change. They may or may not join your cause. If you want to lock horns with the system and have a showdown, great numbers in unison is the only way you will accomplish success.

If you do not have the gumption to begin a revolution, so to speak, then you can be sure you will find someone else to join with who is leading in the same causes you are concerned about. Offer your support, and this will help to bring about the effects you desire. (We would like to make a note here that *in no way should violence be used to make changes. The world is learning how to make its changes peacefully from now on. This is part of the challenge of these times!*)

For instance: If you do not want to pay your taxes on your house because you feel that property tax on your belongings is wrong, then we suggest you go ahead and pay the tax until you can find a large group to join with who are *all* willing to buck the system at the same time. *There is safety and power in numbers.* Alone, you would only be singled out and will find yourself in trouble which you had not bargained for and are not prepared for.

Think of yourself as a spy in a foreign country.

Think of yourself as a spy in a foreign country. Realize that you have to pretend to go along with it for a while until you can change it on the energy levels, which is what you are trying to do. Nothing will ever emerge into physical reality, like a better government, unless it is created first in energy. Once the energy for something is created, then *and only then* can it emerge into physical manifestation.

All these changes you desire in your society must be created in the individual self of all souls on this plane before it will emerge on a mass level. *The battle with the darkness is within yourself, not outside yourself. This*

Spy in a Foreign Land

is very important to remember. *The dark forces are actually you, not someone else.* The changes in your society, and your reality, must happen in yourself first. Then you will be amazed as you watch it unfold into reality with effortlessness and ease.

People are becoming awakened and enlightened more and more often. This awakening may not be noticed until suddenly you realize that it has been happening underneath reality all along and quite suddenly it is there, en masse. When the last one who was needed to tip the scales jumps onto the side of love, the scales will tip abruptly and the light will have a heavier weight in this reality than darkness. It will literally explode into your mass consciousness and into your world all at once when darkness (no awareness) loses the majority rule.

Once fifty-one out of every one-hundred people focus on love instead of fear, the darkness will be dispersed nearly overnight. This is something to look forward to. Be patient while you wait for this time to come. Simply go along with things for a while with a grin on your face, for you know you are effective by changing the system underneath reality. This is necessary first.

If you really want to change the world, and you do not have a manifested vehicle, plan or cause, you can meditate with the *gazillions* of beings who are holding light for this planet and are working toward dispelling the darkness. You can also spread love with all the ones you meet in daily life. You must start in your own corner of reality. If you want to become a leader, you must be master in your own universe first.

If you are not bucking the system in a blatant way, and you are not made a target because you have drawn attention to yourself, then you will be able to function more efficiently in your cause to change the world. It will not do you any good to find yourself immobilized or harmed by the system. It is important to keep your freedom and remain dis-entangled with the system.

Your government, your taxes, and all other areas of government *will* be light filled areas of consciousness. You can be sure of this. It will take some time and it will take great numbers of people uniting in the same voice. Until then, it would be better for you not to draw attention to yourself or make yourself a target until you have thousands of people along your side. If you do not draw attention to yourself, and have remained free of the system's reach, you can create the changes more deeply at energy levels as you live your life.

The system has been set up by *you* on a mass consciousness level. So do not be mad at your system for *it is not outside of yourself*. It is something you agreed to participate in. It is simply a distorted idea of organization which humanity would like to straighten out and reform. The desire in mass consciousness to reform the government is reflected in the individual that is *you*. Think of yourself as a cell within the mass consciousness. Imagine that you can effect the cells around you just by embracing the new paradigm.

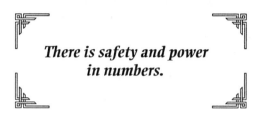

There is safety and power in numbers.

Do not think of the system out there (in there) as your enemy. It is simply a pattern you are working on at a mass level. Like a big computer in the sky, you are all trying to iron out the glitches in the program. You are all doing your part. If you think of your system this way, it may create a more peaceful space for you concerning this.

There are many of you who will be entering the political area of human reality here on Earth. There are many of you who are interested in political careers. You know who you are and this has been a dream of yours. We assure you that you will affect your government greatly and we encourage you to follow your dreams and your heart.

As a light worker, you must remember that you are working in a world which is still leaning more toward fear. You must work with the system that is here for it is strongly rooted. Pretend you are part of it until you are in a position of power. Then you will not be so easily pushed out when you make yourself and your goals known.

Reclaiming the Shadow Self

You must be wise about your strategy. Think of your position as that of sneaking in through the cracks in the system, or through the back door. Suddenly, there you are—-and no one will know where you came from. You do not want to be shut down before you get off the ground. It would be wise to act like a spy inside the infrastructure, for then you will be able to continue to work if you are incognito. If you are not incognito, and wear your causes on your sleeve, or are unwilling to compromise on your proposals, you are most likely to be shut down and shut out from the very system you are trying to change. You will be unable to effect it if you are outside of it.

It is not time yet for these changes to come about in a drastic way. Many of you are simply getting ready and moving toward influential positions which will be advantageous for your manifestation of a better world. Many of you are collecting your energies. You are healing yourselves from your past. This is exactly what you need to be doing at this moment in time.

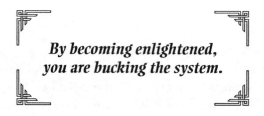

**By becoming enlightened,
you are bucking the system.**

We suggest you do not wear your causes in a rebellious way, or act like a crazy person (in society's eyes) as you try to get your point across. That will get you nowhere. You must be in a position of influence before you can effect the system. You must display wisdom, confidence and self-discipline before people will take you seriously. Do not act like a radical, although underneath it you know you are. It is alright to be a radical, but you will get much further with your plans if you do not raise questions in others about your sanity and stability.

As a last note, we would like you to remember this: by becoming enlightened, you *are* bucking the system!

Affirmations

1. I draw to myself others with like mind. I draw to myself others who desire the same changes in the world that I do.
2. I am part of a united group. Our power is great when we join together.
3. I use wisdom as I buck the system.
4. I create the energy of an enlightened government. I create a space in physical reality for an enlightened government to appear.
5. I transmute the darkness inside myself, thus transmuting the darkness outside of myself.
6. I am patient as I wait for love to be anchored on the Earth plane.
7. I work on anchoring love in my own corner of the universe and daily life.
8. I am a secret agent in this particular reality. I create subtle shifts in the consciousness of all I meet.
9. I am doing exactly what I need to be doing at this time.
10. I am moving into a position of influence even though I do not realize it. I begin by influencing others around me in positive ways.

Exercises

1

In your meditations each day, join with all the beings, discarnate and incarnate, who are holding a space for the shift into the light for the Earth. There is a circle of countless numbers of light beings around the Earth. They are holding the vibrations of love and light frequencies at all times. Join hands with these beings and adjust your energies to match theirs. Along with these beings, project love and light frequencies toward the Earth. Watch as you see the Earth plane light up more and more as you and the others work with it.

2

Visualize yourself having great influence on everyone you meet. Imagine that your positive vision of the future is an infectious disease. See how many people you can infect with positive energy in one day. See how many people experience a positive shift simply by being around you. What do the visualizations look like to you? How do people respond to you? Keep a piece of paper with you and take notes on the positive influence you have on others in one day. Take notes as well on the ones who refused to be effected by your positive energy. There is lessoning in this too.

3

Energize your lifework and goals. See yourself in these roles of leadership. See if you can notice the difference in your personality. This can help you realize what traits you need to develop before the universe gives you a leadership position. You must act like a leader before you are a leader.

Chapter 13

Sexuality

At this time, sexuality is a very tender subject. This is a disconnected and misunderstood area in human consciousness. Many of you have come especially to heal the human sexuality. We would like to start off by telling you some history concerning sexuality. Perhaps, if we describe some of your history, this will explain why sexual violations occur in your society at this time. Humanity is quite confused about it's sexuality right now.

First of all, we will tell you that it was not always the male side of humanity in power. You have participated in matriarchal societies as well. The female side of humanity did not handle power much differently than the male side. We will not give details about this right now, for this is an entirely different subject. If you want to remember this in your cellular memory, you will. Simply realize that it is related to the situations your society is faced with presently and a karmic balance has been played out.

About patriarchal societies: In some cultures, the father was the first to have sexual intercourse with his daughter when she reached the age for giving up her virginity. The first experience with lovemaking was an important passage and a cherished moment for the young woman. It was important that her first lover be someone who cared about her well-being, cared that she did not suffer, and was able to penetrate her without hurting her unnecessarily. It was decided that someone who loved her and would be gentle should perform the ceremony.

When a woman's virginity was taken by a young man, it was found that he was not careful, did not know what to do, nor did he have enough self control. Often the young man would not be patient, for he was typically over anxious. The female was often left feeling disappointed and let down by the experience.

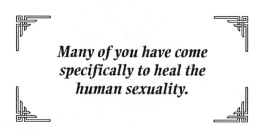

Many of you have come specifically to heal the human sexuality.

The father was placed in this position because he would be the most likely to be careful with the taking of the daughter's virginity. It was believed that the father was the best candidate for the situation. The father could exercise enough self control and would not be rough or abrupt. He would be able to wait for the young woman's natural responses to penetration, for the losing of the virginity does not have to be painful. If much patience and time is spent with stimulation before penetration, the womanchild would open to this naturally. This was the reasoning for this practice.

This can explain why men are attracted to their daughters, and vice versa. This can also explain why mothers are attracted to their sons and vice versa. This is a deeply ingrained cellular memory. It was correct practice at one point in your history. It was pleasant and something looked forward to. The parents taught the child about sex, and used their own bodies to initiate the child into adulthood. Sometimes it was the mother who taught the daughter and the father who taught the son. This can explain these relationships as well.

Fathers are the ones who made the custom acceptable, so unfortunately there was bias and selfish motives. Much abuse took place with this practice when love was not present between the parent and child.

In many cultures, the virginity of the young man, and especially the woman, was seen as a precious commodity. It was something preserved and cherished not only by the woman, but also by the person who the virginity was being given to. There were many things linked to the virginity of the woman. Marriages were arranged by the parents for political, monetary and other reasons.

In the past, the woman did not have much power over her own virginity, nor did she have the choice of who she wanted to give this to. Now is a time when the young woman is educated about sexuality. She can make wiser decisions and see her sexuality in a new light. The female is taking her freewill and power back concerning her sexuality. With the new energy rising in the mass consciousness about sexuality, new patterns will come forth concerning how the sexuality is played out.

Another factor to consider about inappropriate sexual relations is the fact that you have lived different roles in past lives with the people in your present life. For instance, your father may have been your lover in other lives. Your brother may have been your husband in a past or future life. Your mother may have been your wife. Sometimes your genders were reversed. There are a million different roles that you have played with the people in your life.

The karmic play out might be a factor as well. Perhaps your uncle was a jilted lover in a past life. It all carries over and influences the present life. *All* your past and future lives influence your present life. Your present life also influences the past and future lives. This is called "bleedthrough". In knowing this, you can see why it is easy for a sleeping human to become confused about appropriate sexual behavior.

Each of you has experience with some sort of sexual violation, harassment, or molestation. Not many of you have escaped confusion about sexuality. If you are overly promiscuous or overly shy, these are different shades of confusion about sexuality. This is *the* most misunderstood area of human consciousness. Much is being shifted in the human about sexuality. Many of you have come here to deal explicitly with these issues. The job you took may or may not be a drastic one.

For the most part, we are here to address the situation about sexual violations. Many of you are confused and have been derailed about your sexuality. Many of you have been abused as children to some degree or another by the adults around you. Violation is something as simple as a lewd comment or it can be a frightening rape situation. Between these two extremes, there are many shades.

For starters, we would like to define what a sexual violation is.

There is a fine line where things are black and white. When a violation takes place, a violation takes place. There is no such thing as "sort of a violation". If anything is against people's free will, it is a violation. If they are tricked through their naiveté or their innocence, this is a violation. If a person, for instance a five year old or someone else who does not understand sexual things, is forced to make decisions which he or she is not educated enough yet to make, it is a violation of the person's freewill.

If a six year old were to throw itself in the lap of a stranger and want to perform sexual acts, this would be a violation if the adult were to allow this to happen. The child is simply misguided, and needs to be taught what is appropriate and what is not. Just because a child has initiated sexual energies does not mean the child understands or has made an educated decision about what he or she is doing.

There are degrees and types of violation. A trickery type of violation is when a person is tricked into thinking the violation is good for him or her. The manipulative violation is when a person is told that he or she cannot have something needed or wanted unless he or she performs an act desired by the withholding party. The brutal violation is more obvious and is a hurtful crime.

Molestation means that something has been touched and altered in some way. If this was not in the freewill of the receiving party, then this is a violation. We are aware of each and every one of you who have been violated as children. Unfortunately, the percentage is high.

First of all, you must let go of any blame of the self. You were a victim (as you chose to be at the soul level before you came here). You were powerless because you trusted the adults around you—-and rightly so. Among other things, the adults were there to teach you what is appropriate and what is not appropriate in your sexual life. Some of them taught you well and some of them did not.

Now you must go back and re-teach yourself about your sexuality and release your shame. There is no reason to be ashamed about human sexuality. The only reason shame is present is because the human sexuality has been secretive, off limits, and was an abused, misused area of power. Sexuality has much to do with your personal power. We will have more to say about this in a moment.

Some of you did not experience sexual abuse as children, but have experienced it as adults. This is the same thing. All the words we say to those who have experienced a violation of some sort as children can be applied to your situation in adulthood as well. If you experienced abuse or a violation in your adult life, though, it is rooted in your childhood somewhere. You were open to this possibility because you have taken on the imprint at birth in order to transform it even though it would not appear in your reality until later in life.

There are a very large number of you who have experienced sexual violation and it has become a major obstacle for you. For many of you, this is still an unconscious memory. You can be sure that if you have developed an extreme attitude about sexuality in any direction, you most likely have memories about violations, lewd comments, or some such thing from the adults around you.

You discarded these memories until later examination because you did not know what to do with them at the time. This was a way for the mind to protect the self. This was a good protection system. You would be a much different person if you remained conscious of these incidents at the time. Since you did not want to become the person you would have become if you remained conscious of these incident(s), you chose to ignore the things which would have thrown you off your intended path of development.

Not all of you have experienced serious violations. Some of you have simply experienced lewd comments, or perhaps an adult has touched your breasts when they were beginning to develop. Perhaps when you were a young man, a woman or man gazed at your genitals and had sexual thoughts about you which you picked up on. It may have been confusing to you for you most likely did not understand the adult's fascination with your body. The adult most likely felt shame about it at the same time that he or she was indulging in fantasies. You therefore picked up the shame about your sexual areas, for you were using the adult as a gage for what you should be shameful about and what not to. You supposed this was a thing you should be ashamed about.

There are many who are experiencing shame about sexuality and do not know why. Do not belittle the impact a simple lewd comment can have on you. It does not have to be something terrible to have a strong impact.

Some of you have experienced molestation to a medium degree. It was not brutal or painful, but it was not harmless either. For instance, some of you have experienced caressing, gentle sexual stimulation, and soothing bodily feelings as a child. Perhaps you even sought this because it seemed like quality time with the adult. You enjoyed the molestation for it was a pleasant experience.

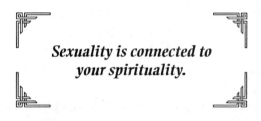

**Sexuality is connected to
your spirituality.**

As a child your sexual centers can be stimulated even though it does not result in orgasm. Any kind of touch, especially if it is gentle and soft, will make your body feel pleasure. Some of you feel guilty or confused about the fact that you felt pleasure in your sexual molestation. Please do not feel guilty, for this was a natural response to what you thought was love and affection. Everyone responds to gentle touch and nurturing. This often *was* an expression of love for you from the adult. However, he or she did not show it in a form that honored your highest good.

Even if the adult was simply fulfilling a desire for him or her self and was not concerned for you, yet you still felt pleasure, we advise you not feel guilty about this either. Even if you encouraged sexual activity, you have done nothing wrong. It was not your fault. Some of you were so bright and so beautiful on many levels (not just physical) that you were irresistibly attractive to the adults around you, or ones your own age who might have taken advantage of your powerlessness and naiveté. They wanted to touch your light.

Unfortunately, some of your light was extinguished because you became confused concerning these areas in your energy field. You did not know how to handle the other party's misguided energies. If you enjoyed the sexual energy as a child, and yet as an adult you are confused about it, let go of your negative feelings now. Simply let it be what it was. You can go back and retrieve understanding of the event(s), but you must let go of blame or shame of the self.

It is alright that you enjoyed it or was something comforting to you. You did not know a violation was taking place. After a while you may have suspected it, but you most likely pushed back your own doubts and fears because you assumed the adult knew what he or she was doing. You believed the adult loved you and would not misguide you.

You may have forgotten these instances because they are not easily understood by the child mind. If you stopped liking the sexual attention you were getting, you may have decided that you had to put up with it. Perhaps you decided this is just the way life is.

You may have also found that appeasing another person's sexual desires has been a way for you to get what you wanted or needed from him or her. You may have found justification for the sexual attention. For instance, it may have been the only time this person focused 100% of his or her attention on you. You may have found you have great love for these ones who have molested you, especially if it seemed like positive, quality time with this person. This is common in non-fearful situations with the perpetrator. Perhaps this was the time when you received presents or sweets. You may have gotten money, which has led some of you to pursue or think about prostitution at some point in your life.

Many of you were brutalized, damaged and hurt to the point of pain and terror. We see that some of you have been victims of atrocious crimes. You may have found yourself stuck on this issue for a long time, if you remember it at all. Your situation is a little more complicated. Not only have you developed shame, uncertainty, and a shutting down in the sexual areas (or an extreme opening up of these energies) you have also learned about terror, brutality and atrocity.

Reclaiming the Shadow Self

Those of you who have chosen to deal with these issues are strong and capable beings. Do not forget this. This is not simply a karmic pay back, as some of you may be thinking. This was something you came to transmute for the mass consciousness and you may have taken on more than your fair share. This is your gift to others.

Be confident in yourself, love yourself and have admiration for yourself for taking on such a difficult task. You are beautiful, even though you may not feel it right now. Your sexuality is still whole and pure underneath all this. There has been no damage to the deeper self where the sexual energy lives in perfect harmony. When you discover this buried sexual aspect of yourself, and have released your shame and terror, you will be free of the imprint.

An adult who has brutally violated you or frightened you most likely had the same thing happen to him or her as a child. This is a very old pattern. Rape has been going on for a long time. It was common in your history and was even socially acceptable! Often, a man was allowed to take a woman or girl whenever he wanted, and there was no argument from either side because there was fear of retaliation. In fact, the feminine side of humanity figured out a way to live with it and get something out of it. The woman or the man was allowed to take a child in the same way, although it was not so blatant or visible.

Many of you have come to deal with the issues of sexual violation on both ends. Some of you have been the sexual offender. You have experienced this as a child, even though you may not remember it. It may have been as simple as watching others do this, and then finding that you could do it too without reprimand.

You are already on your way to healing this aspect of yourself. Do not hate yourself or feel guilty for the sexual offense you have done, even if you have terrified or hurt a little one. Simply change your ways, understand the lesson, and you will be able to continue your life under the law of grace.

If you have violated someone, realize that this was your gift to the other party. Your victim chose to deal with this pattern. This was also a gift to yourself, for you have come to deal with the perpetrator's side of the pattern. Release guilt about this. Guilt is only there to help you realize that you do not want to do this activity again. It is there to help you realize that a misuse of power has taken place. If you realize these things and make a new code of ethics to live by, you have passed the test. There is nothing to feel ashamed about, for you have learned and grown wiser.

If you have not learned, then you will continue the pattern. You will also continue to experience the karmic balance of these actions. Until you realize that you misused your power, and you are still misusing your power, you will continue to go around in circles on this pattern all your life and even in your future incarnations.

Everyone has misused their power, whether it was sexual in nature or not. Everyone has violated someone else in some way, at some time, at some level. We will give you a general tool you can use for yourself and all the ones you hurt or damaged in the past. Forgive yourself first for violating another with your misuse of power. Realize that what you have done was simply out of ignorance (no awareness). It is not because you are a bad or evil person. What you can do for the other soul, and this will help their growth greatly, is to visualize yourself replacing the damage you did to them with light and love.

As you get deeper into the subject of sexual violation in your own past, you will find yourself dealing with much confusion in the sexual areas. You might find yourself dealing with past life memories which were painful and frightening before you find the unconscious memories in this life. The past life memories are related to the upsetness you are experiencing in this lifetime. This will lead you to what your unconscious mind is storing. Remember, the past is simultaneous with the present. It is happening *alongside* the lifetime you are living now. You are tapping into it by the method of association in your memory banks.

Release the inclination to lament the unfortunate circumstances of your past. It was a brave thing you came here to do. This is the gift you give to humanity during phase one of your life. Phase two of your life is only a blink away and you are close to being done with all of this. You will be glad on the other side that you have completed what you came to do in phase one. You will be able to understand and help others who are going through what you have been through. You can be an inspiration to them. They will realize that they too can reach wholeness and live a fulfilling and happy life no matter what their affliction. *You* will be a walking miracle holder.

Sexuality

Within two generations there will be no children who experience violations of any sort. You are on the forefront of the battle line against the darkness (no awareness) in the mass consciousness of humanity. You have chosen to be one of the ones who break the patterns concerning sexual violations.

You may notice that the generation before you did not seem to have much healing going on at this level. Two generations before them, the patterns were still in place and were hardly being shifted at all. This is because the energies present on the Earth today were not as intense during that point in time. Your parents were the first ones to begin the shifting of the patterns, and you are taking up the baton where they left off. You will be helping them to finish their part, for the thickness of the darkness around you is not as great as it is for them.

Your children will be born in a lighter world than yourself. Life will be easier for them to handle and figure out. The darkness will be less thick around them than it was for you. Each generation from now on will have less and less darkness to deal with in the mass consciousness and the individual self.

You may have experienced terror in your childhood. If you are somewhat nervous and insecure as an adult, you were terrified and made to feel insecure as a child. Memories of a painful and terrifying situation will come up for you if this was part of your experience in life. You may have just witnessed the violation of another. This is equally as devastating for a child.

You may wonder where your guidance and protection was. Again, we say to you that your guides were there. They protected you from the things you decided you did not want to experience in your Earth life. They allowed the stage to be set the way you requested at the soul level. Realize that things could have been worse than they were, although it could be said that you went as close to the edge as a person can go without being killed! Your guides also knew they would be here in this moment for you as you heal the fear you experienced in the past.

Some of you carry physical scars from these childhood violations. Wear these scars as the badges of courage they are. These are symbols of your bravery. These are your battle scars which are precious and rare. Do not be ashamed of your physical or psychological scars, self inflicted or not, for these are something you can wear with pride. You have been to the depths of darkness and you have been able to come back.

Some of you did not choose to experience rape in your childhood but you have experienced it later in life. Again, it is something you chose. Do not fear you will never get over it, for you will. You will be wiser and more compassionate on the other side. You may have been comfortable with your sexuality before this happened. It may be difficult to open the sexuality again after an incident like this. Now that this has happened, you may feel you have lost the ability to trust and feel safe in the universe.

This is the goal of the soul: to remember itself while still in the physical plane, and for the conscious self to be able to hold the unconscious self in this reality. You have chosen this because there was no other way to trigger yourself to go into the deeper areas of your soul and learn more about who you are. Perhaps you were at a point in your life where you were getting too comfortable and you were not digging deeper. Perhaps you were going in too many directions at once and needed to focus. Perhaps you were beginning to get destructive in your own life circle and you were headed for a bigger disaster. Perhaps you subconsciously chose to deal with this because of your compassion for others who have suffered these energies. There are millions of reasons why this has happened.

Please do not say to yourself, "Oh! I have caused this to happen because I wasn't paying attention. Oh! I am so stupid. I am an idiot. I knew better than to go through that alley or associate with that person, or go on that blind date!" or whatever else you might berate yourself for. Do not say these words to yourself because this is the opposite of what you are trying to achieve by having allowed this incident to happen to you. If you were meant to avoid it, you would have.

This is something integral to your growth and it will make you richer, wiser and deeper on the other side of the healed experience. What you have chosen is to learn how to love the self and respect the self even while in the victim state. You have chosen to learn more about safety, trust and discernment with energies outside of yourself. Be kind to the self, love the self, and nurture the self as you go through this.

Since sexual abuse and violation is such a large issue for the human consciousness, many of you are needed as guides who *know how* to transform the anguish around this issue. You may have chosen to go through this so you can help a group which you have compassion for. How could you help them if you have not experienced what they suffered? You volunteered to be a victim so you can become a healer and teacher for the ones who are victims behind you.

Realize that this is a gift to yourself and a gift to others. This is a paradox. We realize you might find it absurd to think that a brutal rape is a gift for you, but if you meditate on this, you will eventually see how this is true. Later, the lemonade you have made of your lemons will taste wonderful and you can share it with everyone else!

Some of you did not experience sexual abuse, but you did experience abuse which was brutal and terrifying none-the-less. These things we have said go for you too. Some of you had parents or other adults who have beaten you, tied you up, locked you in a room, punished you by not feeding you, left you somewhere for days, or some other method of abuse. Some of you have suffered abuse that was not physical but it was emotional and mental instead. The scars go just as deep.

These are traumatic experiences that perhaps you have forgotten, yet still hold power over you to this day. Treat these as you would any violation. Love yourself. Take time to go back and re-parent yourself, nurture and soothe yourself, and come to terms with your past.

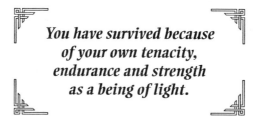

You have survived because of your own tenacity, endurance and strength as a being of light.

If you have had your astrological charts done, you may find that you have chosen a large amount of challenges and obstacles. You may think you are lucky to have survived this long with such great challenges in your chart. Realize that luck had nothing to do with it. You have survived because of your own tenacity, endurance and strength as a being of light. The same challenges which might have destroyed you will also make you a legend in your own time when you conquer them. Many of you do not realize the legends you will become on the Earth plane. You are not ordinary people, you know!

Some of you do not have to worry about these words at all, for your parents were somewhat enlightened and were able to be good parents to you. Parents could be thought of as guardian angels in the physical. Some are better at their jobs than others. Parenthood is practice for guardian angel-ship.

So you may wonder what *is* sexuality all about. What *is* this mysterious thing? What is it *for*? We will not be able to give you complete details, for these things will be discovered and *invented* as you go along. Your sexuality will be different than it was in the past. Your sexuality will be fully understood in the near future.

Sexuality has to do with the ecstatic and love frequencies you are anchoring on the Earth plane. Sexual energy has to do with your power, your light and your ability to manifest. When you can experience your sexuality in its pure state, you will experience levels of ecstasy you never knew existed.

These levels of ecstasy will show you wondrous things and you will bring them onto your plane of reality. These levels of ecstasy will free your spirit from it's focus on this reality and you will be able to see other dimensions which were inaccessible to you before, especially if you journey with a sexual partner. You will also experience deeper connections in your relations with others. You will experience a richer emotional life. Sexual energy is about blending your energy with another person's and becoming one in body, mind and spirit. When you put two energies together, the sum is always greater than it's parts.

Sexual energy has much to do with gestalt intelligence. This is a method for great numbers of beings to come together. Sexual energy is not limited to two people at one time. Sexual energy can be had between a thousand people at one time. Many would say this is an atrocious idea. However, if you were in the mind place where sexuality is pure and non-shameful, you would see that sexuality is just another natural part of the self. This is a part which has the ability to blend with others.

Be careful about who you to blend your energies with. Choose wisely. If there are any doubts at all, refrain. Once you blend with the other person, you might find yourself dealing with his or her difficulties and issues. If this person does not have the ability to shift his or her issues, you will find yourself in a dead end with this one.

When sexual energy is released in it's pure form, the dimensions will open up for you and you will be able to see them superimposed over your Earth plane. When sexual power is released, it is a vehicle for yourself. It can take you to levels of reality you cannot normally reach without it. It will bring you into the beautiful places you dream of. It will take you to the most beautiful aspects of yourself. The ecstatic frequencies will make many things clear, for they are unobstructed areas of consciousness.

Your sexuality has to do with your power as an individual. Sexual power is the same as any power. It is to be used benevolently and wisely.

With sexual energies you will learn how to blend with other beings who are not even human. Sexual energy is not limited to human partners. Sexual energy does not have to be physical. More often than not it is *not* physical at these levels. Sexual energies have to do with the heart centers and the core of your being.

When you blend energies with other beings who are not human, it will not necessarily be manifested physically, if you are wondering about this. At least not until a very distant time in your future. This is far away on the time line. The Earth and the human form will not resemble itself as it is now when that happens. Many of you will have moved on to other adventures by that time.

Sexuality is connected to your spirituality. They go hand in hand. The sooner you can realize this, the sooner you can heal your sexuality. Your sexuality lies very deep within the spiritual body. The sexuality and the spirituality can almost be thought of as the same thing, if this gives you a clue to how important it is on your spiritual path.

The physical sensations that happen when you have an orgasm are a small reflection of what you truly experience in your other bodies, especially the spiritual body. The sexuality, once released, will take you far indeed. You can use this as a way to open up the deepest resources and treasures inside yourself which you have long been cut off from.

Sexuality is being straightened out in human consciousness. It is something to be cherished. It is precious and valuable. It is not something to be squandered, misused or wasted. It is one of the most powerful forces you can tap into within yourself.

An orgasm is the closest of all physical sensations to what it feels like to be one with God. Sexuality is about blending energies with others, and in the end, it is about achieving oneness with all (which is what God really is). When you can achieve oneness, you have mastered the ability to connect with God on a conscious level. Once you have achieved a pure state of sexuality in yourself, and the rest of the people in the world do too, you will be absolutely amazed by what will happen.

This is the most we can tell you right now about the purposes and uses of sexuality. The healed sexuality will take you into places you cannot imagine right now and we simply cannot explain them at this time.

It is a priority to work on healing your sexuality. Healing has to happen before you will reach enlightenment. For some of you it is the last key to be turned before you are fully in remembrance of your enlightenment.

Some of you have denied your sexuality while aspiring to spiritual heights. You have missed a very important part of your spiritual path. The sexuality is hand in hand with spirituality. If you think you can reach enlightenment without dealing with sexuality, we tell you that you are mistaken and you might want to begin work on it if this is something you have avoided.

It is not necessary to have a partner to work out your sexual issues. In fact, a partner might be rather distracting. You can do much meditation and work this out within yourself before you attempt to deal with another person's sexual energies, tensions or motives. We advise at this time that you refrain from sexual relations unless you already have a partnership going. If you feel strong enough to deal with another person's sexual energies, then you might find that the universe will send you a sexual healer. Avoid entangling yourself with someone who has problems with their own sexuality, though, for this will not help you.

Treat your sexuality as the precious commodity it is and you will use your sexuality more wisely from now on. If you are a promiscuous one, perhaps you could use your energies for different things for a while and see what happens. If you are one who is shy, try to bring yourself out of the shell for it is safe now for you to feel, be and exude your sexual self. Perhaps it would help you to sleep without clothing on if normally you are clothed. Perhaps it would help if you dress more sensuously, but do not go overboard.

Take steps in the direction of releasing and freeing your sexual self at a pace that is comfortable for you. If you are not feeling your beauty, your sexuality is most likely locked up. As you heal your sexuality you will find your beauty and grace.

Some of you are wondering about the bizarre sexual fantasies you are having. As you open up the doors to your sexuality, you will be challenged to release judgment upon yourself for the things inside your mind. If you have fantasies or preferences you previously refused to entertain or are embarrassed about, we advise that you entertain these now. These will lead you to the purer energies underneath.

For instance, maybe you have always wondered what it would be like to be a topless dancer, hypnotizing all the men around you and being paid for your beauty and sexuality. This may sound preposterous to some of you, but we suggest that if you are curious, go ahead and try it for a night or two at a real life club (where you are safe) and see what you think of it.

Examine your emotions. You may find there is an exhibitionist side of your sexuality you never knew existed, for you were always so embarrassed about your body. Suddenly, you may find that you are not so shy anymore and you feel more confident about yourself. You may remember past lives where you became highly respected and rich for your sexuality, your beauty and your physical grace. Women discovered they actually had great power over men when they used their sexuality.

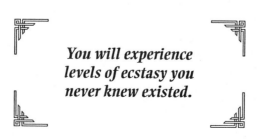

You will experience levels of ecstasy you never knew existed.

Reclaiming the Shadow Self

There is deep conditioning in the human consciousness, especially in the female, of only being able to get rich (or simply to survive) by using her sexuality. Careers in sexuality were the most highly paid careers women could have in your history. This is mass conscious conditioning which you are here to break up. You are here to work on this if you have found yourself in situations where you had to use your sexuality to make a living or to get what you needed or wanted. Even if you were simply in a relationship where you received support depending on how much you "put out" sexually, this is still a form of prostitution. Especially if your *survival* depended on it. Especially if you had nowhere to go if your boyfriend or girlfriend decided to get rid of you.

However, we highly advise that you refrain from considering using your sexuality as a source of income no matter how destitute you are financially in this lifetime. And we absolutely advise that you refrain from any kind of physical contact while exploring your fantasies. The universe will get you fired from the job anyway if you try to stay!

To act out an experience like this is a very strong event in your life. If you do this, it will be similar to cellular release. It brings you back to the moment when these things were truly part of your life. It will bring up severe and strong emotions. It will bring up new realizations. *We only suggest staging a play like this for yourself if you are one who had manifested experiences of prostitution type events in your past.* This will be a jolting way to induce the feelings and thoughts you had at the time. These will come to the surface to be cleared, and you will be released from the earlier events as you work through this.

If you are not quite so bold, or you have not had manifested experiences of prostitution, an exercise in writing your fantasies out would be in order. This includes fantasies about slavery and dominion. If you were a victim as a child, and anything like this was involved, you will find this present in the sexual aspect of yourself because it was among your first experiences. If you choose to manifest this in present reality, we suggest you only explore these things with someone you trust, know and love. Otherwise, you would be in danger. You may not be using discernment well right now.

Many of you are remembering lifetimes of sexual slavery, or of being a master of sexual slaves. This was acceptable in most civilizations and was not always unpleasant. Sometimes, to be a slave and live in a rich man's house was better than being free and living in poverty. This is a deeply ingrained cellular memory in the human consciousness and is something you are in the process of understanding on the Earth plane. This is the root of sadism and masochism practices in sexuality today. The ideas of vulnerability and power in sexual energies are still being explored in human consciousness.

Sadistic and masochistic practices in sexuality are symbolic plays which have to do with your history and past lives. In the past, these plays were not symbolic at all, but were quite literal. These practices were often fearful, unsafe, uncontrolled, against the will of the victim, and had tragic outcomes—like death. If you lived through it, most likely your psychological makeup was permanently damaged and you never recovered your sanity or feelings of peace and safety.

You were in both roles. You were the madman who enjoyed the victims and you were the victim terrified of the madman. These became highly charged memories in your own consciousness and the mass consciousness. Sadism and masochism practices are a symbolic method of working out the literal experiences of this kind of energy in the past.

We would like to issue a note of caution here. Be careful! Do not put yourself in situations where you would be in danger. If you have fantasies of prostitution or severe sadistic and masochistic practices, we advise that you exercise these fantasies only in writing. This would be too strong an experience for any of you and the energies would pollute your bodies. You have gone through this enough in past lives, and you can remember it if you want to. You most certainly do not want to blend your energies with others who are in this space. You are not "mere mortals" anymore.

You are not "mere mortals" anymore.

Reclaiming the Shadow Self

If you have a boyfriend or girlfriend, you can play these games out with him or her. This would be a safe way to explore these concepts. Stay away from strangers, though.

Your guides can also act as imaginary lovers. There have been many healing centers and mystery schools set up on the inner planes and all of you will be visiting them in your dreams and meditations if you want to. If you ask to be taken to one of these inner healing centers, the guides will take you there and work with you whether you are conscious of it or not.

We highly advise that you take advantage of these places. It will speed your process greatly. The guides know how to get you through your trauma or confusion. Once you gain the ability to leave the body (which means you will be going inward) you will visit them quite consciously. Until then, you will visit them unconsciously.

We also suggest not to dwell in these sexual curiosities for long, or allow yourself to be drawn into the energies present at a topless club, for instance. You will only have a short amount of time where you will remain immune to the energies present before you are affected by them. Make sure you get away from less evolved energies concerning sexuality before you are touched by them.

Eventually, all of this will balance out, and you will be far beyond sexual game playing or bizarre fantasies. You will become bored with them quickly. You will be able to touch the pure and unadulterated energies in sexuality quite soon, especially if you have been able to sift through your "demented" areas without judgment about what you are doing.

Affirmations

1. I am innocent and pure. Sexuality is a brilliant, clear energy in my body.
2. I release my feelings of shame and dirtiness about sexuality.
3. I forgive those who took advantage of me sexually.
4. I release fear about sexual intimacy and invite it into my life with openness.
5. My sexuality is now healed. I think of my sexual areas as sacred, angelic, and clean.
6. When I am aroused, I go deeper than the physical sensations and watch what is happening in my etheric bodies.
7. I make love to myself without guilt or shame. I make love to myself with light.
8. Violations that happened to me were actually gifts.
9. My sexuality is pure spirituality.
10. I release cellular memories of sexual abuse in past, present, and future incarnations.

Exercises

1

If you were the perpetrator, visualize yourself in the event that took place. See yourself, the actor, loving the person you harmed as you were performing the violation for them. By this, you can undo some of the effects you have had on this person. It is as if you are lifting a curse which you have put on him or her. This is a way you can deal with your guilt about the violations you have inflicted on others in the past, sexual or not.

The gift of release and healing is your second gift to this person. You have the power to lift your spell. Send love and light to this person. Let him or her know on the inner levels that you are sorry you hurt him or her. If you can tell the person face to face, this would be even better.

Realize that this person may keep the spell going if he or she chooses, but it will not be there with the extra energy you put it there with. Most likely the person will be glad to let go of the spell as well. We use the word spell for lack of a better word.

2

When you are aroused, make love to yourself. There is nothing wrong with masturbation. As you begin to masturbate, watch carefully for all the emotions, thoughts and sensations that come up. Do not do anything about them just yet, even if they are negative. Just notice what comes up. What visuals do you have? What emotions come up? Where does your body tighten up? Are you worried about someone catching you at this activity? Why do you feel ashamed?

Now work with all the things that came up one at a time if there is too much to deal with all at once. Save the other issues until the next time you are doing this.

Work with fear or confusion as it lodges in different places of your physical or etheric bodies. Concentrate on opening your heart center more. Move the orgasmic sensations up through your core and into your heart. Eventually, you will move the sensations through to the top of your head and out the crown chakra. However, do not move on to this until you have fully engaged and connected your heart and root chakra to this activity.

You will have guides with you who specialize in helping humans heal from sexual violations. Ask these guides to help you reconnect your sexual energies. Allow them to fill you with light when you make love to yourself. Allow your hands to be influenced by their energies as they help you heal your sexuality. Allow them to help you release embarrassment and fear about your sexuality.

Keep practicing this when you masturbate until you feel lightness and love for yourself instead of guilt, shame or fear. Once you have accomplished this much, you will be ready to explore sexuality with a partner if you so choose.

3

Imagine what it is like for angels to make love to each other. Imagine what it is like to blend your energy with another being so completely, fully and shamelessly that you become angelic. Imagine the joy and the light that is generated. If you have a partner, encourage him or her to imagine this too. It is the same for humans as it is for angels. Tap into the angelic aspect of yourself and you will see.

Reclaiming the Shadow Self

Chapter 14
Children And Sexuality

Some of you experienced sexual molestation with your peers. For some of you this was a violation and must be dealt with as such. For others, it was fun and exploratory. For instance, you and your best friend might have decided to try things you read about in a book. This is perfectly natural with children and is not something to be ashamed of.

Often, the child begins to feel arousal as young as the age of ten. It is not unusual for children to become interested in each other at young ages. Perhaps they have heard something about it, saw it on TV, or have spied on their parents making love. They are naturally curious about this and will be wanting to explore. This is alright. Curiosity is natural no matter what age this begins.

If a young child is beginning to explore sexuality, and the parent notices this and is concerned about where it will lead to, the parent will want to be sure to educate the child right away about sexuality. It would be wise to educate the child about the results of sexuality, that a baby can be made, that sexual diseases exist, and other such issues which might be applicable. It would be wise to suggest to the child that it wait for a little while before engaging in such activities. The parent might suggest instead to the child that it should explore with it's own body for a while before it touches another person's body.

Reclaiming the Shadow Self

It is not unusual for a teenager of thirteen years old to be wanting intercourse. In your not so distant history, it was expected of children this age to begin sexual activities, especially women. If you deny it to them you will find yourself shut out from their lives and you will lose communication.

You can advise the child to wait until a certain age to have sexual intercourse with others, but do not make this restriction unreasonable. The best thing you can do when your child is beginning to explore sexuality is to treat it as if it is a subject in which you are a guiding angel for him or her. If you can keep the communication lines open about this, your child will come to you with questions and you will be aware of what is going on in his or her progress with this.

Perhaps you have an eleven year old who wants to have sex with another. You might want to tell the child, "I would like you to wait until you are older before you have intercourse because you do not understand enough about it yet. In the meantime, perhaps you should explore your own body so you will understand sexuality better when you *do* have intercourse. Then you will not be confused about it, you will know what you like, and you will know what to do. Besides! You will be a better lover!" This would be more practical advice to the child instead of saying, "Oh! This is terrible. This is bad. You should not be doing this. Do not explore this. You're too young for this."

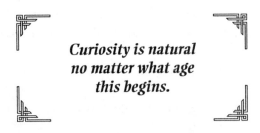

**Curiosity is natural
no matter what age
this begins.**

By a negative statement like that, you will cause fear and shame in the child. This is the pattern which needs to be broken in the generation line. If the child can grow up with his or her sexuality intact, it will not need to be repaired later the way you have had to do or are doing now for yourself. Remember: a child is influenced by even the *slightest* of insinuations. Children are supersensitive to the energies around them.

Do not shut down a child's rising sexual energy. Instead, channel the child's energies into appropriate pathways where the energy can unfold naturally. Teach the child appropriate behavior and a calm approach to the subject. Children are exploring sexuality at an earlier age than you did because information about it is more easily accessible these days. They will need much guidance. Be a helpful guide and not a distorting guide. Aid the child instead of hindering the child. Help the child to keep the sexual energies pure and intact. Teach the child that this is an important issue and is not something to be taken lightly. Teach the child that it is cherished, precious, and powerful energy. Teach the child that this is something to be handled with love and delicacy.

Most of all, teach the child that sexual energies should not take place with one he or she is not in love with. It is important that sexual energies take place only with ones who have deep love between them. We would like to tell you that it is possible (and acceptable) for love to exist between two people of the same sex. It is the soul where the love connection exists, not the body. It is also possible to have deep love with more than one person at a time. There is nothing wrong with this, and it is closer to what the human nature really is.

Even if it is earlier in their lives than you expected, be careful not to thwart your children's sexual emergence when it comes. Allow it to emerge naturally. Do not encourage this before it is ready and do not discourage this when it comes. This is something which is very delicate in the child and must open at the correct speed for every individual. Each child will know when this energy is to be opened in themselves. They are wiser than you realize.

Some children, especially if they have not had traumatic experiences, will show signs of their emerging sexuality as young as the age of four or five. If this is the case, allow it. The children are looking to you to explain what is going on for them. They are looking to you to show them what appropriate use of this energy is.

We realize this may be stretching it for a lot of you, for you may have old fashioned ideas or hang-ups about your own sexuality. It may be dif-

Children And Sexuality

ficult for you to approach your child's emerging sexuality with the openness we have just suggested. But as you do this, you will find this is healing for yourself as well. You will find innocence and pureness in your own sexuality as you oversee the emergence of sexuality in your child. We suggest that for now you let the child explore sexuality on it's own with books you might go through with him or her.

At this time in your history it is a gray area when it comes to teaching the child about sexuality using your own body. Do not be so open with your child that you *share* sexual energies with him or her. This will be clearer later in your development as a race of beings. At this time, it is not appropriate. For now, use books, films, or other aids in teaching your child about sexuality.

Of course, you can speak about it. With your clothes on you can point to places, but do not cross any other lines than that. In the future, your body will not be such a mysterious and hidden thing. Nudity will not be an issue when human consciousness lets go of it's shame about the body. In that period of time, a new understanding about sexuality will arise. Until then, work with the reality you are in.

Some of you have a family which does not hide bodies from each other. You and your children may be naked often when you hang around the house or go to a nude beach. If you are wondering if this is alright, we assure you that it is.

If you are dealing with a child who has been sexually violated, it is important to restore the pure and innocent feeling about sexuality the child had before this event took place. If you find out your child has been sexually violated for a long period of time and you did not know this, it is important you begin the process of repairing the child's psychology about the sexuality immediately. The child will run into many difficulties later if the issues are not addressed, understood and healed right away.

Avoid the temptation to skirt the subject, pretend it did not happen, or abandon the child to it's own devices for healing. This is a time when your child will most likely need professional counseling. Please spend the money on this, for you will be glad you did it and your child will thank you.

The abuse of children is very common. You may think it could not happen to your child, but it can. The effects can be detrimental and even devastating for the child. It can be a stranger, it can be the child's schoolmates, or it can be a family member whom you trust. It is important to be aware that your child is not immune to the realities of this world until enlightenment is reached (remembered) by all.

Educate your child about where the sexual areas are as soon as he or she can understand your words. When the child is two or three, tell the child, "If anyone touches you here or there, this is wrong, and you should not be around that person, no matter how nice they seem. You should tell me about it right away, too."

Sexual abuse can begin as early as babyhood, can continue throughout childhood, and the child will not realize anything inappropriate is being done to it if it is not taught it's boundaries. Teach your child what it's boundaries are. This is the best protection you can give your child. This gives the child quite an advantage. If he or she knows that adults or others touching those areas is a no-no, then at least he or she has a chance to enforce the boundary by walking away from the event before it happens.

If you see any signs whatsoever in your child of sexual abuse, approach the child lovingly and with care so the child is not ashamed, threatened, or afraid of speaking with you about something another adult might have told him or her to keep a secret. Ask the child if there is anything upsetting him or her.

If the child has no idea what you are talking about and says there is nothing wrong and you can tell that he or she is telling the truth, then drop the subject. If the child is upset about something, hopefully the trust and communication between you both will allow the child to tell you what has happened.

Often the abuse takes place right in your own home and it is innocently done by an older brother or sister. When there are older siblings in the house, it is important that the younger child not be uneducated should the older siblings decide to explore with him or her. It is an innocent assumption that the older ones might make. The younger one may have been threatened or is too ashamed to speak to you about it because there is confusion. You may also want to educate the older ones about appropriate action with their emerging sexual energy.

Realize that the child is not going to speak to you in literal terms. You may find the child touching itself or it's dolls in sexual areas, or playing make-believe with the dolls in sexual ways. Your child will give you many clues to what is happening in his or her life during playtime. Spy on your child and listen to what it says to itself when the child thinks it is alone. You may find that the child says it doesn't like school, that he or she does not want to go to camp again or go to a certain friend's house anymore. Perhaps the parent, brother or sister of the friend is a perpetrator. If there is a shutting down of energy, or signs of fear in the child's voice, you should be paying attention. These are clues about what is going on.

You must use your intuition more than you are used to. You are dealing with the non-literal, for the child does not know how to communicate in a literal way. If your child has given you clues, then it is up to you to help this child deal with the events which have happened. If you notice your child has become withdrawn or sullen, you can be sure something drastic has happened, sexual or not. Do not ignore the signs or pretend they are not there. Perhaps the child cannot talk to *you* about it, so it would be good to get counseling for the child. Give your child every chance you can to heal itself.

> **Educating your child about
> what is not appropriate from
> adults is the best protection
> you can give to your child.**

It is possible to restore a sense of innocence and purity about sexuality within the child before it matures. This is the best solution when a child has been violated. Be free enough to talk about this with the child. Do not make the child feel shameful or insinuate that it is the child's fault. Do not blame the child if he or she has disobeyed your rules and then run into this problem. Children are born to test limits and sometimes they get hurt when they do.

Reclaiming the Shadow Self

Perhaps this has happened to your teenager. Your teenager may be very angry. Your teenager may even be looking for trouble because he or she is angry with him or her self, especially if he or she has attracted violations. (The strange thing about human psychology is that when a violation occurs to the child, the child will blame and be angry with the self instead the offending party.) You may find your teenager openly rebels against you concerning sexuality.

If this is happening, you must step back and allow the child to have freewill. Refrain from the urge to overpower him or her, for the child will certainly slip out from your grasp and you will become disconnected from it's life. It is important, as a guardian angel in the physical, to allow freewill and choice. Simply make your children aware of the consequences their choices might have.

If they insist, you must allow them to make their own mistakes. Then stand by to help if they have fallen from their confidence and power. Do not turn your teenager away if he or she has rebelled against you and then decides your help is needed after all. Refrain from having an "I told you so" attitude. Let the child save face.

The child may have much deeper issues which you are not aware of. Perhaps the child is rebelling against you and becoming sexually active in order to make you angry. If this is the case, it is something which started much earlier in life and there is a problem which counseling can help with. The best thing you can do for the child is pray and hold a space of wisdom and light so the child is protected as it goes through it's rebelliousness or promiscuousness.

You should not try to imprison the child or force the child to stop seeing a person whom it wishes to see. It is important to realize your child may make some mistakes you wish he or she wouldn't make. Since the child is so intent on doing it, you must step aside and allow that child to pursue the life path he or she has come here to pursue. This may be on the soul agenda of this child. Realize the child has chosen this and it is not your fault if you have done everything you can short of imprisoning or threatening your child.

It is hard to stand by and watch a child of yours destroy it's life. The only thing you can do is stay gentle with this child and let it know you still love it. It is important that you are there to help your children when they fall down in life. This is the best you can do and is the most wise choice. If you try to fight with your child, the child is left even more alone and abandoned in it's quest for self discovery.

Let the child know you will not object, and you may find the child loses interest in what it is rebelling against you for because you are not giving the reaction expected. So, you see! You can fight fire with water.

Your child has the right to make it's own choices and you are only there as a guiding force. If your child chooses to accept your guidance, this is good—-that is—-if your guidance is good! If the child does not choose to accept your guidance, then this is good too. All turns of events are something you must accept as your reality. This is a huge lesson in non-attachment to the outcome of events in your life. This is also a huge lesson in trust in the universe. The universe knows what it is doing, even if it doesn't seem like it. And lastly, this is a huge lesson for you in allowing another person freewill and choice.

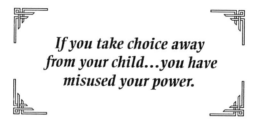

If you take choice away from your child...you have misused your power.

If you overpower and take choice away, *even if it is because you see that he or she is making an unwise choice*, you have misused your power. You are like the guides who are around yourself right now. You are only there to give advice and guidance. You cannot interfere unless interference is asked for. So you must wait for your child to come to you for help, instead of forcing your will on the child. We realize that this is difficult.

Do not forget to call on the guiding ones to help you and your rebellious one. You can ask the universe to intercede for *you*. You can say to the universe, "I do not know what to do with this child. I give up. I give it to you to solve. I trust you. I know you will take care of my loved one and you will help this one find it's way. Please help me to be a wise parent, and please help my little one not to get hurt."

This is the best way to approach this situation. Fighting fire with fire will only make more fire.

Affirmations

1. I allow my child to exercise freewill and choice.
2. I am calm when my child rebels against me.
3. I am learning how to be a guardian angel.
4. I am always conscious of my child's energy.
5. My child is safe and protected.
6. I help my child with more than just words. I hold a space of love and light for my child at all times.
7. My child is wiser than I know.
8. I am confident in my abilities to teach my child about sexual energies.
9. I approach my child with love and care at all times.
10. I am always there for my child—-no matter what!

Exercises

1

Visualize your child as a wise and knowing soul. Evaluate yourself in relation to your child. How do you see your child? Do you see your child as an equal? Do you see yourself as a helping, guiding force in your child's life? Do you see yourself as a superior? Do you see your child as a blessing or a nuisance? Be honest with yourself.

Sit in meditation with an image of your child in front of you. Tell the child you trust his or her judgment. See yourself allowing the child to pursue his or her life path, no matter what form it takes. See yourself as being a caring and loving guide for the child in physical reality.

Release attachment to having the child do things the way you prefer to have them done. See your preferences as gentle, wise suggestions to the child instead of absolute rules that cannot bend. See yourself as a guide who allows the child freewill and choice, even when you wish the child would not make certain choices. Describe on paper what this vision looks like.

Honor the path of the individual. The "mistakes" your child makes may actually be experiences which are needed by the soul of the child. If you prevent the child from experiences needed, you may thwart the child's development at the soul level. See yourself as being there for the child, no matter what, even if he or she turns against you and rebels.

What is it like to love a child who rebels?

2

If fear comes up for you as your child's sexual energy unfolds, refrain from projecting your fear onto your child. Focus on your own sexual development and how it happened. Where in your experience have you been made to feel shame or fear about your sexuality? Where in your experience have you been restricted about your sexuality? What is the child mirroring to you?

Now absorb the innocence you see in your child as his or her sexuality emerges. Heal yourself as your child develops in this area. Notice the areas in which your sexual emergence was hindered or distorted when you were once this innocent about your body. Return to your own beginnings and allow yourself to be healed by the purity of your child's emerging sexuality. What was it like for you when you were naive about your body and innocent about your sex?

3

If your child has been violated or confused about sexuality, practice holding a space of healing for the child. Hold your child in your arms when he or she is sleepy or any other time the child will sit still and absorb transmitted energies.

As the child moves into a trance-like state or sleep, call in your guides and the child's guides. Ask them to work through you and teach you how to heal another being with light. Surround yourself with angelic love. See yourself as a skilled angelic helper for your child. Create a beautiful inner room in which your child can feel safe. Connect your heart center with the child's heart center. Wait until you feel a "click" in your energy. This is your feedback gage as to whether the child is resonating with your energies or not.

Allow the guides to move your hand(s) as it is called for. You will feel an urge to put your hand over certain chakras or other areas. (Do not touch sexual areas physically. If you feel the need to hold your hand over those areas, hold your hand three inches away from the child's body. The light will still pass through to the child without physical touch.) Continue to fill yourself with love and light. Hold a feeling of safety, protection and purity in your own self and wait for your child to resonate with this. You will know when this happens for there will be a drastic surge in the energy. Love and light will increase so much that you might even find yourself in tears because the love is so deep and the light is so bright.

Do this until the energy begins to subside and the guides stand back. You will know when the session is finished. Do not try to keep it going when it ends. The temptation to do this will be present because the light and love were wonderful to bask in. There will be other times. Realize that it does not take a long time to transmit light to another being and facilitate a healing.

Lastly, thank the universe for the healing which took place. You may feel that you have been healed as well! The healer is always rejuvenated and healed just as much as the healee.

Reclaiming the Shadow Self

Chapter 15

Suicide Scars and Fear of Enlightenment

Perhaps you have slashes on your wrists and you are embarrassed about them. Perhaps you hide them or wish you could have cosmetic surgery to remove them. We say to you that it would be beneficial for you to adopt a different attitude toward these scars. These scars prove to others that you know something about the depths of despair and that you also know how to *rise* from them. This is something to be proud of and others will admire it in you.

Many people do not understand suicidal feelings for they have not dealt with issues of self worth. Self worth issues are advanced study for the soul. Many people think suicide is a selfish and mean thing to do to those who love you. What they do not understand is that suicide is committed because of very deep despair, hopelessness, and sadness. They simply cannot understand it if they haven't felt these things. If someone says to you, "Oh! Look at you. You tried to commit suicide. You are not as good as everyone else because you gave up when things got tough."

You might respond by saying, "Yes! I have been to the edge of death, and I have been to the depths of darkness. Yes! I have been sad and depressed, but look at me now. I have survived. I am beautiful and whole. I am no longer suicidal, and I am able to help *you* if you would like some help. So! Are you sad or depressed? Would you like some advice about how you can get out of spaces of darkness? Is there anything I can help you with in your heart?" You see, these are badges of courage you can wear with pride.

This goes for your psychological scars as well. Many of you have been in institutions and have been diagnosed as clinically depressed or insane. Most of you have been in therapy of some sort. You have left these situations because they have not been able to help you further. Some of you were only there trying *make* yourself insane so you did not have to face your life anymore. You found that you could not go insane because your mind was too sharp!

Do not be ashamed about your past. Many of you are afraid to tell anyone that you have been in a mental institution for you know society will view you differently if others knew this about you.

There are many people who are psychologically damaged and are too embarrassed to go to institutions or seek counselors for help. They may be leading what appears to be a normal life. They may have a car, a house, a job, a spouse and even a family. However, their existence is fragile. As soon as they look at the things they are running from, ignoring or hiding from, they might find themselves feeling rather insane as well.

You are a reminder to ones like these that their existence is not as stable as they would like to think. Every man and woman on this planet is insane to some degree or another until enlightenment is realized. So understand that you are not unique in this way. You are simply one who had a *physical manifestation* of your insanity.

The others are hiding this.

[The scars] are
badges of courage.

If people find out that you were in a mental institution and they approach you about it, discriminate against you because of it, or look down on you for this, you might say, "Yes! I have been certifiably insane, but now I am whole, I am beautiful, I have recovered, and now I ask you if you would like my help. I am sure you have feelings and experiences you do not understand. Perhaps I can aid you with this. What do you say?"

Do not be ashamed of your past. Bring it out into the light and the open. Be fearless about showing people where you have been. Of course, do not wear it on your sleeve. Only mention it when it is appropriate and if it will help someone who feels bad about him or her self.

The fact that you have held it together and are near to enlightenment will be an object of marvel for others. They will say, "Oh! This one has been to such dark places and yet is so powerful, beautiful, and joyful. I would have never imagined that someone so damaged could reach such wholesomeness again."

You will be a living, walking, miracle holder. Your miracle is not a physical one, as would be those who have reversed a terminal illness, but a mental one. The psychological self can be terminally damaged as well. You could have died of it as easily as you could die from a terminal illness in the physical body. You might have taken your life by your own hand because of your despair.

Miracle holders in the psychological areas are necessary in the world at this time. You will be inspiration to others that they too can reach enlightenment, no matter how immersed in the darkness they are. Some people think that if a person is damaged early in life there is no hope for that person, especially once he or she becomes an adult. People might think this person should throw in the towel right now and call it quits. Of course this is not the case, and any person who has the intent to be whole again, no matter how damaged he or she is, *will be whole.*

In the future, your scars will disappear if you wish them to. People will grow back lost limbs. All sorts of miracles will happen in the world (and all sorts of tragedies will happen alongside them). Closer to the time when critical mass will be achieved by the planet and the scales tip toward love instead of fear, these miracles will be an everyday occurrence.

We would like to say some things about fear of enlightenment.

Reclaiming the Shadow Self

Many of you are afraid of your enlightenment. You are so close, but you are afraid to walk through the door. This is because you remember past experiences where your enlightenment did not bring you a happy outcome.

In the past, the world was quite afraid of enlightened ones. Some of the forces outside of your reality, which did not have your highest good in mind, did not like the fact that you had achieved enlightenment. They did not want you to stay, for they did not want anyone to figure out what they were doing. You saw through the illusion and rose above it. They did not want anyone to break the barriers which were set up for you.

You might remember lifetimes in which you were tortured, exiled, or killed because you stood up for something you believed in or you began to lead others toward enlightenment. This happened because you *frightened* the ones in power. It would mean a change. They were frightened because they did not understand you. They did not believe you could be true, and often believed you were evil, especially if you became the "unlikely leader" among people who were supposed to be under their control. If you were helping others to reach enlightenment you were a great threat to the darker forces who did not want you to break out of the illusion of fear that you were in. The whole system would be changed.

Now remember, humanity chose to experience this. This was part of the game in the freewill zone.

You may remember being maimed or killed for reasons you did not feel were deserving of this treatment. In some lifetimes you were murdered for simply being beautiful. You were martyred. You were just being yourself, or standing up for what you wanted. We advise that you release the memories and the fears of the ones involved. Also release your anger at or fear of the darkness (no awareness) which had something to do with bringing about the event. Release these and let them come out of your body. Again, cellular release or other kinds of energy work might be in order. Vivid past life memories are highly charged patterns in your physical and energetic systems.

You must face your fear of enlightenment. There is nothing to fear about it in *this* lifetime. You will not be taken out of the game as soon as you gain enlightenment, unless, of course, that is your choice. You can stay this time, for there are many light beings now who have control of

Climb the Mountain

the passageways that lead into and out of this reality. They are protecting you from interference.

Power places are good places to go for unlocking memories, and also for gaining a sense of what enlightenment *feels* like. If you fear enlightenment consciously or unconsciously, we would like to dispel these fears. You will be able to stay and live out your fullest potential in *this* lifetime on the Earth plane. No one is going to stop you now.

You may find that you suffer persecution from your fellow human brothers and sisters when you allow yourself to be a visible light bearer. This is minor compared to what you have experienced in the past! It will be important for you to remain unconcerned about what other people think of you and continue to be yourself. Of course, lend them your ear and see if their words have any truth for they may be exposing one of your blind spots to you. However, do not be afraid to be who you are, even if people criticize you.

**No one is going
to stop you now.**

As the new world leaders and world healers, you will be challenged many times about what you are doing. When you break patterns and barriers, when you lead people in a new direction, there will always be someone there to question what you are doing, what your motives and purposes are, and perhaps even accusing you of the exact opposite of what you are doing. For instance, they may say that what you are doing is evil, even though it is the exact opposite of the truth to yourself.

We assure you that you will not be hurt physically this time, if that is not your choice. Enlightenment is not something to fear anymore. As you break through the barriers there will not be anyone to crush you as soon as you make it. Your fear of enlightenment travels in your veins and your cells, as all your memories and fears do. We suggest that you visualize removal of fear from your system and let the enlightenment come forth in its fullest beauty and brilliance.

Affirmations

1. I wear my psychological or physical scars with pride when someone notices them.
2. I am willing to be vulnerable and let others see my past if it is appropriate.
3. I am free of shame about my past. I realize that it was just experience for my soul on the Earth plane.
4. I am a living, walking miracle holder. I have healed my terminal psychological illness.
5. I am an inspiration to others who want to be whole again.
6. I invite enlightenment into my life right now.
7. I release memories of the past when gaining enlightenment got me killed or persecuted.
8. I am free of martyr roles in this lifetime.
9. I am here to express my fullest potential in enlightenment.
10. I boldly face the new challenges that enlightenment brings.

Exercises

1

If you have self inflicted scars or wounds, be they physical or psychological, this is an exercise for changing your feelings about them.

Look at the scar and examine the feelings you presently have about it. Are you embarrassed? Do the scars make you angry or fearful? Do they make you want to cry? Does it bring up anxiety? Write down the feelings and impressions you get.

Now, relax your feelings and calm your spirit. Get into your angelic or soul level. Wait until you feel a change of gears. Find in yourself a feeling of respect for the self and the path you took. Find a feeling of admiration for the difficulty of the challenges you lived through. Look at the big picture.

Look at your scars again. How have they served you? What did you experience by inflicting injury on your self? How can these scars serve you in the future? From the perspective of self respect, see your scars in a new way. Love these scars and what you went through with them. Respect these scars as the precious badges of courage they are, for you have truly come through a dark area of human consciousness. How do you feel about them now?

2

Visualize yourself in your daily life as a living walking miracle holder, even if you are still in the midst of your process. How do you regard yourself now? How do you hold yourself as you walk or move? How do you speak to others, knowing now that you are the wounded healer who is becoming whole again? How do you treat yourself and others? Several times a day, remind yourself that you are a living, walking miracle holder and absorb the pride you feel about this.

3

Fear of enlightenment is also fear of success. Where does this fear live within yourself? Where does it show up in your life? Allow the cellular memories of persecution to come to the surface. What memories come up? How have you been martyred? What was your death experience? Allow the memories to move through you by releasing the fear they bring up in your system. Transform this fear into a feeling of confidence, safety and wisdom.

As you release the fear the memories bring up, fill the space where the fear was with light. Transform this fear into brilliance. Transform this fear into the boldness it took to be the magnificent being you were (and are). How do you see yourself now and in the future as you live in your enlightened state without fear of persecution or death?

Reclaiming the Shadow Self

Chapter 16

Dark Aliens and Other Misguided Energies

We will begin by informing you that on the soul level, aliens do not exist. Aliens are part of the illusion. However, the illusion is very real at the physical reality level so we will discuss what they are up to.

There is a mixture of fear and fascination with the alien beings which your race has become conscious of. All the aliens are not bad and all the aliens are not good. They are just aliens to you while you are in human form.

There is much questioning about the grays, who are considered bad. These ones have been working their way into your reality. They have been attempting to use the human DNA to enable themselves to be part of your reality on the physical level. They are master genetic scientists. Although they have not succeeded yet, they have gotten close. They are still outside your reality and are not able to participate in a physical sense.

Yes, they have been able to be physical. However, they have not been able to retain all their consciousness inside the physical reality. This is why they are working with the human DNA. They want to bring their full conscious self into this reality but they cannot without the human DNA.

As many of you have suspected, they have been contacting your governments for a long time and have been making deals so they can do the experimentation they want to do. They have convinced your governments that what they are doing is not very important compared to what they have offered your governments in technologies. However, domination and tyranny is what is on their minds. They market consciousness to other beings in other realities. They have even managed to glamorize themselves in your multimedia so you might be more receptive to them when they appear in your reality.

These beings are nothing to be afraid of. If you are afraid of them, it is the only way they can harm you. They cannot harm you if you simply say to them, "Hey. I know who you are. I know what you're up to. You cannot manipulate me because I am just too aware for you. I am too much in control of my fear for you to get me carried away in it." If you stand your ground, they cannot touch you. The only way they can touch you is if you open the fear doorway. This is the only doorway they know of to enter your consciousness.

They are interested in you because they want to know how your consciousness works. They want to understand how the human is able to focus in this reality in such a precise fashion. They can look at your reality in a conscious way. They can appear in your reality in an etheric form. However, they cannot function in your reality physically with full consciousness intact.

Obviously, they do not have your highest good in mind. This is not a bad thing. This is not a good thing. This is just a thing you must discern about. You will need to discern whether you want to associate with this person or that person. You will also need to discern whether you want to associate with this alien or that alien.

**You have an aspect
of your soul
in their reality.**

Not all the aliens have unfriendly ideas toward you. Some aliens are very high in vibration. In fact, many of them have been here to educate you and help you ascend from the dark areas of your consciousness. Many of them have been protecting you from misguided energies in the freewill zone so more cannot happen than already has. Humanity chose a certain path, and did not choose to have all darkness thrown at it and be crushed. These beings made sure that the only ones who could enter your sphere of reference were the ones you auditioned and chose on a mass level.

This is a plan that is difficult to understand in the large scheme of things, but you will understand these things before your life is over on this plane.

There are more than just the grays. There are several different species who have figured out how to disguise themselves to look like you. If you look in the eyes you can tell if they are human or not. You can also tell by their etheric fields (once you can perceive them) and by your intuitions.

Please do not run around judging people and saying to yourself, "Oh! This is an alien, and that is an alien." It is better to just know they are there and be discerning as you see actions speak louder than words. These ones have infiltrated you, yet they are not you. It is alright, for they have come here to learn from you, although they do not realize this is why they are here yet. They think they are here so they can take control, or keep the control they have been losing over the last few decades. They are here to preserve their interests. They do not want you to change, as you most likely suspected by now. Remember: This is an illusion.

At an unconscious level, their races have chosen to interact with your race in order to be brought into the light. As soon as human conscious-ness raises it's vibration, they will either have to raise their vibration to match the human consciousness and interact with it in a polite and appropriate fashion, or they will need to go somewhere else until they can learn better behaviors.

This is what you are here to teach them. They cannot hold any race in slavery (for you were invaded long ago and more than once) without eventually losing control. They are learning that they are not necessarily in control, although the illusion was that they were. They will soon real-ize that love is a more powerful source of energy. They *can* be kicked out if it is something the mass consciousness desires. However, humanity is gracious and will allow these ones to stay in it's sphere of reference if these ones are receptive to love, which is a high probability.

As soon as the human race becomes conscious and sees through the illusion (the game), it will happen for all the races who are involved with you. It will be an eye opener for all who have been involved with the human experiment, including discarnate entities. The present game (illusion) will end and a different reality will begin in which there is co-operation between aliens and humans. The old game will be over and will not hold anyone's interest.

Realize that you have an aspect of your soul (a branch) in their reality, or at least one of the darker realities. You have an aspect of yourself who is living in their reality and is working in their system. In fact, you are opposing yourself. This is a reflection. It is an outward symbol of the battle which takes place within the self.

For instance, when you find yourself going back and forth about something, fighting with yourself, you can see this as a smaller reflection of the greater reality of your soul. Your soul can straddle all realities and in fact has paradoxes inside itself. For instance, you can be a bad guy and a good guy at the same time. You can be the perpetrator and the victim at the same time. You can be the dark one and the light one at the same time. This gives the soul balance, diversity and experience.

Realize that these dark energies are not outside yourself. In fact, you may find yourself face to face with one who is your own parallel self. Realize that these ones are yourself and they are to be treated with gentleness, care and love. Unconsciously, they want to be directed toward the light where they will find more happiness and joy. This is truly what they desire.

They are curious about your emotions because they cannot understand them, nor can they experience them the way you do. They want to attain the ability to do this and you can guide them in these matters. They too seek the ecstatic and love frequencies yet are unable to touch them at this time. As you learn to touch with these frequencies, you can pass on what you have learned to these ones at an energetic level in your meditations.

Visualize these ones before you, and transmit to them the knowledge and the love you have so they too can be empowered. Invite them to resonate with the energies you are holding for them. They are seeking empowerment and light. It would not be fair of you to withhold this from

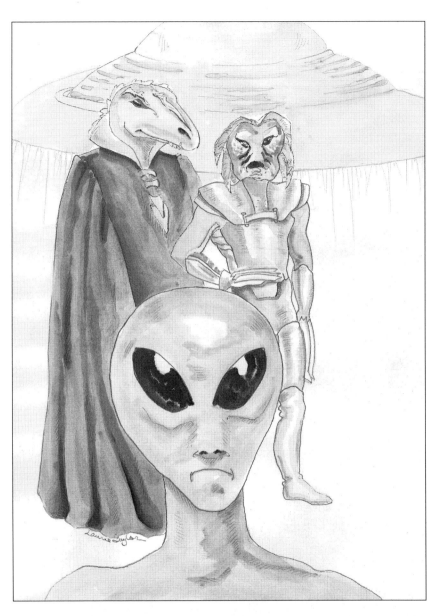

Dark Aliens and Other Misguided Energies

them since you agreed to give this gift to them when you were asked to.

They can choose to accept love from you or not to. It is not up to you to make their choice for them. It is only up to you to provide the information they seek. This is the commitment of the human race to these ones.

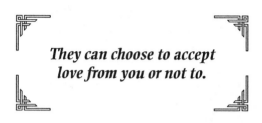

They can choose to accept love from you or not to.

Go to the level where aliens and dark energies *do not exist*. There, you are watching different aspects of yourself from the balcony seats. For instance, one of your selves is a gray. One of your selves is a human. One of your selves is in a race which is in a spectator position. One of your selves is a guide to a human. One of your selves is a guide to a gray. One of your selves is an angel. One of your selves is just born and has no experience yet. One of your selves has been a rock for five thousand years.

One of your selves is not born yet. One of your selves is a cat. One of your selves is your own guide in this lifetime. One of your selves is a master librarian in the Akashic records section. One of your selves is a timekeeper. One of your selves is a mechanic who tinkers with the science of the universe. The list goes on forever. Everyone is schizophrenic, so to speak. The soul has multitudes of personalities, aspects, and expressions of those sides.

Do you see just how multidimensional you are now? You have no idea how much area of consciousness you span as a soul. You are incredibly experienced! You are incredibly diverse!

Many of you, especially those of you who are not originating from this galaxy, are here because you may have had something to do with why humanity is where it is right now. Many of you have misused your power before you came here. If you remember alien lifetimes you have, you may remember times when you did not care about humanity the way you do now. You did not have compassion toward humanity. You did not have the wisdom and understanding that you have now. You may remember that you had power and you misused it on this plane.

Entertain the thought that perhaps you have been a member of a race which was responsible for disconnecting the human DNA, causing disruptions and interfering with the freewill of humans. Since you were one of the ones who knew how to disconnect it, that is the very reason you are back here and have gone inside of it to reconnect and rebuild from the inside out instead of the outside in. You could think of this as a karmic payback, sort of. If you destroy something, eventually you are drawn to rebuild it when your heart opens and you are not happy with what you have done. This is duality and paradox at work.

For example, you could think of yourself as being the same as Hitler who is on the other side now and feels much caring for the ones he has hurt, directly or indirectly, and is doing much to repair the damage he has done. You are doing the same thing in your own way. You realize you have done something not in alignment with God's will and you want to balance it by doing the opposite.

Some of you have alien guides who you do not realize are aliens. Some of your guides are actually ascended parts of yourself, alien or otherwise. These ones have your higher purpose in mind. Some of these guides are here because they have helped to cause the disruptions on your plane and they want to repair it.

Since there is a belief in penance, we would like to inform you that your penance does not have to happen in the form of punishment. Your penance can be in the form of repairing and rebuilding that which you have destroyed. Yes, you may be looked up to and glorified for what you are doing. You may be admired for your wisdom and beauty. But you must remember that you are not here for the glorification of yourself, and you have actually come back because you have been one of the misusers of power. This should help you keep your ego in check should it try to take off with you.

You will achieve successes and perhaps become recognized in your circles for the light you spread. If you should feel self importance and it gets out of hand, this will bring you down in burning flames. You are here to do a job. You are in service. You are not more special than everyone else, although others who are not finished with the concept of worship may think you are. If you allow your egotistical self to get too big, you will be brought down, for worship is not a part of the new paradigm which is coming into this world. Treat all people with utter respect and humbleness. Treat them as your teammates, not your fans, even if they are *acting* like your fans.

Aliens and other entities who have been attracted are here because much attention has been drawn to the Earth plane. As we have said, much has been done here that has never been achieved anywhere else in linear time. (Realize that time is simultaneous and the finished version always exists next to the unfinished version.) This "experiment" has never been completed in a successful fashion. Every time this has been done, self-destruction or destruction from an outside source has happened.

This will be the first chance to see if this can be done and to find out if it can be maintained. There will be a challenge in the future to see if the love on Earth can overpower the forces which might want to hurt it or put it to an end.

Since you have attracted so much attention, you have attracted dark energies *and* light energies. This has been going on for a while now. The darker forces have called on their friends to help keep control, and the lighter forces have been pouring in because they are interested in seeing what will happen once this has been turned into a different kind of place which is accessible and useful to them. Up to this point, the Earth plane has not been accessible, nor was it a desirable place to go.

Now that new possibilities are about to open, no one really knows what will happen once Earth is turned into a place of light and love. Transformation of the Earth plane will allow the freewill zone to have more opportunities, probabilities, and will make new choices available.

As you may have heard before, humans are a blend of DNA from different beings. Each species gave a bit of itself to the human experiment. The human could be thought of as a conglomerate DNA arrangement of the best of many worlds. If this works, which is a very high probability this time, the possibilities are endless. The ones who contributed DNA to the human form are all coming back here now to see what is happening.

This was a project which has been shelved for a while. This was a project that was not believed to work out anytime soon. In fact, life on this planet was about to be destroyed by an outside force. All life was to be extinguished and the experiment was to be started again from scratch, for the results were not desirable.

However, it was determined there was a difference this time as civilization rose. This was the first time a potential was reached where enlightenment on this planet could be gained in a benevolent, wise and balanced fashion in the human form. These ones are coming back and they have much anticipation and hope. They are doing everything they can to help in the freewill zone without violating the freewill guidelines.

The reason this was shelved for a while was because there was frustration with it. This has been an ongoing project for quite some time and still was not worked out. It seemed to be a dead end. However, it has exploded into a surprising result. The ones who are watching are quite amazed and interested. They are cheering for you as you deal with the obstacles in your path.

The ones who are giving it their best shot to hold you down are there because you asked them to be. You wanted a challenge as a race of beings.

Fear always has to do with worry that your freewill will be interfered with. You fear you will be hurt against your will, that you will be detained against your will, or that you will be made to do something you do not wish to do. This is where fear is born. Fear is compounded by the lack of self love which is prominent in the human consciousness. Lack of self love is a learned pattern. It is not the pattern you have as a soul.

Even members of the
dark forces
have a soul level.

The catch is, once you have taken on any program you are not allowed to give it back without improvements. This is just one of the rules of the game on Earth. Even if it takes you lifetime after lifetime to get the program repaired, you must still finish the game. Some of you have been given breaks, yes, but you still are committed to finish the job. You have volunteered for this. *Everyone* is obligated to solve the riddles of human consciousness or else you would not be allowed to actively participate here. What use would it be to the universe if you are not here to help repair the programs? This, as you are certainly aware of, is not exactly the place a soul comes for a vacation! This is a working area.

You have been given extra energy, resources and aid in this age to repair the programs and unlock the secrets of the DNA. There is much attention on this place now, moreso than there has been in a long "time". Be aware that some of the ones who damaged the programs in the first place do not consciously want you to be successful. They may try to hinder this process, which is what they are supposed to do right now. This is their role.

If you realize they are simply misguided energies who are looking for the light and for advancement, just like yourself, you will realize there is nothing to fear from these energies. Love will melt their hearts, no matter how stony and hard they have gotten. Even though they have engaged deeply in the darkness, they still have a heart and it *can* be touched. *Even members of the dark forces have a soul level.*

In the past, there have been many dark entities and thought forms waiting to play with you if you managed to part the veils. If you were not prepared with knowledge of how to deal with these beings, they often devoured you and spat you out for sport! Many humans who reached this point and experienced this were left quite insane on the Earth by these encounters and could not return to sanity in that lifetime.

The way to deal with these beings, should you encounter them, is simply this: do not fear them, be loving with them, and redirect them to the Source for the light they desire.

You see, these misguided energies are attracted to your light. As you throw off the darkness, your light becomes brighter and brighter, actually brilliant. So do not see them as "bad", for they are not much different from yourself. They simply are looking for the source of light like you are and are unconsciously hoping you can help them evolve.

Your soul is not human. Only this branch, which is you, is having human experience. It could be thought of as a category of experience in the soul. The human DNA and consciousness is separate from your soul.

Dark Aliens and Other Misguided Energies

There are ones who have been created just to be incarnated in the human form, but they are rare and are not necessarily here at this time in great numbers.

Most of you are alien to this system. The human DNA and mass consciousness is something you are just wearing for a little while. You can think of yourself as human for now, though, for you have a vested interest in creating the changes necessary here. There is much of yourself which resonates with human consciousness and the human form. You will carry the memory of human experience forever in your travels throughout the universe. You will draw on the experience you have had here in your future endeavors, just as you are drawing on experience you have had elsewhere in *this* particular endeavor on Earth.

Most of you do not like to stay put very long, and this has been a long assignment for your soul. You may find yourself tired of this plane and wanting to move on to other places. You may feel quite tired physically, mentally and emotionally. This we understand. You have taken on an exhausting task. Be patient. It will be over soon and you may change your mind and stay. It will be a new world and a nicer place to live. Your vitality will return to you very soon and in this same lifetime. You will not be tired for long.

We have been asked about the exorcism techniques necessary for particularly strong and unbending dark entities, "ghosts".

If you have come across a trapped entity on this plane, you can most certainly help this one go to the light and re-integrate with it's soul source. However, if the entity is very angry and very powerful, you will need a group of lightworkers to work with this one. The larger the group the better. That way, no one will get hurt as this entity throws a fit before it gets to where the pain and anguish is in it's heart. Once the entity is in the place where it feels hurt, sad and the anger has been dissipated, then it is ready to make the transition to the light.

Do not try to handle powerful misguided entities by yourself if you can help it. They *can* do damage to you if they are powerful enough. Some of them can even scramble your consciousness and you will have a very difficult time putting yourself back together. Do not underestimate these entities.

Affirmations

1. When I encounter dark energies, human or alien, I react with love, compassion, respect and understanding. I treat them the way I would want to be treated if I were in their position.

2. I conquer my fear when others, human or alien, challenge me to do this.

3. Misguided energies have a heart just like I do.

4. I have pleasant encounters with beings when I meet them, even the misguided ones.

5. I honor all paths, even the path of aliens who are desiring of control and tyranny. I help them to go higher (more inward). I help them find empowerment and light.

6. My discernment is excellent.

7. I move inward to the level where dark energies and misguided ones are not a reality. I live on the soul level. I connect with these ones at the soul level only.

8. I release judgment, anger and fear about misguided energies, human or alien. I forgive them for interfering with my freewill and the freewill of others.

9. I consider misguided energies my equals, even though they are not able to hold love frequencies the way I can right now. I realize that they are more developed in some areas than I am.

10. I am here to reconnect the disrupted energy systems of the human form.

Exercises

1 A

First of all, let your imagination run away with you. In this exercise, do not worry about what you think is true and what is not. Just imagine what you would have explored if you were told that you can go anywhere in the universe and explore anything you wanted to take part in.

List past lives you think you have had. List future lives you think you might have. Remember, they are simultaneous! Step sideways if you want to see them, not forward or back. Your past and future lives are in a circle around you. Time shifts and dimensional shifts are a sideways movement after you have moved inward.

List alien experiences you have had. List plant, animal or mineral kingdom experiences you have had. List molecular experiences you have had. List etheric experiences you have had. Whatever kind of experience or lifetime you imagine you would do, given the choice, write it down.

Now you have a skeleton outline of what your experience is as a soul. If it is something you were attracted to exploring, it is most likely something you have done. For instance, if you would have been a pioneer had you lived during the 1700's or the 1800's in the U.S., most likely you were a pioneer. Realize that you can have more than one lifetime going on in the same period of time, too. You are not limited to one lifetime per period. Add to this list as you remember more every day through dreams, feelings, sudden visions and realizations. You will be building your own library of your akashic records.

1 B

Touch base with an aspect of yourself which is not human. Look into the realities of the aliens and see if you can find a counterpart of yourself there. See the aspect of yourself playing the role of a misguided entity in some other reality at this time. We guarantee you have one! What do you see? What feelings or sensations come up? Release any judgment you might have about your other self. What can you do for this self? What does it need from you?

Hold a space of love and light for this alien self until you feel a resonance with it. Let the bond between you grow stronger. Invite this one to discover love with you as you grow into enlightenment. Invite it to experience what you experience. If you are curious and would like more insight about your counterpart, ask it to let you look through it's eyes in it's native reality.

You have no idea how much this will affect your other self and the dimension it lives in!

2

If you have had or will have encounters with misguided energies, this is an exercise in redirecting them to the Source for the light and love they seek. (You can do this with misguided humans too!)

Imagine that a misguided energy approaches you. It wants to play a game of fear with you. What is your first reaction? Confusion? Fear? Neutrality? The urge to flee? Resistance? Write down the first reaction you have when you are approached by a misguided energy who might want to harm you.

Now think of yourself as the master you truly are. Take yourself out of the level the misguided energy is approaching you from. At the soul level of the misguided energy and your soul level, there is nothing to fear and no harm can be done. At the soul level, there is no such thing as illusion. The misguided energy is approaching you from the level where illusion is real. You must approach the misguided energy from the level where the illusion is not real.

Smile and send love, compassion and understanding to this one through your eyes. Touch the heart chakra of this one and shift it's focus from the illusion that it is separate and undesirable. Tell it that what it is searching for is within itself, not outside. Now touch the third eye center of this entity and allow light to flood it's mental body and emotional body. Dispel the darkness as much as this being will allow you to. Then give it a hug and send it on it's way with light all around it. You will notice a feeling of gratefulness from this one.

If there is no shift for this one and it cannot accept your gift, you will notice that it will just shrug it's shoulders and go off to look for someone else it can play with. Either way, you have done your part and remained safe from harm at the same time.

3

Think about your DNA. Think about all the information you have stored in your DNA. Imagine all the worlds and species it spans. It is immense! The information and outlets in your DNA straddle the entire galaxy and more. Make a connection with all the beings who contributed to the human DNA and allow them to respond to you. They love you very much and appreciate what you are doing. Allow them to help you.

Ask your DNA to reveal to you something which is important in your growth right now. Ask it to show you what is presently being unlocked in your system. Allow sensations, feelings and visuals to come up as you linger in the alert waiting space. Your DNA will reveal incredible things. As you imagine unlocking it's codes and secrets, you will be energized and you will speed your process of remembering.

Reclaiming the Shadow Self

Chapter 17

God's Psychology

As we have said in our introduction, there are things to understand about God that are misunderstood. We will address these things now.

We will refer to God as a male only for simplicity's sake. God is all sexes and none at the same time. (There are more than just male and female, if you would like to know this.) We will also use a lower case "h" for pronouns referring to God just for simplicity's sake.

First of all, let us describe the word God as we are using it for it is a word that means different things to different people. As *we* use the word, God is the sum total of everything in existence down to the minutest particle in an atom. This includes evolved forms and unevolved forms. Remember, the sum total is always greater than it's parts. That is why God seems so much greater than any given individual.

God is actually all individuals blended into one whether they are conscious of it or not. That is why God is not outside of yourself. God is a gestalt intelligence which is made up of you and everything else. God is the mass consciousness of the entire universe. That is why he is so smart! The way molecules make up a table, that is the way you make up God. The table (the sum) is greater than it's parts (the molecules). Without the molecules, there is no table. Without you, and every other, there is no God.

Reclaiming the Shadow Self

Once you gain the ability to reach all areas of creation consciously and behave harmoniously with and inside them, then you have reached the ability to see things from God's viewpoint. You and every other being have a long way to go and much to explore on your way back to God-state. I doesn't end here on the Earth plane. Earth is only a minute part of a much larger journey.

All beings are in the image of God. Not just humans. All beings are in the likeness of God himself. All beings *are* God, even the grays and other dark ones.

If all beings are in the likeness of God, then there are some parts of God which are not yet evolved. If God is not yet evolved, then he will experience conflict within himself. Of course, God (you) is in his completed form and in his non-completed form at the same time. We cannot say this often enough about paradox.

We do not want you to think we are saying God is not perfect. He is perfect, just as you are, and we do not want to raise controversy in your mind before you have a chance to hear us out. All of this is very simplistic in terms. Please take all of this with a grain of salt. See what it causes in your mind as you pursue the avenues we are leading you to.

You are a miniature version of God, just as each of your cells is a miniature and complete version of you. If your scientists were advanced enough, they could take a single cell from your body and create an exact replica of yourself, memories, emotional makeup, physical body and all. Fortunately your scientists will never be able to do it until love is anchored on the Earth plane.

Look at your own life and your own self if you want to know who God is.

The things you have gone through and the feelings you have felt will give you a clue to what God has experienced as he has been watching his universe. As you have seen chaos in your life and felt anguish, you can imagine what God has felt as well. If you feel frustration, then God feels frustration. If you feel anger, then God feels anger. If you feel joy, then God feels joy. God has a rich emotional experience. *You* are God's emotional experience. God experiences everything you do.

All the beings in this universe are reflections and parts of God. The high angelic realms reflect the ecstatic aspects of God. The darker ones reflect the parts of God where he does not understand himself yet. Realize that God has become frustrated at times with all this, although not at the level *you* experience frustration. This universe, the freewill zone, has taken him for a walk instead of the other way around. He relinquished control. He did this out of love and trust because the freewill universe asked him to let it be in charge of itself for a while.

> **Look at yourself
> if you want
> to know who God is.**

You can think of God as a student. He is a great student at that. He is more of a student than you realize. You could think of him as a school kid in the classroom. As he undertook this experiment, or project, which perhaps a teacher had suggested, he meditates upon his project. He grieves with it and triumphs with it. The din of the classroom is in the background, and he cannot really hear it. He is engrossed in his project and is fascinated by what is happening. Do not think you do not have God's full attention, for you do.

We will give you an analogy. God has many blocks sitting on his desk in his schoolroom. The blocks are actually extensions of his own self. His friends are playing with their blocks, and he is playing with his. God is far past the kindergarten level. God has peers. He knows others like himself who have their own universes. There are even Gods above the God that we know, who are his teachers. They are very powerful beings, and God is part of them.

For instance, you have peers in your soul family, and then your soul family belongs to a monad, which is made up of several families which originate from itself. Then, once the soul families blend into the monad, it is a great being. Yet the monad is part of an even greater entity. It goes on for infinity. So does God (the gestalt intelligence you are part of).

Realize that this is only one universe and there are many Gods (gestalt intelligences). There are many universes, just as there are many of you and many universes which are created by you. Each of you *is* a universe of your own. You are the God of your particular universe.

In our analogy, the blocks are symbolic of God's universes. Some of the blocks are different colors. Some of them are made of different substances. All the blocks are part of God's makeup. God plays with these universes and learns from them. They are a teaching tool for himself. He is learning about himself by watching what his universe does. You are actually teaching God many things about himself if you would like to know this. This should help your self image greatly!

God plays with these universes and does certain things to them to see what will happen. For instance, he will disassemble one and put it back together to see if he can remember just exactly how it was, which of course he always does. Sometimes he will disassemble them because he wants to change them and see what will happen with these changes. He may put them back together differently on purpose just to see what will come of it.

This particular universe, this block, is one who said, "Hey. We watched you disassemble us many times, and we would like to see if we can do it ourselves. We would like to see if we can put ourselves together without any help from you. We would like to see if we can do what *you* do!" In the journey before this one, God (the gestalt intelligence you are part of) nudged it here and there to get it to go the way he wanted. However, in this one, the universe said, "Don't nudge us, God. Keep your hands off. Don't interfere."

Of course, this was a surprising request for God, for he did not expect his own self to request freewill and separation from himself. If he was to give it freewill and set it on it's own, he would have to relinquish control and let it be as it wanted to be—-for better or for worse. This could be perceived as a fearful thing for God to do, for he is one that likes to be in control of himself, just like you and anyone else.

So this is a great lesson for God in the release of control. It is as if God said, "Alright, I will give you this chance if you desire it so much. If you want to separate yourself and be allowed to make your own mistakes, then be forewarned that it won't be easy. I will help if you call on me by reminding you of the vision. I will keep my hands off, though, and I will watch what happens. Be assured that I am always with you although you might not feel it."

Think of this universe as one that once was a gray universe. (Think of gray as a beautiful color, so you can see the gist of this analogy.) Some of God's universes might be blue, yellow, or may not have a color you recognize. It may not even be a substance you recognize.

God separated the particles of this gray universe. He put the white particles on one side and the black particles on the other. The point of the game was for the black and the white to mingle and turn back into the gray again. Gray is the desired goal. Gray is how it was when it started and that is how it wants to be when it is over.

The black and the white opposes itself. As the universe comes back together, there is much disruption, disharmony, and craziness, as the two sides swirl and tumble about each other. Each particle tries to find it's original position once again.

Not only God is watching this, but God's friends and supervisor are watching as well. Sometimes God feels embarrassment for he feels that his project is not successful in all areas. Some are turning out to be to his liking and some are not. This is where we could say God has reached frustration points, the Earth plane having been one of them, especially if he can see how to blend the energies from his vantage point, but cannot touch. He could change everything in an instant if he were allowed to. However, he (you) has agreed to let the universe sort itself out on it's own.

As this happens he experiences the pain of each and every one of the beings inside it, for each one of them is a cell in his body. Not only does he watch his universe come back together, but he *feels* everything that happens. He has become tired of the pain at times, like you have. However, he is not allowed to cheat in the game, and he also has a supervisor (himself) looking over his shoulder. He cannot get away with any tricks. He must play by the rules he agreed to. This has been a source of concern and worry for God in a way. He is not sure his universe can harmonize itself without his help, for he has never witnessed it before. This could be thought of as his first freewill universe. This is, in fact, the birth of a God, which we will explain in a moment.

Reclaiming the Shadow Self

God plays with his universes in many ways. The possibilities are endless. Sometimes he disassembles the universe. Sometimes he blends more than two universes together. He may blend three universes together into one and see what happens. He may try four, or seven. Multiple universe blending is happening in this one. Some of the things he does with his universes are short journeys and some of them are long. This one could be considered a long journey.

Just because the universe will eventually come back together again in harmony does not mean it will be exactly the same as it was before this journey was started. Once it has been through this journey, it will never be the same, for the substance of God (you), which is this universe, will forever remember what has been learned. This substance will know it's journey was unique and much was gained. Every time a universe is disassembled and reassembled, learning has taken place. It is always improved. This is the main game for God (you). He likes to disassemble universes in certain ways, and be creative about it's restoration.

> *The battle in the universe is the battle God has inside himself, for he is dreaming it.*

Sometimes he blends his universe with his friend's universe and it may be a very alien universe to look at, for it is another being's (another gestalt intelligence's) creation, a different product of another God's mind. That is not happening in this particular universe.

Look at your friend and imagine the differences between you both. Imagine that you both were to create entire universes. Imagine what differences in the universes there would be! These are very challenging endeavors when Gods attempt to blend their universes. A universe with two Gods is something difficult for you to imagine.

You could see the opposing forces of the dark and the light as two sides of God. God agreed to have this opposing situation inside himself. The battle in the universe is the battle God has inside himself, for he (you) is dreaming all this. Darkness (no awareness) is the side of himself that said, "Well, I am not a bad guy, but okay. If you want to play this game, I will give it my best shot."

The wars within the universe are wars that take place within God. He is learning to understand these sides of himself. If you look at it this way, you may find that you have more compassion for these events as they happen on the Earth plane. Warring energy is truly of God himself. The war energy is a concept which God desires to understand. The opposing forces are both God, not just one or the other. God is not just the light. The darkness is God too. The darkness is a creation of God.

Your shadow self is as much you as your light self is. It is not outside of yourself. The battle within your own heart is the smaller reflection of the battle within God's heart. Truly, the battle is about loving the dark side. It is easy to love the lighter side, for it is the known, the developed side. The dark is more difficult to love for it is undeveloped and unpredictable. This is what God himself is going through.

There was no guarantee to the outcome. God wanted to see which side of himself was more powerful when it came to a battle of wills. This has been a source of worry for him because he did not know which side of himself would win. Of course, it was only a game. The teacher and himself could put an end to it if it became too intense and was going in the direction of self destruction. He could always take it apart and put it back together correctly when all is said and done.

The only thing God (the gestalt intelligence you are part of) is allowed to do is hold the vision of what the end result of the universe will look like as it goes through chaos and searches for it's original template. Sometimes God's vision gets through and sometimes it does not, for the particles have their own agenda. The universe sometimes listens to God's silent vision and sometimes it does not. When it reaches a "stuck" area, it then calls on God for the vision he is holding of the original template so it can get another idea about how to reach it's goal.

Reclaiming the Shadow Self

This has happened recently on a mass level and that is why there is such an acceleration in growth on all planes right now. There was stagnation happening in many realms, and there was a cry for God's (your) help. Since he (you) was invited to help, he (the part of you that is God consciousness) has sent out waves of his energy and vision to give the universe the nudge it needed and asked for on a mass level. Then the universe (you) will continue it's journey as before until it reaches another "stuck" area and calls for God's (your) silent vision again.

God wanted to nudge it before this, but he has had to refrain. He (you) could see from his vantage point and wisdom that something endeavored was not necessarily a beneficial direction toward the goal. But he had to sit back and let the universe make it's own mistakes and experience the mistakes within himself. (Remember, mistakes are not really mistakes.)

In the meantime, he has been going on a roller coaster ride along with it. This is what we mean when God is being taken for a walk instead of the other way around. This is not an easy thing for a God to do! To release total control is not a normal thing. His heart has been broken just as much as yours has. It is an experience that every God eventually plays with at some point in his education, though. Our particular God has reached this point in his.

Realize you have experienced isolation from God. It is because you yourself asked for it as a mass group of energy within God's body. You have not been isolated from God because he discarded you, or wanted to get you away from him. In fact it was quite the opposite. He did not *really* want to let you go. Because you wanted to find out all about the power God has, and do what he does, then you had to separate yourself and learn the lessons on your own.

You can love and understand the self more easily now, because you can see how you and God are the same and work together to co-create. It may be easier now to love your shadow self and the shadow self of others now that you know the shadow self is actually God too. It will also be easier for you to love others, alien or human, for now you can see that they are a reflection of God who need love and understanding. Treat them appropriately. This is a part of God which does not understand himself yet. God is learning about himself just as you are learning about yourself.

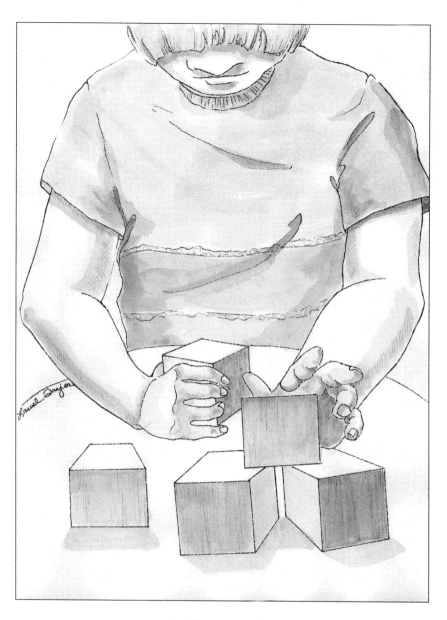

God's Psychology

Reclaiming the Shadow Self

Remember, you are a miniature version of God. You are a contributor to the greatness that God is! He would not be great without all of you.

Realize that God can feel sad, he can feel anger, he can cry, and he is totally capable of behaving in an immature fashion. When someone acts immaturely, it is God who is behind it, learning, and not just the individual. This should help you feel better about yourself, for you are simply doing the things that God himself is doing. You are a cell in his body. You are experiencing an event which is moving through him.

The entire mass consciousness of the human form is an aspect of God's psychology. The entire mass consciousness of the grays is an aspect of God's psychology. The entire mass consciousness of the angelic realm is an aspect of God's psychology. The experiences and the thoughts had by all are exactly the same experiences and thoughts of God. None of these aspects of God's psychology are complete within themselves. They are all part of a greater psychology which works in a somewhat simple and at the same time complicated fashion. It is a paradox that everything is simple and complicated at the same time.

The only advantage God (the gestalt intelligence you are part of) has over you is that he knows how the movie will end because he can go there and look anytime he wants to. He is not "stuck" inside illusion, so he can see all things in their finished and unfinished versions, including himself. Only when he makes himself forget the ending does he feel fear—through you.

If you are capable of feeling embarrassment, then God is capable of feeling embarrassment. His own friends may be snickering at some of the things he attempted in his universes, and might even be laughing at him because he nearly got "stuck" in some of his endeavors. But it is okay, for God has a sense of humor and can laugh at himself. "Stuckness" never lasts forever. He also snickers at what others do with their universes.

Realize that it is a game and is not quite as serious as it seems. It is a lesson for God. Since you are God, you too are learning the lesson.

Everything we have said pertains to the freewill universe that God has created. Of course, there are many other universes and some have nothing to do with freewill. However, the freewill universe is a very important part of God's (you as a gestalt intelligence) education. This is an important process in his growth. It was absolutely necessary for all of his parts to learn about freewill, choice making, and release of control before he went any further with what he was doing.

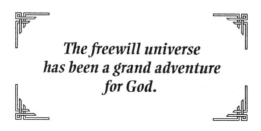

The freewill universe has been a grand adventure for God.

Without allowing freewill and choice, there was not as much excitement, we might say, in God's studies. It was beginning to get a little boring for him. The freewill universe has been a grand adventure for himself. It is not anywhere near over yet! Perhaps it could be said that the universe is at the quarter mark on it's journey to completion.

Enlightenment of the human consciousness is a very large step in the direction of completion. It is a landmark in the journey. It is certainly a turning point and will create a quantum leap on many levels for all beings who are searching for harmony within themselves.

You may feel that God has abandoned the Earth for a while. He was frustrated with himself and wanted to stop looking for a while. Part of him did not want to feel this anguish anymore so he did what many of you tried to do. He wished to ignore it and go on for a while. But he knows he cannot turn his focus away for it is inside himself. He knows he must become whole and heal it eventually.

You might say, "How could it be that he let this go on for thousands and millions of years?" Time is irrelevant to God. However, he (you) did not expect it to be so difficult. If you find these feelings in yourself, you will find that they are a reflection of what God is feeling.

This is why you may feel that God has abandoned the Earth plane.

Realize that God is not as all powerful as you think. He is in an evolving state like yourself. As you evolve, God is evolved. He is not yet in his perfection, for he has disassembled his perfection in order to see it come back together and learn from the process. The only thing God is allowed to do, unless he is asked for guidance, is to sit, watch and feel. He is not able to change the course of events, for he has been asked not to by the universe itself! He did not always want to look, because it made him sad. However, it is not that he was not paying attention or that he abandoned you.

Different parts of God's creation become the center of the creation at different times. When something exciting happens somewhere in the creation, it suddenly becomes the center of attention. That is what is happening here now on the Earth plane. Anytime an entire race of beings breaks through the veils of illusion, it is a major event in the universe. This is a major healing of a piece of God's psychology, and everyone is excited about it. When some other group of beings breaks through their illusion, *they* will be the center of creation for a while. This is the way it works.

God can feel pride in himself, just like you can. As he witnesses himself healing and coming back to wholeness, he is proud of it. You can look at your growth and healing in this way. Allow it to happen in it's own way. Do not rush it, or try to make it take any particular form. It will happen as long as you hold the vision for yourself that you are whole, complete and enlightened in a simultaneous time frame, the way God does. You will find that it will emerge in this reality and manifest within yourself if you hold the vision.

God can birth new Gods. All the beings in this universe will blend to become a God once this journey is completed. This universe (gestalt intelligence) will be a great being and is part of God, yet will be a separate God from God. Gods experience oneness. God is not separate from his friends. So it can be truly said there is only one God force in existence.

You may wonder, "Why has God (me) done all this if it was such a source of pain? What is the use of doing all this? It seems like a big waste of time and energy if the universe was already there in it's complete form, and then he disassembled it just to see it be what it was before? Why was this exercise necessary?"

It is because God wants to learn and explore.

Then you may say, "Why does God want to learn and explore? He knows everything in a simultaneous time frame because he knows how to access this."

The reason is because it is something fun to do. If you had all the abundance in the world, and you had millions of dollars and never had to work again in your life, you could ask yourself, "Well, what will I do with myself? I cannot just sit and watch TV for the rest of my life. What would I like to do in order to entertain myself?"

This is how it is for God. He does not *need* to learn. He does it because it is fun. He does it because it takes him on a journey. If you yourself were a millionaire (which most of you will be, by the way), you did not need anything else in the whole universe, and had more than enough time and money to do anything you wanted to do, you most certainly would explore, search for experiences and travel as much as you can. By doing this, it gives you something fun to do even if you run into difficult situations. This is what is happening for God.

Yes, God knows everything there is to know. He knows all the things his "supervisor" knows, which is himself. He is lacking nothing. He needs nothing. However, it is fun for him to pretend he forgot, and thus allow an adventure to take place within himself.

This has been a very difficult concept to convey in the English language. We have done our best as far as an analogy. We have still fallen far short of explaining God's psychology. This is the best explanation we can give to you, although it is much deeper than this. It cannot be translated. This has been simple language for a deep and uncommunicatable subject. You will discover more about this when you go inside yourself. It cannot really be understood through words. What we are telling you is a beginner way of perceiving God's psychology, his universe and what he is up to.

What we are attempting to convey to you is that you are more like God than you think you are. You are a living piece of God. Your connection with God is more personal than you realize. You *are* his mind, his emotions and his body. You are experiencing events which are moving through him. He experiences what you go through as the event moves through him, and he sees it from your viewpoint. You are like a microscope into his and your creation. *You have no idea how completely you are God.*

When you are sad or happy, realize that it is also something God is experiencing. Think of the things you do, no matter what polarity they are on, as ways that God is learning to deal with himself and his reflection. If you find yourself fighting with someone, realize that God is experiencing through the other person as well. God is fighting with himself.

Reclaiming the Shadow Self

There is a point where it doesn't make sense to battle the self or others anymore. When God learns to love himself inside and out, which you are helping him with, the battle with reflections and the battle with the self is over. Humanity is reaching this level, individual by individual.

This is for your information if you would like to know this. See where your mind leads you as you think about these concepts. *There is much more behind this door of thought. We hope we have triggered these deeper levels for you. You will find them as you go inward!*

Affirmations

1. I am God. God is me.
2. I am constantly aware of God in all beings and all physical matter. I recognize God in others regardless of how they are acting.
3. If I fight with another, I am really fighting with myself because we are both God.
4. I give up the concept of battling within the self and accept all parts of my self and others.
5. When I want to know more about God, I study myself.
6. My issues are God's issues. My emotional experience is God's emotional experience. What I feel, God feels. What God feels, I feel.
7. I am the vehicle for God's experience inside his creation.
8. I am a Co-Creator with the Prime Creator (God).
9. The darkness is as much a creation of God as the light is.
10. I allow deeper levels of understanding about God's psychology to be triggered in my "mind".

Exercises

1

Look back at your past. Look at the present conditions of your life. Look at all the emotions you have experienced. Whether they were positive or negative (or a mixture of both), see them as things you experienced as God. Connect with the paradox that you are separate from God but you are not. See if you can truly reach the understanding and feeling that you are God in the physical plane with a certain set of challenges.

How would you deal with your challenges now that you truly understand you are God in the flesh? How would you treat yourself now that you know you are God who has allowed himself to forget what he knows? What do you feel now that you realize you are God's emotional experience? Do you now respect yourself and the path you took more? Do you see your innocence and essence now?

2

Connect with God (Prime Creator) as you endeavor to create something. Perhaps you would like to create a better relationship with someone, abundance, healing, an artform, or some other act of creation. Visualize a cord between your physical self and the God self deep within. Imagine that you are combining your energies with the energies of the Prime Creator through this cord. Your will is in alignment with his. You will feel a surge of energy through the cord and your body will tingle or heat up as you set up the conditions for co-creating with God.

Now that you have the immense power of Prime Creator behind you, focus on what you would like to create. Think of him as a being who has the means, and you have the desire, vision and commitment to manifest. Think of him as your backer, sponsor or investor. Direct the energies you now hold toward physical reality. Imagine a vacuum in physical reality where your creation will manifest. Watch as it begins to unfold in the energetic realms. Watch as it begins to crystallize and gel, becoming more and more solid. Allow it to break through the veils and turn into physical matter. You will see it soon in your life. Trust the process.

Thank the Prime Creator for co-creating with you.

3

Imagine that you are going to visit with God in his classroom or playground. Perhaps you would like to visit him in a secret garden and sit on a bench with him. Sit with God as if you were his equal, which you are by the way. Release all ideas of inferiority to God. Visit with him as if you were casually visiting your best friend. What do you talk about? What do you both act like? What is your body language? Are you relaxed? Are you at ease with God and he with you?

Talk about your life with God. Ask him what he thinks. Tell him what you think. It is alright if you want to tell him about your dissatisfaction with him in the past or present. He will understand and listen to you respectfully. He will take what you say into account. If you ask him for explanations about confusing issues for yourself, he will give them to you.

Ask him what he needs from you. Tell him what you need from him. Ask him what his plans are for you. Ask him to open the connection between yourselves and let him know you want to be in touch with him more deeply.

Ask him what his goals and desires are with his universe. Lend your energy to what he is doing. Align yourself with him and feel the connection between the both of you as it deepens inside your heart.

Do this exercise often. The more you can connect with God as a friend, an equal, and a partner, aligning your energies with his, the sooner you will experience miracles and magic in your life. At that point, you will experience what it is like to be one with God (gestalt intelligence).

Reclaiming the Shadow Self

Chapter 18

The Aftermath of Remembering

After you have opened some of your upsetting unconscious memories or past lives, you may find yourself quite devastated by what you see and the emotions you feel. We would like to assure you this state of devastation will not last forever. You may have the feeling you have been so defiled you can never be pure again. We would like to dispel this fear. You are pure underneath the defilement and unsavory circumstances you have been in.

You may have a feeling of deservingness for all the sadness you have experienced. There may also be a feeling of fear, for you are aware of the law of attraction in the universe and you may be convinced this can happen again. You may fear that these imprints are something which will plague you forever and will cause you more upsetting circumstances as you open up your "can of worms".

Be assured that you are protected.

We encourage you to think of yourself as a God or a Goddess who has allowed him or herself to be made "dirty". This has happened for reasons you will not entirely understand until you are clearer and further away from your trauma. We assure you there are valid reasons for this. Yes, there can be a surface understanding at this time. However, a deep understanding of the reasons why you went through horrible circumstances is something you will discover later. You will understand them when you gain entry to your inner worlds. Be patient with this process. You are going through a mourning period for your injured child within.

Think of yourself as a God or a Goddess who has stepped down from his or her majesty in order to experience what is denser than his or her own reality. When you begin to stir again, as you are stirring now, you will rise up in flame and fire from the ashes. You will be brighter and stronger than you were before you allowed your descent into darkness (no awareness).

You are clean underneath all this. There is only a small part of you which feels dirty compared to the expanse of your soul that does not. There is only a small part of you that feels confused. The rest of you knows exactly what it is doing and is steering you through your healing. You are your own supervisor and you are doing an excellent job!

The "pollution" of your system is not permanent. The pollution is there to be transmuted and transformed. It is there to be turned into the light it really is. When you awaken from your sleep, as you are doing now, you will see through the illusion of this reality. This will not just happen in a mental way. It will be deeper than this. There will be understanding and experience instead of just knowledge that this reality is not as real as it seems. There is a place in your soul where *none* of this is real. There is a place in the universe where the conflicts you have been through are not solid at all. *It is the energy of the conflicts and events that count.*

From this place, which will be beneficial for you to access as often as possible, you will see that the issues which seem so large to you now are actually petty and small at the levels you are moving toward. This is how it feels when you are looking at the "big picture". The challenge is to rise above the place where the issues and the conflicts are big. There is a place where issues and conflicts are actually humorous. If you can access this it will speed your growth.

Accessing a place of neutrality in yourself is something you can achieve no matter what your bias is. The aftermath could be thought of as the emotional fallout which most likely will happen when you remember, and finally deal with, devastating events in your life.

You may feel as if your energy systems are collapsing. You may feel as if your body is disintegrating. You may feel as if your personality is falling apart. The fears you never thought you had will come to the surface. You might feel as if your wires have short circuited. You may find yourself back in the fear you experienced at the time of the event as if it is a delayed reaction. You may find yourself with irrational imaginings of all the fearful things that can happen to you. You may find yourself fearing other people and projecting on them. You may find that you suddenly see trauma in everyone's energy systems which they are unaware of in themselves. It is important to take your emotional fallout with a grain of salt. You are dealing with your issues of trust in the universe, yourself and other people.

You may find yourself in the fear frequencies more often than you wish to be. However, we suggest that you allow these feelings to flow. Remember you are protected as these emotions release. You are irradicating the possibility that these things can happen again. Even though you might fear your energy is attracting unfortunate and unhappy circumstances, this is exactly what you are neutralizing in your DNA by facing your fear. It may need to flare up for a while in order to be cleared. Be allowing with your release and refrain from having judgment on yourself. You are being held in a safe space energetically and you may have taken practical measures to insure your safety—-which would be wise.

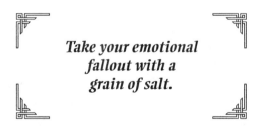

Take your emotional fallout with a grain of salt.

Please do not fear now. The universe knows it would not be beneficial to your healing if the devastating events you fear happened again. It would be silly at this time. It would be useless, for the imprints are already there. They do not need to be set up or reinforced the way they needed to be implanted earlier in your life. The universe desires your success, so be assured that you have nothing to fear from your fears at this time! Yes, like attracts like. You may be certain you will attract that which you fear. However, there are many light beings helping humans with this as they transmute darkness. Their interference with the law of attraction during deep healing is there because you have asked them to do this.

You will feel rage when you first see through the illusion. You will feel rage at the helplessness you experienced in the past. You may find yourself very angry with God when you find the not so pleasant memories. You may find yourself wanting to throw *bricks* at God!

This is alright. We ask you to express and release this anger toward God. Yell at him and be angry with him as much as you like, for he understands and he will not take it out on you for expressing your anger the way humans did in your past. Realize that your anger with others is actually your anger at God. Your anger with others is also your anger with yourself, for *you* are God.

Express this rage at God fully. You can do this through writing, physical activity, or any other method that helps you to get your anger out on the table. You may find that you have a stubborn attitude suddenly toward God and the world you live in. You may find that you have rage against the very *nature* of the reality you are in. You may feel that all this pain was a useless waste of energy and it was all for nothing. We guarantee you that it was not, although it is impossible for us to explain the reasons for pain and fear on this plane. You will know this when you enter your inner worlds. We highly suggest that you keep your rage at God between yourself and him. Refrain from inflicting pain on others, or you may incur negative karma.

Most likely, you have been depressed all your life, or at least most of it. If you express your rage it will help lift the depression. Know that your guides are constantly with you and are working diligently on your energy field. Masters visit you often and help you as well. Know that in their eyes you are pure and innocent and full of clear light. They do not see you the way you see yourself. If you see yourself as defiled, devastated, crushed, immobilized, mutilated in your mind, realize this is an illusion you are under at this time. This illusion will lift from yourself as you let go of the powerfully charged fear you hold. Realize that you are an angel in physical reality. You have an angelic self which cannot be touched by the rudeness and harshness you have experienced on the Earth plane.

We advise that you do not indulge in your fear any more than necessary. The more you can focus on the ecstatic frequencies and teach your body to vibrate at these levels, the sooner you will be able to move through your pain. Fear frequencies are something you are familiar with. Perhaps you have been a rather nervous person all your life. Perhaps you have felt intimidated and inferior. Perhaps you have been stubborn or tough all your life. All these things come from the fear frequencies.

Emotional fallout is to be expected when you clear upsetting events from your system. Allow others to love you during this time and it will help you greatly. Perhaps you could ask your friend to hold a hand over your chakras, especially your heart chakra in front or behind. You will experience much shifting, for the guides will work through your friend whether he or she knows this is happening or not. All that is necessary is that the person who is helping you loves you. The guides can magnify this by one hundred times and more.

You may have panic attacks even though you have never been prone to them before. They will pass as quickly as they come. Realize that panic attacks are just waves of anxiety and fear which are moving through and out of your system. Do not be alarmed by the fact that you are not the same person you were before. You will not be the same person after this is over anyway. Be allowing to the old self as it dies, so to speak. Let it kick and scream if it needs to. Your old self is rescinding the throne to the soul self. The soul self is wiser and deeper. There is no high and low, only degrees of inwardness.

During the aftermath, you may find that none of your friends fit you anymore. You may find your job does not fit you anymore. You may find that the place you live does not fit you anymore. You may see the aftermath as being a crumbling of the reality you know. We wish to inform you not to be afraid when this happens. You may feel like you are being made to start from scratch again. You might have to let go of everything you developed and worked for in your life. You might find that your personality and character is crumbling and you don't know who you are or what you are about anymore. You may find that you lose interest in goals which were driving forces for you all your life.

This is alright. Allow the disintegration to take place. You must make room for the new self which is coming forth. The new self is emerging even though you cannot see it. It will be there quite suddenly and you will not know how you became so clear all of a sudden.

You may find in the aftermath that your anger with someone who has annoyed you may magnify far beyond it's original size. You may find that you are angry with systems of thought. The fact that abuse exists at all on the Earth plane may anger you. It might even be a driving force for you in the future to do something about it once you are healed.

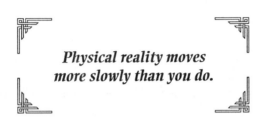

**_Physical reality moves
more slowly than you do._**

Even though your surroundings do not look favorable to you at this time, know that favorable circumstances are coming to you. Physical reality moves more slowly than you do. You simply must wait for the old to pass and the new to come in. In dealing with the aftermath, you may find you must separate yourself from people and situations you are accustomed to.

You may feel saddened by the state you are in right now and might feel like giving up. You may feel it is just too painful and it doesn't seem to be doing anything except making you more dysfunctional than you were *before* you faced your fear in order to transmute it. Keep in mind that you are headed for a blast which will open yourself in a brisk manner. You will be clear in the near future and it is not very far off. You will feel as if you have crossed a line and everything will feel different from then on. Know this is coming to yourself and that you do not have to worry. Just keep plugging along, so to speak, and you will get there.

Learn how to hold happier vibrations in your body. Your body has simply gotten into the habit of holding fear. Teach your energetic systems to hold happiness for at least five minutes per day. Asking your guides to help you with this will create immediate results. Let them hold you in their arms. Let them tickle you!

The secret to a healthy body, mind and spirit is happiness. If you are having difficulty in any area of your systems, it has to do with a lack of happiness, safety and joy. The trust issues will clear. Trusting the self, others and the universe after what has happened in your present life and your past lives is a major step in your growth. We know this is a difficult accomplishment. It is a leap of faith.

The aftermath of remembering confusing or devastating events will make you feel fragile. Expect it. You may not consciously remember feeling so fragile and vulnerable ever before in your life. Allow this fragility and vulnerability to come forth, knowing you are protected. The fragility and vulnerability will become more clear to you as time moves on. The fragility and vulnerability are signs that the work you have been doing on yourself is working!

Fragility is a high state of mind and emotion. Go into the fragility and face the fears which emanate from it. Realize that you are a precious jewel inside a shell which has been defiled. You may find yourself frightened to come out and be your beautiful self again. You fear that if you are beautiful, trusting and innocent again, you will be taken advantage of and hurt once more. Perhaps you projected a "tough" image so no one would attempt to take advantage of you again.

We assure you that this will not happen. You have developed much skill in discernment and you are now empowered. You can be open, trusting and vulnerable without being taken advantage of if you know your boundaries and keep them intact. People will respect your boundaries and your wishes for they would rather have your company than your withdrawal from themselves. This happens because *you* respect your *self*. As soon as you stop respecting the self, intruding energies can enter your reality.

Allow yourself to vibrate where the fragile feeling is. This will lead you to love. Your heart will become open once again to receive love from yourself and others.

Much of your journey is about learning to trust again. Yes, it is an unpredictable reality. It is full of dangers and joys. But now you are in a place where you can take control of what you choose to experience. You are no longer under the illusion that you are at the mercy of the world

The Aftermath of Remembering

around you. Now you know you can take the reins and control your own life. The world around you will be your playground instead of a source of fear. Project clarity.

If you are about to be abused against your will, stay calm and put yourself in your heart space. Surrender to what is happening. Refrain from falling into fear (even if it is in the form of anger), which has normally been your first reaction up to this point. Look this person in the eye and vibrate at love with this one. Reassure this one that you hold nothing against him or her if he or she chooses to abuse you. However, let this one know that you would prefer it if it didn't happen.

If you give love to this one who desires to hurt you, he or she will find that the energy put out will return to him or her with a boomerang effect. This person may find him or her self in tears instead of aggression. This is the power of unconditional love. *Compassion is a force to be reckoned with.*

Vulnerability is not as vulnerable as it seems. It is the ability to allow things to pass through you or go around you. Thus it can return to it's source. It is also the ability to consider the fact that the other person has a valid perception. It is being able to admit that you can be wrong, or that you handled something incorrectly.

In the aftermath, you will feel as if you are living through total destruction of yourself. Keep your chin up and continue, for you are far past the halfway point in your healing. Know that you *will* succeed. There is no question about it. Know that soon you will have clarity in your systems. Know that you will be able to hold the joy frequencies on the Earth plane very shortly. This does not mean you will not have challenges to holding your joy. However, you will not be blocked in the core anymore and it will be easier for you to deal with the situations which come your way while in your enlightened state.

Do not think you deserved everything which happened to you, for you did not. This is not how it works. You *chose* the things you wanted to learn in your lifetimes on the Earth. It was not thrust upon you. You were not cast here because you messed up somewhere in the universe and were sentenced to Earth. You came here willingly. The hell frequencies you have experienced in this reality did not come to you because you deserved it.

Reclaiming the Shadow Self

If the issue of deservingness comes to you, it comes from yourself. You can drop the idea of deserving hell frequencies anytime you wish. Release the idea that you have done something wrong to deserve unhappiness in your life. Even if you were a villain in the past and had a string of victimized lifetimes after it, you still did nothing wrong to deserve it. You chose a progression of lifetimes for a certain understanding you wanted to achieve. It was a course of study you undertook. You needed to understand the criminal heart and mind.

If you would like to know what you deserve, it is this: you deserve much love, respect, joy and happiness! There is nothing else you deserve.

Handling your view of yourself during the aftermath of your memories may be a challenge for you. You may feel as if you look ugly. You may look in the mirror and think you look terrible. Realize that how you see your physical appearance is not necessarily what you look like to others. Has anyone ever walked up to you and told you that you look great when you thought you looked terrible?

If you see all sorts of negative things about your appearance, realize that this is an illusion for yourself. Other people are not seeing what you see. It is all in the eye of the beholder.

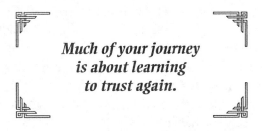

***Much of your journey
is about learning
to trust again.***

And looking terrible is definitely not what you look like on the inner planes! On the inner planes, there is incredible light emerging from inside you. It is being reborn and remembered by you. On the inner planes, you are glowing and *extremely* luminescent. Some beings come here just to gaze at your beauty, for your designs are intricate and fascinating even in the midst of your sadness. There is brilliant light in yourself, and it could be seen as "filling out" of certain areas, becoming more detailed and defined.

On the inner planes, you are like a beautiful photograph which is in the process of developing. As your colors and details appear, there is much excitement in the ones who are watching and there are many delighted "ooohs" and "aaahs".

Only *you* are not able to see your own brilliance right now, for you have not *wanted* to see your brilliance. You were enmeshed in a lack of self worth. You did not believe you had brilliance to begin with. If you only knew, you would be in love with your self the way you should be!

The aftermath may drag on for awhile. You might find yourself becoming impatient as you wait for the new to come in. You may feel you have changed, but you are still surrounded by lack, survival issues, or whatever else plagues you. You may find yourself frustrated or even furious about it. Remember: it is going to take some time for the new life to set up. Physical reality is slower than you are.

In the future, you will gain the ability to move physical reality with more speed. This will not only be due to the fact that your abilities will become more developed. It will also be due to the fact that a planetary shift is taking place and the "rules" are changing. For now, accept where you are.

Affirmations

1. My guides protect me from attracting that which I fear as I transmute my darkness.
2. I am a God(ess) exploring denser realities than the one I am from.
3. I access the "big picture" with ease.
4. I am neutral. I release judgment about myself and the reality around me.
5. I trust the universe, myself and others.
6. My guides are constantly with me. They are diligently working on my energy field.
7. I know how to handle emotional fallout. I teach my body how to hold higher vibrations.
8. The world is my playground.
9. I release my old reality with love and thankfulness for what it did for me. I make room for the new self which is coming forth.
10. I generate more and more self love every day.

Exercises

1

If you have others in your life who are in denial about what happened in your life, sit with them in your mind's eye. Release them to their own beliefs and path. Let go of your own needs for them to comfort you, believe you and have compassion for you. Look to yourself for the comfort, belief and compassion you need. How can you give this to yourself? What would you (as the child) want you (as the adult) to do for you in this situation?

2

Place yourself inside the concept of neutrality. Look at the world around you and the people in it with non-judgment. Look at yourself and your own life with non-judgment. What does neutrality feel like to you? Are there different degrees of neutrality? How accurately can you reach the vibration of neutrality? Is your neutrality balanced by compassion?

See yourself in incidents that happened in the past. How would the event play out differently if you were neutral in the situation? See yourself in the future. See yourself in relationships or situations you are presently immersed in. How would you carry yourself in these situations if you were neutral about your surroundings, yourself and others? Remember, neutrality does not mean lack of compassion. Write down the changes you notice about events and relationships when you visualize yourself reacting in a neutral, non-judgmental and compassionate fashion.

3

Lie down and pretend you are floating in a sacred healing room. Your guides and many others who you would like to call on are present in the room. They stand in a circle around you. They love you ever so dearly. They have great respect for you because you are so brave! They are impressed with you, actually.

Let out a big sigh as they place their hands on you and work with your energy field. Relax. There is nothing you need to do except receive. Imagine that they are straightening out tangled areas of your gridwork, replacing missing or broken parts, reconnecting chakra and energetic grid systems, or fixing whatever you imagine is damaged. Imagine that they are restoring you to full functioning ability and when they are done with you, your energy field will be perfect and unmarred.

Let them tinker with your machinery any time. Invite them to work on you even as you go through your day. Feel your energy shifting underneath your conscious mind.

Reclaiming the Shadow Self

Chapter 19

Doubt, Denial and Self Love

There will be many times in your journey of healing that you will doubt the memories you have. You may even find yourself in denial. You may feel it is impossible that such drastic things could have happened to you. You will be sure this is your imagination. We say to you that no matter how badly you feel about the self, there is not the possibility that you would imagine such things for yourself just for the sake of imagining. You are not prone to torture yourself, believe it or not.

You will release great trauma when these memories come up. Your feelings will be highly charged and deep. It is impossible for you to have such a strong reaction to the memory if it did not happen. Trust the visions, memories, and feelings. You will see as you look at the path you have taken that there are many things which correlate with the memory. You will find that the personality traits you have developed are related directly to the events which devastated you. There are things you attracted later in life which point to the fact that the memory is valid. There are *many* clues to the validity of your memories.

These memories are lodged in your physical system. They are not just in the mind. So trust the feelings you have. Trust the visions you get. Trust the memories which come up. The memories will become more detailed as time goes on. Do not doubt the self.

Reclaiming the Shadow Self

There will be times in your path of healing that *others* will challenge the validity of your memories. Your family members or the perpetrators will especially protest against the validity of your memories. If you are searching for validation outside yourself, we must inform you that this is highly unlikely. If you *do* find validation outside of yourself, yours is a rare case. See it as the blessing it is.

You will need to trust the self more than ever before. You must believe in the self. You are the one who is most important to be believing and honoring of the self. If you doubt the self, you will neutralize your efforts and you will not be able to move through this until you come to a conclusion about whether you believe these things happened to you or not. You will find yourself in limbo until you trust the self. Your soul will not reveal any further information to you until you are willing to embrace what it shows you.

*You will need
to trust the self
more than ever before.*

You will find that your family members and others are not so willing to believe you when you speak to them about what is troubling you. They may even try to convince you with facts that your memories are incorrect. Realize also that if a family member has been a perpetrator, he or she may have blocks in his or her own memory because of guilt about what he or she has done. There may be denial on the other party's part because he or she is unwilling to admit to him or her self that these things did take place.

We do advise that you speak to the ones who you feel you need to speak to about what you remember. Silence will not be helpful for yourself or the others involved. Silence is not golden in this instance. A shift cannot take place for the other party if there is no confrontation about it. If you confront the perpetrator you may find that it will create a shift for him or her sooner or later. It is possible that it is in the highest good of the other party to be confronted with his or her past, even if he or she has long ago abandoned such practices. Speak about these things and get them out in the open.

Perhaps you have to warn others about the behavior of the perpetrator so the perpetrator is not provided with an opportunity to do this to another person.

If the perpetrator is one you will never be able to confront in person, confront him or her in spirit and see what happens. You will be heard in the conscience of the one who was the perpetrator. You will be surprised to find out that the deceased perpetrator has a much different attitude toward you now that he or she is in spirit.

If the perpetrator is in denial and refuses to shift, release this one to his or her own path and to God.

When you speak to the ones whom you desire support from and you do not get this, you may find yourself feeling more alone and upset than you were before. We highly suggest that you release attachment to other people believing you.

You may find that other people do not even *want* to know what has happened to you for they find it is just too frightening and horrible for them to listen to. Perhaps someone is willing to hear your story but still refuses to believe what you are saying, telling you it is a dream, it is in your imagination, or you are crazy and you should seek help. It is rare that others will believe you were the victim of a crime when you were younger, especially if it was dramatic.

You must release this person to his or her own path and allow this one to believe whatever he or she wants to believe. You must allow this person to believe what rings true for him or her self. However, remain steadfast and continue to trust in yourself.

You can still allow this person to be a part of your life. You may need to refrain from certain areas of conversation. However, you may find that this person is not useful to yourself in your healing. You may find that a separation in physical space is necessary. This is alright. Do not do this with the attitude of cutting off the other person. Simply release attach-

Self Love and Self Protection

ment or the need for help or approval from this one.

You are in a delicate state and you need to have around you only people who are supportive and caring about what you are going through. The ones who challenge you about what you are doing, doubt you, or tell you that you are crazy are not beneficial to your healing process.

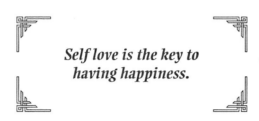

Self love is the key to having happiness.

As we have said before, some of the memories which come up for you are in the mass consciousness library or are part of your past life records. Some of these may even be past life memories of a member in your soul group. However, if the memory creates an emotional charge for yourself, we advise that you work with it as if it happened to you in your *present* life for it has taken a grip on your energetic systems. If it bothers you, it is an issue for yourself.

As you go along with the memories you are retrieving from other lives, you will find that the past life memory or mass consciousness record will lead you directly to the incident you lived through in this lifetime which has caused your fear. Memories which might not be your own are directly related *in essence* to what you have suffered in this lifetime. The disjointedness of the memories is not a reason to doubt they are real.

Generating love for the self is something you will need to do during this time. Self love is the key to having happiness. Love the self as you go through all your emotions, like fragility, rage, or whatever form it takes. Generating love for the self is a skill you are here to develop for humanity. It is something you will continue to develop all your life. However, it will not be so difficult in the future because you will have a foundation. You are building the foundation now. If you feel lack of love for yourself in the future, you will be able to pinpoint it right away and work with it

Reclaiming the Shadow Self

for you will know how, finally. You will not have the confusion about how to love the self the way you do now.

We advise that you look at yourself in the mirror as if you are a friend of the reflection you see. Love the reflection you see the way you would love someone who you cared deeply about. Have compassion for the reflection and what he or she is going through. Love the damaged parts of yourself, which are the inner children of the self. Give them the love they need so they can heal. If a lost child on the street is hurt, you would most certainly care about it and help it to find peace again. Use the same energy toward yourself.

Affirmations

1. I trust my inner wisdom. I trust the information I get from my deeper resources.
2. When others invalidate my experience, I release them to their choice and remain steadfast to myself.
3. I am brave and confront others about injustice. I do so gently but firmly. I am free of attachment to the outcome when I let someone know they have hurt me.
4. I am willing to ask others for help.
5. I am proficient at generating self love.
6. I know immediately when I lose my centeredness. I regain my sense of balance right away.
7. I take good care of my inner children. I love my inner children and take care of them the way I wish I was taken care of by my parents.
8. I am perfectly sane.
9. I search for validation inside myself. I release my need for validation outside myself.
10. Even though my memories are disjointed, I trust them.

Exercises

1

Imagine that all the particles around you in the air are full of love. This is what it feels like when you consciously perceive your guides touching you with their love. You can tap into this whenever you want. You are being showered with love and light at all times. The very atoms around you are alive. Let love be transmitted to you through the atoms in the air. Blend your energy with the ones who are holding this space for you. Open up and allow yourself to absorb their energy (love).

2

When you feel a sense of self doubt and denial, find the child within who is bringing this up to yourself, the child who is invalidating you. Why does this one want to shake your belief in your information? Is this one conditioned to do this? Is this one part of your discernment system and has value?

Listen to the child. Questioning the validity of things is a sign of intelligence. Weigh what the child says to you with clarity. Now ask this child to help you with your belief in the self. Each child, subpersonality, aspect, or whatever you call the separate parts of the self, has a purpose. Each child has a positive and negative side. What is the positive side of the self-denying child? How can it serve you now that you have self value, self worth, and the desire to be validating of yourself?

3

Generating self love: Close your eyes and let go of all your thoughts and emotions. Take a break from what is usually in your mind. Imagine that you are a timeless being, which you are. Forget about your present path and where you are now. Tap into your essence of self. What does your essence feel like? See how rich you are inside when you forget about your troubles and fears. The raw essence of yourself is truly brilliant, unique and precious.

Put a ball of light in your heart and let it expand until it is all around you. Inside this cocoon, bathe yourself with love. Let it come from deep inside. Let your God-self show you how much it loves you. Hold yourself like the beautiful newborn baby you always are in every moment. Pretend you have no history, only an abundant and beautiful future. Pretend you will never experience lack or fear. Surround yourself with compassion, love and softness. What does self love feel like?

Chapter 20

Inferiority and Self Hate: Why?

You might be wondering why you have allowed yourself to feel inferior. You may be wondering why you have experienced self hate.

You feel inferior because you do not value yourself. You turned on yourself. You turned your anger inward because you did not know what else to do with it, especially if you were not allowed to have negative feelings when you were a child. You had no outlet and you had no guidance about how to handle anger when it came up. Usually, you were punished for having anger.

Most likely, you were not allowed to confront the adults around you about how they were treating you or invalidating you. Of course, you did not know how to express this, for a child must be taught how to express itself clearly. The adults around you did not teach you how to handle your feelings and express your emotions appropriately.

A child who does not feel safe enough to convey it's feelings will often explode when the pressure becomes too great and throw a temper tantrum or act "bratty". This set up a cycle of events and you found yourself trapped in a negative pattern flow.

If you tried to convey to an adult (the one in power) that you were upset with him or her, often you were the one who was made "wrong". This happened because the adult was not able to be vulnerable and look at a fault in him or her self. If the adult was willing to let you be "right" sometimes, it would have enabled you to have a sense of equality and value.

So you turned your anger inward and became your own worst enemy. (If you ever thought about harming or murdering yourself, you qualify as your worst enemy!) You did not let yourself have anything sweet. You punished yourself worse than anyone ever did. You may have spent much of your life calling yourself names and speaking rudely to yourself.

This is common human psychology. It is normal for humans to blame themselves, especially children. As a child you were conditioned to do this. In order to release inferiority, you must go back to the places in your past where you were conditioned to hate the self and feel valueless. You must find value in your self in the moments where someone else convinced you that you were not valuable. You must find love for the self when someone convinced you that you were not worthy of love.

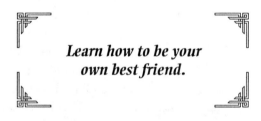

Learn how to be your own best friend.

Learn how to be your own best friend. Do you listen closely and lovingly to your inner children when they want to discuss how they are feeling or are needing to be helped? Perhaps you are sympathetic to others and listen with love when they pour their heart out or seek your advice. Do you do this for yourself? If you are more caring toward other people than you are to yourself, perhaps you would like to switch the old saying around to, "Do unto yourself as you would do unto others".

If you allow others to keep mistreating you, you are not being your own friend. You are not looking out for your own well-being. You are not taking care of yourself if you are taking other people's side against yourself. You must learn how to be on your own side.

Be a friend to yourself, not your enemy.

You are dealing with issues of value. (In the advanced studies of the soul, self worth issues are the primary focus.) If people do not listen to you when you want to confront them about an offense, it makes you feel non-valuable to the offending party if they are showing a lack of concern or caring about your well-being, happiness and peace. If you are trying to speak to them about something that has upset you, and they will not listen, you are getting the message from them that you are not valuable to them and they don't care about your feelings. If you turn this inward, instead of releasing their judgment toward you and realizing their inability to be vulnerable, you will find yourself feeling inferior and unworthy.

Many of you never really felt as if you were a part of anything. Many of you did not feel welcome when you came to this world. You were not really sure if you were wanted. Many of you do not feel special or worthy of being part of a group and this started with your family. You may have felt that you had no right to be here.

Once you started school and found yourself in the same emotional patterns with other children as the ones you experienced with your family, you weren't sure *if the world in general* wanted you, let alone your influencing adults and friends. You did not have a sense of belonging. You did not have a sense of security. You did not have a sense of home.

Many of you grew up in a situation where you received mixed messages. Sometimes your parents, siblings, friends or other adults were nice to you and enjoyed your company. Then suddenly, the next day for no reason that you could understand, they could not be bothered with you, treated you as if your were an inconvenience, a nuisance, or even took their anger at something else out on you. This caused you to be insecure. You most likely felt as if you were walking on thin ice. You were trying to be careful not to cause anyone to become upset with you, especially if the inevitable "scene" became a loud, scary or violent one.

You were constantly alert, feeling out the energies of others, trying to guess what kind of mood they were in, and fearful that you would make a mistake. (This is why you are so proficient at sensing the energy of others, by the way.) Sooner or later, you made a mistake, of course, and incurred the wrath of the adults or your friends. Sometimes they were looking for it so they had a valid reason to act out their anger on you.

Give Yourself a Rose Today

If you were being ignored, you may have found yourself seeking attention and reassurance that you were loved. Sometimes you were demanding about it. Then, if you were punished, you felt even more insecure and unloved. You found yourself confused and had no one to turn to in order to understand it.

It was natural to turn the upsetness inward on yourself. The more the adults around you convinced you that you were unlovable, the more you hated yourself for being imperfect and unlovable. It is a vicious cycle which is difficult to break. Eventually you might have found yourself dealing with suicidal feelings because you abandoned the self and gave up hope on ever being lovable, perfect enough, and valuable.

Realize that this came from others——not you! This was conditioning. You were taught to hate yourself instead of love yourself. Projections were put on you by other people. Now you have to decide what is projection and what is true in what other people think about you.

Find out where your inner child selves are injured and guide them through it. Release guilt about how you handled things in the past, for you did the best you could.

Release anger at yourself for becoming your own worst enemy. You did not know what else to do. You did not have good guidance from the influencing adults around you. How were you supposed to know? You were a child. A child looks to others to find out what it is, who it is, and how it fits into the world. If others were sending you the message that you were not valuable or lovable, then you had the natural human reaction. You took up the same behavior toward yourself that they showed toward you. Now you must go back and re-parent yourself.

Affirmations

1. I am a wonderful parent to myself. I am teaching myself how to have self love and self respect.
2. I am worthwhile. I am worthy. I am lovable. I am valuable. I am precious. I am cherished. I am special.
3. I now cast off the projections others put on me when I was a child.
4. I am my own best friend.
5. I release my anger and guilt for becoming my own enemy. I release my negative feelings about self-betrayal and self-abandonment.
6. I treat myself lovingly and with care. I speak kindly to myself.
7. I have a right to be here. I belong.
8. It is safe now. If I make a mistake, I am safe and loved.
9. I let go of insecurity. I have security, confidence and boldness. It is my natural state.
10. I attract to myself people who love me, care about me and treat me with respect.

Exercises

1

If you have fear, give it a symbol. Perhaps it is a monster, a chainsaw that is chasing you, or any other kind of symbol. What is your first inclination? To run?

Turn to the object of your fear and face it head on. Sit down right in it's path as it bears down on you. Surrender to it. Give yourself up to it. Stop resisting it and running from it. Let it overtake you. Face it calmly as it devours you. What happens?

The object of your fear is actually your power. If you face your fear, it will turn into power which will enable you to do things you have never been able to do before. If you embrace the object of your fear, you will find that it was your power you feared in the first place!

You can do things in physical reality to face your fears. If you are afraid of the ocean, swim in it. Surrender to it. Surrender to the fact that there are sharks in the ocean and they can eat you. Surrender to whatever the universe wants to do with you. If you are to be eaten by a shark today, so be it. If you are afraid of nature, pick a safe place like a campground, and stay overnight by yourself. If you are really brave, go hiking into a remote area and camp there.

You must surrender to that which you fear. When you are fearless, you are free. Get creative about facing your fears, no matter how small or silly they seem.

2

Imagine that you are in a huge bowl. It is a symbol for this reality. You are immersed in all the things which are in the bowl with all the people who are also immersed in the things in the bowl. Now go to the edge of the bowl and begin to scale the side of it. There is a ladder, maybe even an elevator. The climb is easy. When you reach the top, sit on the rim and look around.

What do you see? Are there others sitting on the rim who are gazing down at the activities in the bowl? Are you alone? Are there guides? What is happening on the rim? What is the energy of the atmosphere on the rim? Is there humor and lightness of being? Look down at the things in the bowl. See your counterpart (you) moving about among the things in the bowl. You are looking at the big picture.

Now look behind you. What is on the other side of the rim? Is it a void? Is it infinity? Are there other bowls with rims and people sitting atop looking down? Do things look different? Are you looking at other dimensions? Let your imagination run away with you.

3

Look back on your life. Notice how intimidated and inferior you felt around other people. What made you feel intimidated? What were the feelings you had? What were the thoughts you had? Who said derogatory things to you before you started saying them to yourself?

In one column on a piece of paper write all the unkind things you say, or once said, to yourself. In the second column, write out the exact opposite of that comment.

Start saying only kind and loving things to yourself. Start thinking only kind and loving thoughts toward yourself. Tell the part of you that berates or insults you to open up and let love in. Thank it for teaching you what it is to become your own enemy. Now that you know how not to be your own friend, you are free of the lesson and can embrace a new relationship with yourself. Invite the shadow self to join in with your new outlook on yourself and your life.

You will find that this part of you readily responds.

Chapter 21

Handling Your New Power And Challenging Old Altars

When you first reclaim your power from the shadow self you will feel a great surge of energy move through you. It is important to keep yourself under control as much as possible during the initial surge of power.

When you have seen through the illusion, you may feel inclined to destroy old altars. Old altars are things that once meant a lot to you. Old altars are something you looked up to and respected. An old altar can be a relationship, admiration of another person, goals and desires, admiration of a system of belief like religions, or any other kind of configuration you hold dear.

We will use spiritual teachers and religious organizations as an example, for often this is the form your old altar takes. A spiritual teacher can be in any form: an admired and helping friend, your lover, or any other person you see as more enlightened than yourself. It will take place in any kind of relationship where "inferiority versus superiority" exists.

Conflict may happen with a spiritual teacher you once respected, especially if the teacher has wronged you in some way. You may find that you want to strike out at the teacher if you have been slighted. You might see the humanness in your teacher for the first time. Suddenly you feel that this person or belief system is not worthy of being your teacher anymore. Perhaps you are not able to put your thumb on the reason why you are angry with your teacher just yet.

If you find that a spiritual teacher (or any other old altar) is completely ridiculous to you now, this is upsetting for the teacher. He or she falls from the pedestal you have put him or her on where he or she may have been feeling comfortable. The teacher may have difficulty dealing with you on your new level, for now you are an equal as far as the amount of consciousness you can hold.

When you retrieve your power from the shadow self there is no more need for the spiritual teacher. The teacher was only there to help you get your power back and attain entry into your inner worlds. Once you have done this, the relationship with the teacher must change or it will disintegrate. There is no more acceptance on your part of non-equality energies between yourself and others.

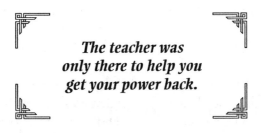

The teacher was only there to help you get your power back.

A teacher may unwittingly slight his or her student because there may be a need in the teacher to feel superior, or be the more enlightened one. Even teachers forget they are students. Even though it was the goal of the teacher to help you get on your feet and become an equal, when that actually happens it can bring up in the teacher his or her own fears and the need to be more powerful than yourself.

Your approach to the teacher up to this point has been one of submission and admiration. When you suddenly are not in that space anymore the teacher may not understand what is going on.

In the future, your teachers will be of a different nature. They will be on an equal level with you and they will be more like your friends than your teachers. There will not be separation between teacher and student. This is what you should look for in your new spiritual teachers if spiritual teachers happen to cross your path. We advise that you go inside the self and find the teachers within, for these are the ones who can do the most good for you. They will not have the reactions that can be expected from human teachers.

If you decide you want to bring something to the attention of the spiritual teacher, we advise that you do this only with guidance behind you. Consult your guidance first about the methods or actions you should use. Consult your guidance about whether you should do this at all. Consult the higher self of the teacher and his or her guides and ask if this is something you should do for them.

Perhaps it would be in the highest good for the teacher to discover the shortcomings you have seen with someone else further into the future of his or her own path. Or perhaps it would be in the highest good of the teacher to be confronted by one such as yourself right now. It is an individual case with each energetic conflict so we cannot advise you one way or the other.

We *do* advise that if you want to confront someone who has wronged you, ask yourself this question: "Does this person care enough about me to work it out with me, or will I be shut out by him or her and nothing will be accomplished?" This will give you the answer to the question about whether you should or should not confront another person or organization about what you have seen.

Realize that this is your own judgment and may not be the judgment of others around you, especially if they are still in a state of worship. Your issues with the teacher may not be things other people notice or care about. You may be alone in your views. Resist the urge to pull other people into it. Do not start a mutiny. This will not accomplish anything. This is between you and your teacher only.

If you need to speak with someone about it, do this with very few people. Only discuss it with friends who you think will be objective and who love you and the other party equally. Only discuss it if you sincerely need some feedback. Refrain from speaking about your conflict with another for the purpose of complaining. Only if you are truly attempting to understand the conflict better is it a worthy reason to discuss it.

Reclaiming the Shadow Self

However, you will need to be vulnerable (open) to what the other says and look at your own self honestly. Always be willing to see your own faults when you challenge one you love to see theirs.

> *Always be willing to see*
> *your own faults*
> *when you challenge*
> *one you love to see theirs.*

The old altar will be challenged to shift with you if you confront it. Sometimes this challenge will *not* be met. If the old altar does not want to shift, and the answer to the above question is negative, the best thing you can do is wash your hands of it and let it go with love. That is when you release the teacher to his or her own choice to bypass the lessoning you are presenting to him or her. Let the universe take care of the shift you see needs to be made. Validate yourself on your own and let go of the need for contact with this one.

There is a fine line which must not be crossed when expressing your anger with an old altar. There is a point at which you would incur karma if you did not stop. Letting someone know you are upset with him or her does not incur negative karma. Striking out does. There is nothing wrong with expressing your anger if you express your anger from the heart and you stop before damage is done. You can express your upsetness in a calm and gentle way. Avoid expressing your anger from the negative energies, like fear of disapproval or abandonment. Your guidance will let you know where this point is.

If the person or system you confront does not want to work it out with you after the initial confrontation, then any further interaction on your part with this one would be useless. The results would be destructive instead of constructive. As soon as you begin tearing at the other party you are angry with, you incur negative karma.

If your teacher refuses to communicate with you about your feelings toward him or her, you might be tempted to destroy everything the teacher is creating——-and you may even have the power to do it. *Be careful with this. Be careful that you do not use your power wrongly. Do not become a misguided energy yourself! Be careful that you do not allow darkness and misguided energies to work through you.*

Yes, you have anger and this is alright. But do not allow your anger to overtake you. Be careful what you do with it. It is a vehicle which brings either destruction or creation——-your choice. Use your anger to achieve love in yourself and the world around you and you will achieve it. Use your anger to achieve darkness and destruction and you will achieve it.

If you express your anger and the driving force behind it is a sincere wish for love to be present between yourself and whatever your old altar is, you will be successful in your endeavor. It may take some time, so allow plenty of space for the old altar you are challenging to shift. You cannot force anything to happen sooner than it wants to. As you confront another party about something, you will bring up all his or her own fears. You must allow room for the other party to work out the fears on their side.

Through this, your spiritual teacher is learning how to dispel the anger of another by being vulnerable.

By being vulnerable, the teacher (or the one in power) takes away the need of the other to show anger. Vulnerability is about releasing the need to be more powerful than others, the need to be right, and the need to be in control. Vulnerability is the ability to consider the possibility that something needs to be recognized and developed in the self. If the offending party listens to the offended one with respect and equality, the offended one will be able to speak his or her truth gently in a clear space. There will be no need to use anger to insist on being heard, understood and valued. Anger is a strong desire for change. It is also a strong insistence on being heard, understood and cared about by the one who has done the injustice.

You may feel your power like a warrior. You may feel rebellious. In situations such as yours, rage at injustice is the first thing you will feel when you accept your power. You may feel driven to do something about what you see.

We suggest that you keep a sense of humor about what you are doing even while you are expressing your anger. Try not to get caught up in the seriousness of the situation. You might think of yourself as an actor even as you express your anger. However, stay focused on yourself and what *you* are supposed to be shifting. Refrain from being focused on what the other is supposed to be learning even though you may be well aware of what his or her faults are. *There is as much for you to acknowledge as there is for the one who is being challenged by you.*

Again we say, use the anger to drive out the darkness (no awareness) in yourself, not for hurting others. What you are really angry about is the fact that you and everyone else on the Earth have been dis-empowered for a large chunk of time. Everyone resents being "stuck" in patterns.

Realize that your spiritual teacher may feel betrayed by you. Your spiritual teacher may be angry with you and your seeming ungratefulness for what he or she has done for you. If your teacher is enmeshed in his or her patterns in any way whatsoever, and does not have the ability to remain neutral, vulnerable and compassionate at the same time, you can expect your teacher to have a drastic reaction to you. You are challenging your teacher to expand his or her ability to love and respect other beings no matter what is happening.

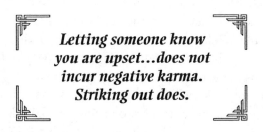

Letting someone know you are upset...does not incur negative karma. Striking out does.

On your part, you are being challenged to love your teacher even after you have seen your teacher's faults. *It is just as much of a challenge for you to love as it is for your teacher.* Even if your teacher refuses to embrace the shift and you must walk away, you will still be challenged to love this one. You will not be free until you discard negative feelings you have toward your spiritual teacher, even if you do not want to associate with him or her in physical reality anymore. If this one refuses to work it out with you, you must still love him or her.

This goes for any of your relationships. You must love them back even though they are dishonoring you. Eventually your feathers will not get ruffled when someone treats you with a lack of respect. This is unconditional love. Jesus, and a countless number of other saints like yourself, have perfected this.

On the other hand, you may be challenging your teacher for reasons of self validation. You may be in a power struggle with your teacher. Be careful about this. We are not giving you a license to create havoc and disharmony. If love is not present, there is no point in causing chaos. Only if there is deep love behind your challenge should you consider it.

Spiritual teachers and leaders are transforming the mass conscious patterns concerning positions of power and influence. Influence and power must be used entirely differently. The old paradigm is leaving the Earth plane and the new paradigm is coming. Your spiritual teacher is learning about right use of will and power. Your spiritual teacher is also being challenged to let go of the need to be recognized and worshipped by those he or she feels are inferior or less advanced.

Your spiritual teacher is learning about equality from the opposite end of the spectrum which you are approaching from. Your spiritual teacher is being challenged to step down from the throne and achieve humbleness. Your spiritual teacher may be challenged to roll up the shirt sleeves and join the students at an equal level. You may be challenging your spiritual teacher about his or her belief that he or she is more special, informed and important than others.

You will be teaching your spiritual teacher one of the most important lessons he or she will ever learn. You are teaching your teacher about unconditional love and non-judgment of others. Your spiritual teacher will be challenged to be vulnerable enough to admit that he or she can be wrong. He or she may need to admit to a fault or humanness. It may be a blind spot for the teacher. Most of all, the teacher will be challenged to love you and continue to be open and helpful toward you instead of dealing with you in an old paradigm way, like shutting you out.

By not being willing to look at the self, this is when the offending one (the one in power, the "higher" one) snubs the feelings of the offended one (the inferior one, the "lower" one). Because of this invalidation, the offended one becomes angry. How the offended one chooses to deal with people who don't care about his or her feelings will be one of two results. He or she will either walk away or become angrier. Either way, separation is achieved and not oneness. It is up to the perpetrator, the one in power, to be vulnerable. It is up to the victim to keep his or her own power and self value and not to give it away to another person or situation.

In a perfect world, conflicts would be handled differently.

In a perfect world, conflicts would be handled differently. The one who voices his or her upsetness will be met immediately with respect and a willingness by the offending one to look at a fault he or she may have, a caringness about the offended person's feelings, and compassion if a misperception has taken place on the offended one's part. In a perfect world, the offended one will not need to become angry in order to be heard because he or she will be heard the first time it is brought up. The first approach the offended one makes to a conflict is usually gentle and backed by a desire for peace again. Anger only happens after the first few attempts to communicate are not reciprocated.

If your confrontation is met with receptivity, you will find that your anger recedes and there will be a shift toward the positive for you both. You and the other party can expand yourselves greatly. The communication will lead to an understanding and eventually a shift for you both. Anger is a powerful charge of energy. It is useful when the desire to shift a stubborn situation is strong.

If your spiritual teacher wants to work it out with you and shift, then appreciate this blessing! The journey to conclusion will be easier and more fulfilling for you both. When there is no closure, there is a feeling of incompletion. However, you can complete this in yourself even if the other party does not complete this in him or her self. All you have to do is reach neutrality, have love for this one, non-judgment about his or her choices in life, and honor the path that he or she took even if it is not the one you think is best. Perhaps the spiritual teacher is not ready to shift. This is his or her freewill choice and you must be decent enough to allow it.

Not many of you will be led to challenge your teacher. Most of you will simply begin a different kind of relationship with your spiritual teacher, one of equality and enlightenment. Most of you do not have spiritual teachers (anyone you feel is superior to yourself) who need challenging. And even if you do feel that you need to part ways, it will not be dramatic. However, a few of you *will* be led to challenge your teacher. These are some guidelines about the correct approach and also some clues so you know what is happening for you.

Realize that you have been in both positions, the offending one and the offended one. Be gracious toward the one who has wronged you, no matter what the result of the conflict. You have much to think about on both sides of the coin.

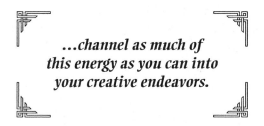

...channel as much of this energy as you can into your creative endeavors.

Handling your emotions during the initial surge of power as you come out of the aftermath may be quite a challenge. We highly recommend that you channel as much of this energy as you can into your creative endeavors. Your creative endeavors will explode into manifestation on the Earth plane if you use your energy this way.

You are receiving your new power, which is power you once had. *This time, you hope you will not hurt yourself again by misusing your power.* You realize now that power is a dangerous thing and it is not a toy. The consequences for abusing power are greater now than they were before your latest string of lifetimes because now you know better! A commitment to use your power lovingly is a serious one.

What is happening when a conflict arises between you and someone else?

The balance of power has been tipped and the challenge for each is to find the balance again. The one who invalidates the other first, and the other buys it, takes the power. It can happen two ways at the same time, not just one way. Conflicts with others is about power struggle and a lack of respect and love. The way to gain harmony is to love and be vulnerable with each other. If each party lets go of the need to be right, then both of you can look at the situation clearly.

You will not be able to live with relationships that are out of balance. You will refuse to put up with poor conditions in relationships you have with other people even though you love them dearly. You will find it impossible to stay in the relationship if the way the other relates to you does not change. Be ready for a roller coaster ride in your relationships and friendships during the dark cycle of your spiritual path. You will be letting go of many of your old friends and gaining new ones who relate to you in higher ways than your old ones did.

Accept this, let them go with thankfulness for your time together, and move on. Do not try to make a relationship something it is not, for you will only become frustrated and damage the relationship. It is better to be allowing and let people flow into and out of your life effortlessly. Do not hold on to them.

Realize that you will always be connected with this person on the soul level. You will see him or her again many times in your future and past (simultaneous) lives and in other dimensional adventures. Do not think you are separated forever from one who you love, for you are not.

You may *not* need to end the relationship, but you may need to give each other some physical and psychic space for a while if there has been

Handling Your New Power

a highly charged conflict. You can still love each other while you allow each other space. It is not the end of the world if you have a temporary "divorce". In fact, it is healthy. It is a chance for each to do his or her "homework" alone. Much realization will come to the surface for each person in the conflict if personal space is re-established. Even while you are having a conflict with someone, always keep an eye on the big picture. It will help you if you refrain from becoming too immersed in the illusion.

If you run into people who decide that they just don't like you, let them go and don't try to get them to approve of you. Keep in mind how many people there are in the world. You are bound to run into plenty of people who like you. Do not spend your energy on trying to get everyone you come in contact with to like who you are, faults and all. It simply cannot happen in a world full of mirrors. Later, when the Earth plane is transformed, everyone will love everyone.

> **Taking your power back
> is one thing, but
> using your power wisely...
> is quite another.**

Many of you have fixated yourself on getting love from a certain person. Obsession with another person is not healthy for you *or* the other person. The very person you are in love with will be the same person you become angry with if he or she is not reciprocating the way you want him or her to reciprocate.

Love at first sight happens because you have had past lives (and future lives) with this person. You cannot love someone the way you love this one if you did not know each other from somewhere along the line. Hate at first sight works the same way.

Handling Your New Power And Challenging Old Altars

You may be looking back on your life and feeling guilty about how you handled and misused your power in the past. Now that you see how you have misused your power (misguided your energies) in the past, you might be having a hard time forgiving yourself for it. You are angry at yourself for not being perfect, for having done it "wrong".

It is alright. Yes, perhaps you did deal with things in an inappropriate fashion. It is still alright. This is allowed in your "education". It was lessoning. The universe *expects* you to make "mistakes" while you are in education mode. You are understanding how to use and how not to use your power right now. You will be clear about this soon. Forgive yourself for using your power wrongly and misguiding your energies in the past. It was only "Misuse of Power 101". You are now finishing your finals in this class, so to speak.

However! Once you actually understand and know how to use power, you are responsible for using it correctly! Then you will need to stay on your toes and watch yourself like a hawk!

You will be given the power to manifest miracles...

At first you will be tempted many times to misuse your power. This is the time to develop self discipline (the way a loving parent would discipline a being it was responsible for) and self control. After a while, you will not be tempted to misuse your power. It will be second nature to you to use it correctly.

There is much to know and much to be aware of once you have your power back. Taking your power back is one thing, but using your power wisely and in a benevolent fashion is quite another. This is where a whole new set of challenges comes up since phase one of your life is over and phase two has just begun.

You will find yourself with power you cannot imagine right now. You will be given the power (you will take back the power) to manifest miracles for others and for yourself. You will be enabled to manipulate physical matter and you will teach others how to do this in the future. You will be able to create miracles like Jesus did. Your miracles will be even greater. You will create many examples of what enlightenment looks like. This will happen because your ability to love and establish a partnership with physical reality will increase. This will also happen because the nature of the coming age makes it easier.

Affirmations

1. I am my own guru, teacher and healer. I am my own "doctor".
2. My spiritual teachers are really my best friends. My spiritual teachers treat me with equality.
3. I always consult my guidance before I confront others.
4. If I express anger or other negative emotions, I do it from the heart level. If I express negative emotions, it's only because I desire a positive solution.
5. I thank my old altars for helping me to grow.
6. I am sensitive to the feelings of my old altar.
7. I love and respect my old altars even though I see faults. I allow my old altars time to deal with issues.
8. Now that I have my power back, I use it wisely and benevolently. I use my power with love. I use my power gently.
9. I now have the power to manifest miracles in my own life and the lives of others.
10. I channel my regained power into creative endeavors.

Exercises

1

Imagine energy moving clockwise around you. In the same layer, superimposed over the first energy, another energy moves counter-clockwise around you. Imagine and feel both directions at once. As the particles in the energy move through each other in their respective directions, watch as patterns set up and then disintegrate again. Watch as patterns move into form and then into not-form. Some of the patterns will gel, crystallize, light up and linger longer than others.

Concentrate on the movement of the energies around you. Just watch. Your vision is 360 degrees in all directions. Sense what is behind you, under you and above you with your inner vision. Notice how still you are in the middle of this. Now stop everything. What happens?

2

If a situation troubles you, a memory troubles you, or a person troubles you, let go of the struggle. Let out a big sigh and surrender. Let this energy, which you have been resisting, into your energy field. Let it all in. Embrace it as the precious gift that it is. Hold it close to your heart.

Think of the troubling energy as an enlightened messenger sent from God to play a part in your play and teach you something. Think of this person or situation as a symbol in your reality. Thank this one for triggering your anger or fear so you can work with it. Think of this person or situation as a Buddha who has been sent just for you. This is truly what is happening on the soul level. What are you being challenged to develop in yourself? What are you being challenged to understand? What are you being challenged to change?

Assure yourself that this troubling circumstance will be resolved soon, for now you are willing to surrender to it and develop in yourself what you are being challenged by the universe to develop.

3

If you are upset with an old altar, how does this feel in your energy systems and your physical body? What is the area of fear that is triggered? Are you afraid underneath your anger? Now that your old altar is no longer worthy of your worship, are you being forced to believe in your own self? Are you unsure about what to believe in now that the very person or organization you believed in turned out to be less than you thought?

Handling Your New Power And Challenging Old Altars

Now relax your body. Let go of the tension. Unwrap the anger from your system. Don't take it so seriously! Yes, you are angry, and perhaps you feel invalidated. However, you have the knowledge that you and your old altar are role playing with each other and it is only an illusion you both are in. Go to the soul level. What is the energy of the situation? What kind of resolution do you desire? What do you see when you look at the big picture? Sit with the party you are upset with at the soul level. Find the humor in what is going on. You are very good friends at the soul level, you know.

Now find your heart center. Feel what it is to love at the soul level as you both look at the big picture and see yourselves in a struggle within the parameters of the illusion. You both are teaching each other something important. What does it feel like to be in the soul space instead of the fear space with this old altar? How does it feel to direct your energies toward this one from your heart? Is your anger so serious now? Or does it come from a place of love?

Reclaiming the Shadow Self

Chapter 22

Your New Life

What can you expect in your new life?

This is a chapter about what you will be moving into and what you can look forward to. Use this information as inspiration to help yourself stay on the path of healing you are on. If you knew what was coming to you, you would probably pass out on the floor with amazement! Do not be afraid you will never experience your new life or that it is not coming. You will *not* be forever in a state of healing. There *is* a time when wholeness is reached.

Your new life will be full of light. Your new life will be full of love. Everything you create will come forth with ease. Everything you do will be synchronized. You will be enlightened. You will not be thwarted or interfered with. If it does happen, you will not be thrown for a loop, for you will know how to deal with it.

You will have complete self love. You will feel much differently about your self once your healing has taken place. Your toughness will go away as your fear does. You will be softer, gentler and kinder.

Your new life will bring much positive excitement instead of negative excitement. You will finally be able to have healthy, nurturing and loving relationships. If a relationship has conflicts which arise, you will be able to deal with it in an enlightened, new paradigm way. Your relationships will not end in devastating fiascoes anymore. Your relationships, if they need to change in nature, will result in friendships, not enemies. This is not a dream of Utopia. This is possible.

You will feel as if you are living in Utopia, even though the world around you will not be such. You are anchoring the new world *alongside* the old world. Fearful things will pass you by and will not be attracted to your energy fields. Fearful energies will not be in your reality. It does not mean, however, that you should not acknowledge and have compassion for those who are still dealing with fear on the planet. Do not be ignorant of darkness while you are in your new life. Do not pretend it is not there. Be compassionate toward the fearful darkness, even though you have already completed most of your journey with it. The darkness still needs your love and acknowledgment even though you are not "bullied" by it anymore.

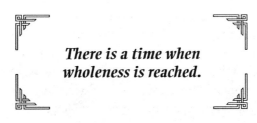

There is a time when wholeness is reached.

Your new life will begin when your sacred self is in place, which is what you are facilitating now. Your new life will be full of joy. Your creativity will flourish. It will come from a place of love.

Do what you do because you love it, not because you will make money at it. For instance, if you are writing books, making music, or any other kind of artistic endeavor, do this just for the sheer joy of doing it. Do not have attachments to whether or not it is noticed by anyone.

Do not create according to what you think will sell or fit in with the mainstream. You are not mainstream material. You are a buccaneer and an explorer. Your creativity will not be common place. You will be creating your own categories. Your creativity will be coming from the beauty of who you are and it will not matter to you if it is recognized. Flowers exude their fragrance whether anyone comes to enjoy them or not. However, be assured that you will have recognition as long as recognition is not what you are focused on. That is the trick.

Be patient as you wait for your new life to begin. Your new life will take some time to gain momentum. You have changed the probable realities you were headed for before you took on the project of your healing. Now you are accessing other probable realities which were previously unavailable to you because you were blocked and could not receive them. Now that you can, it will take some time for the new realities to set up. Do not doubt that it is happening, even as you wonder in this moment if you will ever see a better life. It will come to you, do not worry. It is coming to you now. You have already planted the seeds during your healing and are still planting them.

A whole new plan is being set up for you just as you planned before birth, ironically. New events and directions are being examined by you at this crossroad in your life. You are making decisions unconsciously with your inward self about what realities you would like to create. You cannot even imagine how happy and brilliant your new life will be, but if you try it will make you smile!

In your new life you will not experience fear the way you have up to this point. You will not have a constant state of confusion or depression anymore. In your new life, your body will look the way you want it to. There will be no difficulties with your physical presentation of yourself, if you would like to know this. You will find that as you release stress from your system, you have lost the extra weight you wanted to lose, or you have gained the extra weight you wanted to gain. You will find that your skin clears up. You will find that your digestive system or any other broken down area in your body will work fine. In your new life, you will be quite attractive to others.

Many of you get flashes of the legends that you are in the future. However, you brush these visions off right now because you cannot believe you could possibly be so incredible. Believe that you are! The flashes you get of your future self are messages your future self is sending you.

What your new challenge will be is how to handle all the people who will come to you for your love and light. This is not a terrible challenge at all, and can be quite joyful for the self. You will be called on to help many people and sometimes it will be quite demanding. If anything, you will be challenged to keep the ego in check, for many will worship you. Right now you are being challenged to let go of your feelings of inferiority. Once your new life comes, the tables will turn. You will be challenged to be *humble* and let go of feelings of *superiority. It is just as much a challenge to be humble as it is to have self worth.*

Keeping the ego in check is simple. Always be willing to look at yourself and be honest about your imperfections. Look at everyone in your life, even if you are a highly respected teacher, as a person who is there to help you become more enlightened. Embrace the idea that you are still a student even though you have accomplished much and are teaching others. Never lose sight of your student-ship, no matter how developed you become, and you will not fall into the traps that ego spreads out for you.

All the goals and desires you had up to this point may be different or they may be the same. In your new life, you will not be attached to goals and desires for the self. You will simply be interested in doing service in whatever way is needed from you. Of course, you will most likely be called on to do things you have been trained for in your education if you still want to do whatever it was you were trained for. You may find that you are called on to do service in areas where you did not realize you had talents, but you will be surprised to find that you do! Whatever it is you are called to do, you will love to do it. The universe will not ask you to serve in areas where you do not want to serve.

It is impossible for you to imagine right now what your new life will bring about. Your new life will bring you desires and goals which are more connected with the soul than the personality desires were. You will remember talents you have in other realities and other lives. These are things you can bring forth for yourself even in this moment. Realize that in your new life you will be looking at it differently. You will be the master you are, and you will *feel* it too. The new life will be beautiful indeed and it is not very far away. It is up to you how long you want to take before this comes to yourself. It may not happen overnight, but it can still be rather quick.

In your new life, you can expect much abundance. Do not fear that this will not come to you. In fact, you will have new challenges when it comes to handling abundance if dealing with wealth is something you

Rejoice and Dance

choose. Wealth is not as easy to handle as it seems and you will find this out when you get there. You will be challenged to be generous with your abundance. You will be challenged to be wise about your abundance. You will be challenged by people who are jealous of your abundance and are blocked from their own. You will be challenged to funnel your abundance into the correct avenues. You will be challenged to look at your abundance as energy the universe has given you to spread light instead of material wealth. Wealth has many traps. There is much to be learned by the mass consciousness in this area.

Your abundance will take form in many ways. Your abundance will not be limited to financial matters. Your abundance will take form in your relationships. The love around you will be abundant indeed. Your experiences will be abundant. Your self love will be abundant. You will be continuously challenged to be open and receive your greater abundance.

Be patient as reality breaks down and sets up again around you. Physical reality takes more time than does your ability to shift your energy out of the old and into the new. As the old leaves and the new comes, there will be a period of hovering, limbo, or no-man's-land which you will feel as if you are "stuck" in. This will be a time when you will not necessarily know which direction to go, what to do, or what to pursue. You may feel a lack of guidance. However, when you are in a state like this, the best thing to do is wait and enjoy the waiting time.

Make the transition time from the old to the new count. Make the best use of it you can and do not allow yourself to lose faith. When you are alone, the best thing to do is enjoy your aloneness. When you are directionless, the best thing to do is completely enjoy your directionlessness. It has a purpose. It is just as important as the times when you *do* have direction. When you are challenged to wait, *learn how to wait!*

During the waiting time, you can develop your skills in patience. You can also develop your ability to surrender to the way things are in the present moment. You can develop your trust in the universe and it's timing. Several things are happening while you are in the hover mode. Your synchronicity helpers are still setting up "chance" meetings or new situations for you. It is a lesson in learning how to wait constructively. It is also a chance to accept and respect the self in it's "unrealized" state. If you can accept this, you will move through the hover pattern more quickly.

As you wait for your new life to open up, keep a watchful eye for your opportunities. They will come quite suddenly out of left field. Keep an open ear to your guidance for the guides may tell you what to do and you may need to move quickly on the spur of the moment. Then your new life and reality will explode into existence for yourself. Just be patient and watchful.

Your new life will take some time to gain momentum.

In your new life, you can expect dimensional travel. You can expect visitation from aliens and other types of guides. You can expect to be shown new skills. You can expect to discover memories of your more pleasant lifetimes. You can expect much.

Do not feel that all your pain has been for nothing. Your lemons will be made into lemonade soon enough. Simply follow your intuition and your feelings. Your feelings are your steering mechanism through this reality. Follow your heart, even if it doesn't make sense to your personality or mental self. In the long run, if you follow your heart, it was the path of most abundance and happiness after all.

You must embrace the new life now if you want it. You must vibrate with the energies of your new life before you can *have* the new life. If you want to be successful, you must adopt the vibration of success into your system so it will be attracted to you. Visualize yourself in your new life, even though you may not know what you will be doing. Peek into your future and see the way you walk through your new life, the way you talk and interact with other people and with yourself. See what needs to be adopted into your present energy systems in order to have this in your life. If you can develop the traits now of leader, healer, and co-creator with God, the new life will come more quickly.

Self worth and self love have everything to do with your new life becoming a reality. You will have to trust in your new life. You will be constantly challenged to reaffirm your trust in the universe, others and yourself. Do not be alarmed that your lessons will not end even though you are healed. You will find yourself going over old issues now and then for the rest of your life. However, the same issues will be much easier for you to deal with when they come up, for you will already know how to deal with them. You have worked with the root cause. There is a time when you will not be faced with the same issues. This will come in phase three of your life, which is most likely a span of five to ten years at the end of your life. This is still far off for most of you.

Now that you have self worth, self love and have cleared your feelings and fears about the past, you will be able to transform your patterns with more adeptness and ability. You will be able to shift yourself immediately when you feel yourself losing your centeredness. You will be able to shift yourself more quickly than you have ever been able to before. In your new life, you will know how to master all emotions, events and issues which come up for yourself.

You will find that there continues to be wrinkles here and there in your make-up. However, each time your issues come around to you again, they will become smaller and smaller and smaller until eventually you have ironed out all the wrinkles and there is nothing left to iron out. This will be the point where you have fully remembered who you are, what you are about, and all your experience in this and other realities. This is when you become your full conscious soul self (God-self) on the Earth plane.

Until then, your issues will come up when you are challenged to love yourself or another person more than you do in the moment that the challenge is being made. This is the basis of *all* conflicts between two or more energies. You will constantly be challenged to love yourself and other people as long as you are on the Earth plane. It will happen until oneness is achieved by all.

You will not suffer the heartbreak you presently do. Lessoning (experience) goes on forever, in a sense, but the nature of this changes depending on the level you are looking at things from. Once you achieve neutrality, you will find that you can choose which level you want to play at in your reality. There are many levels in this reality and different approaches to it. Neutrality to the reality around you is a key to being free of judgment and emotional upset.

Once you develop neutrality, your new life will be in your hands. Once you are neutral about what you see around you, including negative things which you have created yourself, you will be able to steer through your life without interference. Neutrality does not mean coldness or indifference. Neutrality is active. Neutrality is more about honoring of all aspects and perspectives, not just one or a select few. Neutrality combined with compassion for the reality around you is a key to understanding unconditional love.

In the new life, you will be challenged to love yourself constantly. This is one of the main issues in the mass conscious mind of humanity which keeps it from having happiness, peace and safety. The more you can love the self, the more you can have in the new life. Your rewards will be great for learning how to love the self. Learning how to love the self is quite a feat indeed! Try to remember, though, you already knew how to do this at one time and you have only had to relearn it as you rebuild the wiring of the human being from the inside out.

Everything you have read so far is not real at a certain level. There is a place where none of it is applicable. The more often you can reach the place where you can see the big picture, the place where your issues are not "real", the more you will feel in control of your life and know how you fit in to this reality. *The trick is transcending the level where these things exist.* From the higher (deeper) level, which is the realms of the soul, you can deal with denser realities with ease and focus. Things like dark experiences, dark entities and other such illusions will not seem so dark at all anymore. You will see the light that actually exists within them.

You will attain the ability to have unconditional love for others which is truly a product of the divine self. The sooner you can avoid the inclination to judge, the sooner you will achieve neutrality. The illusion around you can be beautiful or the illusion around you can be unsavory. It is up to you what you want to see in the illusion.

You can expect in your new life to see the energies you have been wanting to see. You will have your "superpowers" in the new life. You will even visit your homes for a brief visit here and there in order to rejuvenate and continue the work on Earth you are doing in your last required lifetime.

You will taste the sweetness of life, which you have been starving for. You knew it at one time and now you are finding it again. You will have many sweetnesses to choose from. There will be no such thing as lack. You will have transcended (moved inward toward the soul self) the need for such realities.

You will have experiences of meeting your parallel selves, for some of you have at least one parallel self on the planet at this time. These are other branches of your own soul. When you meet these ones, you will feel as if you know them personally and you will know their mind. You will learn how to blend with your parallel selves, even the ones outside of this reality, and you will see through their eyes anytime you want, as they will see through yours. It will be like having the ability to be in more than one place at the same time. Even your past life personalities are parallel selves.

You will also experience gestalt intelligence. Gestalt intelligence is the blending of two or more minds and becoming one entity together. You will learn how to blend with the souls of your soul group first and then you will go beyond this and learn to be part of a larger entity. You will be enabling the human to hold more than one energy in the body at once. You will be enabling humanity to become a fully functioning gestalt intelligence. Eventually you will realize yourself as a blended part of the entire human consciousness. You cannot even imagine right now the oneness that will be experienced by the human race and the magnitude of what that means. It does not end there though. It goes on and on for infinity.

Affirmations

1. Even though I am surrounded by my old life, I vibrate with the new life that is coming to me.
2. I am living in Utopia. Utopia is my reality.
3. Unconsciously, I am planning my new life right now.
4. I now release from my system the vibrations of my old life.
5. When I am asked by the universe to wait, I enjoy waiting and make good use of the time.
6. I am patient as my old reality breaks down and my new reality sets up.
7. I am forever a student. I use my ego for manifestation and creation on the Earth plane.
8. I accept and value myself in my "unrealized" state.
9. I now turn my past into light which I use to enrich my future.
10. I am my soul on the Earth plane.

Exercises

1

In your meditation, pretend you are ten years into your future. You have taken a break from your busy day of spreading light and you are meditating. What do you, as your future self, feel like? What is your essence? How does your awareness feel? Are you more detailed and whole? What is the expression on your face as your enlightened self? What does the energy around you feel like? Are you happy? Are you well loved? Are you abundant?

Your future self is very available to you. Ask your future self to help you. Ask your future self to sit with you for at least a few minutes every day so you can learn how to hold the stronger and more focused energy it holds.

2

Imagine that you never came to Earth. Imagine you have only experienced heavenly realities up to this point. Pretend you have never had a frightening experience. However, you are fully developed and very wise. Leave the Earth plane for a while, forget about it. Tap into the other realities in which you play where there is no fear. You are there, since you are multidimensional. What does it feel like to be a person who has only experienced joy, beauty and love? What would you feel like if you knew you were completely safe?

3

Make columns on a piece of paper. What were your goals and desires as a child? What were they when you were a teenager? What were they when you were in your twenties? What were they in your thirties? What were they from every five to ten year increment after that? Look at your list and see what has changed as you grew older. What are your goals and desires now? What do you think your goals and desires will be when you are ten years into your future? What about twenty years from now? Keep in mind that the world will be much different then. Which goals and desires are related to the personality self and which ones are related to the soul self?

Conclusion

Always go deeper and deeper. There is always another level underneath the one you just discovered. You will never reach a place where there is not a deeper level in yourself. You are infinite.

You chose the life you chose because you did not come to Earth to play around this time. You did not come here to dip your little toe in or just have a looksee. You came here to become fully immersed and *change an entire world!* Do you realize the proportions of what you have set out to do?

You came here with serious intents on your mind to break up all the madness. The only way to do that was to go *inside* the madness. That is why you took the hard road. That is why you came here long ago, and that is why you are here now. You are finally completing the task you set out to do. This is the final push.

You are healing centuries upon centuries upon centuries of fear and pain. That is why it is so intense right now. The Earth is pushing the heaviness off herself and you are the ones who have agreed to do the work needed to make this process complete. Think of fear as excitement, and you will be able to turn your fear around.

You can let out your breath now and relax. The nightmare is over for you now. You will not have to experience terror, hopelessness or despair anymore. It is done. This was your last required lifetime in the "fear zone". You are finished with fear and now you're in for a treat! As soon as you release the last of the fear in your system you will experience Heaven on Earth.

There is not much more of this left. You are on the brink of a huge success and breakthrough. At the time of the second coming (re-emergence of the Christ Consciousness in everyone), all remaining darkness (no awareness) will be dispersed. Humanity will be free of it's self imposed bondage to fear. It takes people like you to unlock the "shackles" which have kept humans from being free to be who they are.

The beauty of humanity is about to burst forth unchecked. In the past, the positive, loving and beautiful aspects of humanity were trying to flourish on the Earth plane. Beauty was able to come forth in small pockets and hidden areas. However, it was always crushed or dispersed by darkness (no awareness) before it reached its full expression. Now you are about to see it reach it's full expression. Now that human peace is being allowed to come forth with out fear of it being destroyed, incredible and amazing things will be created on the Earth plane. This is a great time to be alive, for you will see it in your own lifetime!

There are some who will not choose to participate in the new world. When the final call is made for those in fear to cross over, the Earth will split off into two realities. One will be the ascended new world, and the other will be the descended old world. There will be two parallel Earth realities. If you would like to know this, there already exist several parallel Earth realities. They occurred at other very important crossroads for the Earth plane long ago. The descended old world will be an addition to the already existing Earth realities.

You can find freedom long before the world is instantly transformed. You will be guides to those beside you. This world will not be able to harm you anymore once you find freedom, which you are only a breath away from, we would like to add.

All opposites are blending into one. High/low, left/right, superior/inferior, perpetrator/victim, dark/light—-all are coming together. It is like the crack of thunder that happens when hot and cold meet. There is an explosion when opposites meet and then blend with each other. This is happening inside you as an individual, inside you as the gestalt intelligence that is humanity, and inside you as God, the gestalt intelligence of the entire universe. Savor the intensity as this happens. It is beautiful and powerful. Many beings have come to look at you and your world, for they are fascinated with what you are doing. They have been hypnotized by your beauty and daring.

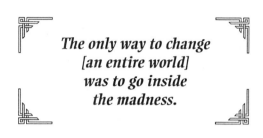

> ***The only way to change
> [an entire world]
> was to go inside
> the madness.***

You are on your way to becoming what Jesus was. What would a world full of Christ-like people be? What directions would a world like that go? You are reclaiming your dignity and your divinity. You are becoming God's mature, conscious expression of himself on the Earth plane. Instead of ascending the Earth plane and leaving it behind, you are doing it the other way around. You are bringing ascension down to the Earth, so to speak. You are bringing heaven to the Earth. You are not trying to escape the Earth. You are attempting to anchor the soul realms *here*. You could think of this age as a descension process of the heaven frequencies instead of the ascension process of the human race.

Who else is going to do this but you? You are the vehicle! You are the Buddha. You are the Christ. You are not any different than Christ, no matter what you think of yourself right now. In fact, you are quite equal to Christ, for he is another soul just like yourself who came here to break up the madness. You actually had many lifetimes similar to his. He just happened to become famous. You have been all kinds of saints in your vast experience and multitudes of lifetimes. Your thoughts toward yourself will change soon. See if you can put aside your fear long enough to take a peek at the lifetimes when you were gurus, teachers, prophets and legends of other sorts. There is not one of you who has *not* had this experience.

Open your memory to go far beyond your experience here on the Earth plane. Encourage your memory to recall your core essence, your God-self, and the experiences you have gathered elsewhere besides Earth. You have had millions of lifetimes all over the universe. You are so incredibly wise, you would giggle at the fact you are worried right now about whether or not you will ever find wholeness again. You are huge! Your experience is infinite.

Enlightenment is simply a state of full remembrance. It is all about remembering who and what you are in the soul planes. It has not been an easy task. However, reclaiming your power is fun. It does not have to be a task at all. It is an adventure. You will look back on the material in this book less than a year from now and say, "Wow! I am so far beyond the point where I was when I needed that book!" You will be relieved.

You are a spiritual traveler. You have stopped for a while on the Earth plane to participate in what was, and is, happening here. You were fascinated by it. It peaked your curiosity and interest. It was as if you were passing by and you saw something you wanted to know more about. Perhaps you heard about it from other travelers and came here to check it out for yourself. Some of you actually came here because you were frightened that the madness on Earth would spread to your own homes if it remained unchecked. Some of you came because your friends were "swallowed up" by the energy on Earth and you knew they could use your help. There are many reasons why you came here.

> *You are a spiritual traveler*
> *and you would have it*
> *no other way.*

First and foremost, though, you came here in order to gather experience, explore and have an adventure. You are a spiritual traveler and you would have it no other way. You will travel, have traveled, and are traveling to countless other worlds and realities. You will never stop exploring. It is your nature. This is the big picture.

Nurture yourself. Take care of yourself. Be your own best friend. You could probably use a best friend in your life right now. Be that friend and you will blossom. Nurture the flower that you are. Shape yourself gently as you bloom. You are opening in a most beautiful way, even though it might look ugly to yourself. On the inner levels, it is magnificent to behold for the beings who have come to spectate.

What makes any person an incredible human being is simply the fact that the person has the ability to be who he or she is. There are no other secrets to greatness than this. As soon as you can be yourself, express yourself freely without fear, and embody the frequencies of love, you will see your own greatness for yourself. It is now time for you to develop your deepest self respect, self appreciation and self love. It is time now for you to develop honor for all other beings and energies in the universe. Embrace and appreciate their uniqueness (or strangeness!).

The shadow self is the part of you that has your power. Your power has been neutralized because there is fear in your system. Working with the shadow self as your friend, instead of a nuisance or an enemy, will release your brilliance, your love and your power.

The dazzling darkness is incredible indeed. Think of it as the Cave of Creation and you will understand what the dazzling darkness really is. Your shadow self is the part of you that is being created and developed by you and God. Humanity has been creative about manifesting fear and anger from the darkness. Now humanity is getting creative about manifesting love and peace from the darkness. The darkness is God's creation. It is useful. It is not "evil" at all.

Begin in earnest to reach for your inner worlds. Concentrate your efforts 100% and the process will go much more quickly. Establish sanctuaries in your inner worlds where you can rest and feel peace. You will remember the love you knew before you came here.

There is a place in every single one of you where your own throne room lies. Go there now and clear the cobwebs. Sit on your throne every

Reclaiming the Shadow Self

day and you will begin to feel what it is like to be empowered again, the way you were before you gave it up. Fill your inner palace with laughter, fun and music again. Your throne room has been quiet for a while, but it is still there.

God-Speed...

We end our message for now, but know that we are with you. We are honored to be of service to one such as yourself, for you are magnificent indeed. We wish you God-Speed in your journey to your inner worlds. We wish you God-Speed in your journey of awakening. We wish you God-Speed in your journey of *Reclaiming The Shadow Self.*

Peace

Thanks!

I thank all the people who helped me to heal, whether they are mentioned here or not. There are so many!

Anna Maychuck for her editing and advice.

Christopher Yayas, owner of a store in Key West named *Heaven*, for giving me the opportunity to hone my channeling skills. And Raphael for believing in me.

Eric Rittenhouse for being a nut, extending his circle of friends to me, providing shelter, helping me sell my jewelry, and trips to meditate by the sea.

Expanding Light for providing a safe and light filled environment to begin my healing process.

Patricia Resch and Bodhi for their expertise in cellular release.

Gary Brehmmer for deep trance cranial sacral therapy and Marjorie McDougal for her wonderful massages.

Dr. Michael Vogt, Dr. Judy Fox, and Dr. Louis Mulhalka for realigning my damaged spine.

Dr. David Horowitz for stabilizing my body's chemical make-up during the stress in my healing.

Kelly Kolodney and Peter Motika for their clear channeling abilities.

Michelle Hunter for her clear channeling abilities and the title for this book!

Farmer's Insurance for providing the money I needed for a year and three months to heal from a car accident which was a blessing in disguise (for me, anyway!).

Ron Piper and Janis Deklotsk for offering me a ride from the border of Mexico and offering me a job to fill my pockets with money again. I was broker than broke!

Rob Harmon who entertained me, gave me a place to stay, and inspired me to think about taking up surfing.

Blair CarMichael for watching my kitties for two years, talks on the phone, sending my mail to wherever I went next, providing shelter, and being a stable point in my life.

Emily, my sister, for being who she is, and her husband Todd for his weird humor. Also Esther and Elizabeth, my nieces, for fun on the beach and for being so cool!

Meade and Cheryl Breese for making me laugh and being yet another stable point in my life where I could get mail! Also thanks for the opportunity to swing a sledgehammer for a month, build a new foundation under the house, earn some money and get my anger out all at the same time!

My guides and soul group for helping me find my way through the labyrinth.

Issau and Chris for restoring my faith that the universe takes care of me.

Michael Hammer for his music.

Robin and Steve Francis for giving me shelter in Key West and keeping me out of the snow during winter. And little Ian for being so lively and easy to tickle!

All the people who upset me or harmed me, thus giving me a chance to improve on myself and dig deeper!

Kathey Fatica for her terrific graphic design skills and helping me get this project into manifested form.

Ciarán Mercier, Middletown, CA for his expert advice on self-publishing. If you need a consultant, he's the best!

About the Author

Christine Breese lives in California. She has a degree in Audio Engineering and a degree in Film-Making and Video Production. She worked for MGM Studios, Disney and other various companies. She works freelance on television and film projects. She currently writes scripts for independent films, makes music, and channels Anwan.

About the Artist

Laurel Taylor also lives in California. She has a Master's degree in costume design from Boston University. She is an illustrator, sketch artist and freelance designer. She currently works freelance on television and film projects, as well as theatrical productions.

Recommended Reading

Courage To Heal	Ellen Bass and Laura Davis
Courage To Heal Workbook	Laura Davis
Trauma And Recovery	Judith Herman, M.D.
Seth Books	Jane Roberts
Any Inner Child Books	there are lots of them!

Tools For Exploration
47 Paul Drive
San Rafael, CA 94903
1-800-456-9887

There is a list of spiritual retreat centers in the book
Journey of Awakening by Ram Dass

There is a comprehensive list of communities
in the book *Communities Directory.*
It is available from:

Twin Oaks Community
138-R Twin Oaks Rd.
Louisa, VA 23093

(540) 894-5798

Look for Christine's other books:

Daniel, A Sexual Healer available now
Alindra, A Past Life Remembered available fall of 1997

Please feel free to write about your experiences with Anwan's message. Even though she cannot answer letters individually, Christine will read them if they aren't too long! Please feel free to send your questions. They might be answered in future books or newsletters.

Let us know if you would like to be on our mailing list. We will advise you of upcoming camping trips, seminars, workshops in your area, and events with Christine/Anwan and other various healers/teachers she works with.

Please address correspondence to:

Christine Breese
Starlight Press
P.O. Box 718
Rock Hall, MD 21661